Cambridge Latin Course
SECOND EDITION

Unit IVB

D0682536

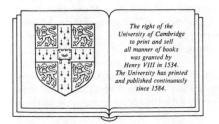

The right of the University of Cambridge to print and sell all manner of books was granted by Henry VIII in 1534. The University has printed and published continuously since 1584.

CAMBRIDGE UNIVERSITY PRESS

Cambridge
New York   New Rochelle
Melbourne   Sydney

Published by the Press Syndicate of the University of Cambridge
The Pitt Building, Trumpington Street, Cambridge CB2 1RP
32 East 57th Street, New York, NY 10022, USA
10 Stamford Road, Oakleigh, Melbourne 3166, Australia

This book, an outcome of work jointly commissioned by the Schools
Council before its closure and the Cambridge School Classics Project, is
published under the aegis of the School Curriculum Development
Committee, Newcombe House, 45 Notting Hill Gate, London W11 3JB.

First published 1973
Second edition 1988

Printed in Great Britain at the
University Press, Cambridge

ISBN 0 521 31279 5
ISBN 0 521 31280 9 North American edition

DS

Thanks are due to the following for permission to reproduce photographs:

pp 11, 109 Fototeca Unione at the American Academy in Rome (negs FU 960, FU 2281);
pp 17, 149, 153, 163 The Trustees of the British Museum; p 26 Deutsches Archäologisches
Institut, Rome; pp 36, 52, 79, 96, 98, 113, 120, 160, 171 The Mansell Collection; p 41
Viscount Coke and the Trustees of the Holkham Estate; p 44 Somerset County Council,
Museums Service; p 51 photo Vatican Museums; p 67 Soprintendenza Archeologica di
Roma; p 75 Elisabeth Ayrton; pp 76, 135, 146 National Archaeological Museum, Athens
(invoice no A15163); p 80 Fitzwilliam Museum, Cambridge; p 88 Patrimoine des Musées
des Beaux-Arts, Brussels; p 94 Capitoline Museum, Rome; p 144 courtesy, Museum of
Fine Arts, Boston; p 173 Kunsthistorisches Museums, Vienna.

'Musée des Beaux Arts' reproduced by permission of Faber and Faber Ltd from *Collected
Poems* by W.H. Auden. Copyright 1940 and renewed 1968 by W.H. Auden; reprinted from
W.H. Auden: Collected Poems by W.H. Auden, edited by Edward Mendelson, by permission
of Random House, Inc.

Richmond Lattimore's translation of Homer's *Iliad* is reproduced by permission of the
University of Chicago Press, copyright 1951 © 1962 by the University of Chicago, all
rights reserved.

Drawings by Peter Kesteven, Roger Dalladay, Joy Mellor and Leslie Jones
Maps and diagrams by Reg Piggott, Jeff Edwards and Celia Hart

Contents

Bīthȳnia

For about four hundred and fifty years, the Romans controlled an empire that stretched from the Atlantic Ocean to the edge of Russia and from Scotland to the Sahara Desert. The empire's provinces were ruled by an enormous and complicated organisation of governors and their staffs.

As a rule, we know very little about the day-to-day running of this vast network; but in one case we have an unusually large amount of information because the provincial governor's letters to the emperor have survived, together with the emperor's replies. In about A.D. 110, Gaius Plinius Caecilius Secundus (Pliny) was appointed by the Emperor Trajan to govern the province of Bithynia et Pontus (roughly equivalent to northern Turkey). It was an abnormal governorship: Pliny had been personally chosen by the emperor himself; he was given special authority and status, and he had a special job to do. Stage 41 contains five of Pliny's official letters to Trajan, together with Trajan's replies.

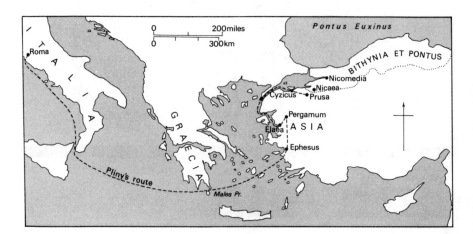

Pliny's route

adventus

I

GAIUS PLINIUS TRAIANO IMPERATORI

navigatio mea, domine, usque Ephesum saluberrima erat; inde,
postquam vehiculis iter facere coepi, gravissimis aestibus atque
etiam febriculis affligebar; Pergami igitur ad convalescendum
substiti. deinde, cum navem iterum conscendissem, contrariis
ventis retentus sum; itaque Bithyniam intravi aliquanto tardius 5
quam speraveram, id est XV Kal. Octobres.

navigatio *voyage*
usque Ephesum *as far as Ephesus*
saluberrima: salubris *comfortable*
vehiculis: vehiculum *carriage*
gravissimis: gravis *severe*
aestibus: aestus *heat*
febriculis: febricula *slight fever*
Pergami *at Pergamum*
ad convalescendum *for the purpose of getting better, in order to get better*
substiti: subsistere *halt, stop*
aliquanto *somewhat, rather*
XV Kal. Octobres *17th September (literally 'fifteen days before 1st October')*

1 How did Pliny travel to Ephesus?
2 What change in his method of travelling did he make when he got there?
3 Why was he forced to stop at Pergamum?
4 What method of travel did he use for the final stage of his journey? What delayed him?

nunc ratiōnēs Prūsēnsium excutiō; quod mihi magis ac magis
necessārium vidētur. multae enim pecūniae, variīs ex causīs, ā
prīvātīs cīvibus retinentur; praetereā quaedam pecūniae sine iūstā
10 causā impenduntur. dispice, domine, num necessārium putēs
mittere hūc mēnsōrem, ad opera pūblica īnspicienda; crēdō enim
multās pecūniās posse revocārī ā cūrātōribus pūblicōrum operum,
sī mēnsūrae fidēliter agantur. hanc epistulam tibi, domine, in ipsō
adventū meō scrīpsī.

Prūsēnsium: Prūsēnsēs *people of Prusa*	opera: opus *work, building*
excutiō: excutere *examine, investigate*	revocārī: revocāre *recover*
necessārium: necessārius *necessary*	ā *from*
pecūniae: pecūnia *sum of money*	cūrātōribus: cūrātor *supervisor,*
iūstā: iūstus *proper, right*	*superintendent*
impenduntur: impendere *spend*	mēnsūrae: mēnsūra *measurement*
dispice: dispicere *consider*	fidēliter *faithfully, reliably*
mēnsōrem: mēnsor *surveyor*	

5 What is Pliny doing at Prusa? From lines 8–10 find two reasons
   why Prusa is short of public money.

6 What kind of assistant does Pliny ask Trajan for?

7 What job does Pliny want this assistant to do?

8 What impression does Pliny give by the words 'nunc' (line 7) and
   'in ipsō adventū' (lines 13–14)? Can you suggest any reason why
   Pliny is so anxious to impress Trajan in this way – is it, for
   example, to make up for any failure on his part?

II

TRĀIĀNUS PLĪNIŌ

cognōvī litterīs tuīs, Secunde cārissime, quō diē in Bīthȳniam
pervēnissēs. brevī tempore, crēdō, Bīthȳnī intellegent prōvinciam
mihi esse cūrae: nam ego tē ēlēgī quī ad eōs meī locō mittāris; tū
efficiēs ut benignitās mea sit manifesta illīs.
5 prīmum autem tibi ratiōnēs pūblicae sunt excutiendae; nam satis
cōnstat eās vexātās esse.

4

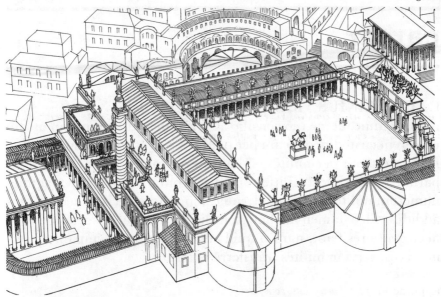

mēnsōrēs vix sufficientēs habeō etiam eīs operibus quae aut Rōmae aut in proximō fiunt. (lines 7–8)

mēnsōrēs vix sufficientēs habeō etiam eīs operibus quae aut
Rōmae aut in proximō fiunt. sed in omnī prōvinciā inveniuntur
mēnsōrēs quibus crēdere possīmus; et ideō nōn vereor nē tibi dēsint.
sī tū dīligenter excutiēs, inveniēs. 10

[handwritten interlinear translation:] for I have scarcely enough surveyors for those works which take place whether in Rome or in nearby. But in all provinces. surveyors are found which we can trust. I'm not worried that you are lacking. If you investigate carefully — you will find them.

Bīthȳnī *Bithynians*
meī locō *in my place*
efficiēs ut: efficere ut *bring it about that, see to it that*
benignitās *concern, kindly interest*
vexātās: vexātus *confused, in chaos*

sufficientēs: sufficiēns *enough, sufficient*
aut . . . aut *either . . . or*
in proximō *nearby*
omnī: omnis *every*
dēsint: dēesse *be lacking, be unavailable*

1 What phrase does Trajan use to emphasise that Pliny's job in Bithynia is an important one?
2 What impression of himself does Trajan want the Bithynians to have?
3 Why is Trajan unable to agree to Pliny's request for a surveyor? What steps does he suggest Pliny should take instead?
4 On the evidence of this pair of letters, what special task has Pliny been sent to Bithynia to perform? Can you suggest reasons why Trajan should have chosen Pliny for this task?

carcer

I

GĀIUS PLĪNIUS TRĀIĀNŌ IMPERĀTŌRĪ

rogō, domine, ut mē tuō cōnsiliō adiuvēs: incertus enim sum utrum
carcerem custōdīre dēbeam per pūblicōs servōs (quod usque adhūc
factum est) an per mīlitēs. sī enim servīs pūblicīs ūtar, vereor nē
parum fidēlēs sint; sī mīlitibus ūtar, vereor nē hoc officium magnum
5 numerum mīlitum distringat. interim pūblicīs servīs paucōs mīlitēs
addidī. videō tamen in hōc cōnsiliō perīculum esse nē utrīque
neglegentiōrēs fiant; nam sī quid adversī acciderit, culpam mīlitēs
in servōs, servī in mīlitēs trānsferre poterunt.

usque adhūc *up till now, until now*
parum *too little, not . . . enough*
fidēlēs: fidēlis *reliable, trustworthy*
officium *task, duty*
distringat: distringere *distract, divert*
utrīque *both groups of people*
sī quid *if anything*
adversī: adversus *unfortunate, undesirable*
culpam: culpa *blame*
trānsferre *transfer, put*

1 What problem is causing Pliny difficulty? What disadvantage
  does each of his two alternatives have?
2 What step has Pliny taken for the moment?
3 Is Pliny satisfied with his present solution? If not, why not?
4 What reply would you expect from Trajan? Would you expect
  him to agree with what Pliny has done? or to prefer another
  solution? or to snap at Pliny for bothering him with trivialities?

II

TRĀIĀNUS PLĪNIŌ

nihil opus est, mī Secunde cārissime, mīlitēs ad carcerem custōdiendum convertere. melius est persevērāre in istīus prōvinciae cōnsuētūdine, et pūblicīs servīs ad vigilandum in carcere ūtī; tū enim, sevēritāte ac dīligentiā tuā, potes efficere ut servī fidēliter hoc faciant. nam, sī mīlitēs servīs pūblicīs permiscentur, 5 rēctē verēris nē utrīque neglegentiōrēs sint; sed nōs semper oportet hoc meminisse: mīlitēs Rōmānōs in prōvinciīs nostrīs positōs esse nōn ad carcerēs custōdiendōs, sed ad pugnandum.

nihil opus est *there is no need*	ad vigilandum *for keeping watch*
convertere *divert*	sevēritāte: sevēritās *strictness, severity*
persevērāre *continue*	permiscentur: permiscēre *mix with*
cōnsuētūdine: cōnsuētūdō *custom*	

1 In Trajan's view, who ought to guard the prisoners?
2 Why had Pliny been reluctant to adopt this solution, and how does Trajan answer his objection?
3 Which of Pliny's fears does Trajan agree with?
4 What aspect of the problem does Trajan seem to feel most strongly about? Is it the unreliability of the public slaves, the disadvantage of sharing the work, or some other aspect?

Language note

1 In Stage 40, you met the gerundive used with 'ad', meaning 'for the purpose of . . .':

Quīntus ad Salvium accūsandum surrēxit.
Quintus stood up for the purpose of Salvius being accused.
  or, in more natural English:
Quintus stood up in order to accuse Salvius.

iuvenēs ad pompam spectandam advēnērunt.
The young men arrived for the purpose of the procession being watched.
  or, in more natural English:
The young men arrived to watch the procession.

2 In Stage 41, you have met sentences like these:

pontifex ad **sacrificandum** aderat.
The priest was present for the purpose of sacrificing.
  or, in more natural English:
The priest was present in order to sacrifice.

līberī ad **lūdendum** exiērunt.
The children went out for the purpose of playing.
  or, in more natural English:
The children went out to play.

The word in heavy print is known as a *gerund*.

Further examples:

1 puer in fossam ad latendum dēsiluit.
2 senex ad cēnandum recumbēbat.

3 Further examples of sentences containing gerunds and gerundives:

1 mīlitēs ad imperātōrem **salūtandum** īnstrūctī erant.
 (*gerundive*)
2 mīlitēs ad **pugnandum** īnstrūctī erant. (*gerund*)
3 Plīnius ad **convalēscendum** in oppidō manēbat. (*gerund*)
4 haruspicēs ad victimās **īnspiciendās** prōcessērunt.
 (*gerundive*)
5 servus ad **labōrandum** ē lectō surrēxit. (*gerund*)
6 dominus ad pecūniam **numerandam** in tablīnō sedēbat.
 (*gerundive*)
7 clientēs ad patrōnōs **vīsitandōs** per viās contendēbant.
8 amīcus meus ad **dormiendum** abiit.
9 multī āthlētae ad **certandum** aderant.
10 cīvēs aquam ad incendium **exstinguendum** quaerēbant.

In sentences 7–10, which of the words in heavy print are gerundives, and which are gerunds?

aquaeductus

I

GĀIUS PLĪNIUS TRĀIĀNŌ IMPERĀTŌRĪ

in aquaeductum, domine, Nīcomēdēnsēs impendērunt sestertium
|XXX| CCCXVIII, quī, imperfectus adhūc, nōn modo omissus sed
etiam dēstrūctus est; deinde in alium aquaeductum impēnsa sunt
CC. hōc quoque relictō, novō impendiō opus est, ut aquam habeant,
5 postquam tantam pecūniam perdidērunt. ipse pervēnī ad fontem
pūrissimum, ex quō vidētur aqua dēbēre perdūcī (sīcut initiō
temptātum erat), arcuātō opere, nē tantum ad humilēs regiōnēs
oppidī perveniat. manent adhūc paucissimī arcūs; possunt etiam
exstruī arcūs complūrēs lapide quadrātō quī ex priōre opere
10 dētractus est; aliqua pars, ut mihi vidētur, testāceō opere agenda
erit (id enim et facilius et vīlius est). sed in prīmīs necessārium est
mittī ā tē vel aquilegem vel architēctum, nē id quod prius accidit
rūrsus ēveniat. ego quidem cōnfīdō et ūtilitātem operis et
pulchritūdinem prīncipātū tuō esse dignissimam.

aquaeductus *aqueduct*
Nīcomēdēnsēs *people of Nicomedia*
|XXX| CCCXVIII *3,318,000:* [ ] *= multiply by 100,000;* [ ] *= multiply by 1,000*
imperfectus *unfinished*
adhūc *still*
omissus = omissus est: omittere *abandon*
dēstrūctus est: dēstruere *pull down, demolish*
CC *200,000*
impendiō: impendium *expense, expenditure*
opus est *there is need of (literally 'there is work (to be done) with')*
perdidērunt: perdere *waste, lose*
perdūcī: perdūcere *bring, carry*
arcuātō: arcuātus *arched*
humilēs: humilis *low-lying*
quadrātō: quadrātus *squared, in blocks*
testāceō opere: testāceum opus *brick work*
in prīmīs *in the first place*
vel . . . vel *either . . . or*
aquilegem: aquilex *water engineer, hydraulic engineer*
ēveniat: ēvenīre *occur*
ūtilitātem: ūtilitās *usefulness*
pulchritūdinem: pulchritūdō *beauty*

1 What happened to the Nicomedians' first aqueduct?
2 What has happened to their second attempt?
3 Why does the aqueduct have to be carried on arches?
4 What three suggestions does Pliny make in lines 8–11 ('manent . . . agenda erit') for the providing of arches?
5 What request does he make to Trajan?
6 How does Pliny attempt to make his idea more persuasive to Trajan?

II

TRĀIĀNUS PLĪNIŌ

cūrandum est, ut aqua in oppidum Nīcomēdiam perdūcātur.
cōnfīdō tē summā dīligentiā hoc opus effectūrum esse. sed medius
fidius! necesse est tibi eādem dīligentiā ūtī ad cognōscendum
quōrum vitiō tantam pecūniam Nīcomēdēnsēs perdiderint;
suspicor eōs ideō tot aquaeductūs incohāvisse et relīquisse, ut inter 5
sē grātificentur. quicquid cognōveris, perfer in nōtitiam meam.

cūrandum est *steps must be taken*
medius fidius! *for goodness sake!*
vitiō: vitium *fault, failure*
incohāvisse: incohāre *begin*

grātificentur: grātificārī *do favours*
perfer: perferre *bring*
nōtitiam: nōtitia *notice*

1 Does Trajan give permission for the new aqueduct?
2 What is Trajan especially concerned about? What does he suspect?
3 What does Trajan do about Pliny's request for a water engineer?

lapis quadrātus

testāceum opus

supplicium

I
GĀIUS PLĪNIUS TRĀIĀNŌ IMPERĀTŌRĪ

Semprōnius Caeliānus, ēgregius iuvenis, duōs servōs inter tīrōnēs
repertōs mīsit ad mē; quōrum ego supplicium distulī, ut tē
cōnsulerem dē modō poenae. ipse enim ideō maximē dubitō, quod
hī servī, quamquam iam sacrāmentum dīxērunt, nōndum in
5 numerōs distribūtī sunt. rogō igitur, domine, ut scrībās quid facere
dēbeam, praesertim cum pertineat ad exemplum.

ēgregius *excellent, outstanding*
tīrōnēs: tīrō *recruit*
distulī: differre *postpone*
sacrāmentum dīxērunt: sacrāmentum dīcere *take the military oath*
numerōs: numerī *military units*
cum *since, because*
pertineat ad exemplum: pertinēre ad exemplum *involve a precedent*

1 What has Sempronius Caelianus discovered? What action has he
   taken?
2 What does Pliny want Trajan to decide?
3 Why is Pliny particularly hesitant?
4 Why does he think the case is important?

II

TRĀIĀNUS PLĪNIŌ

rēctē mīsit Semprōnius Caeliānus ad tē eōs servōs, quī inter tīrōnēs
repertī sunt. nunc tē oportet cognōscere num supplicium ultimum
meruisse videantur. rēfert autem utrum voluntāriī vēnerint an lēctī
sint vel etiam vicāriī ab aliīs datī. sī lēctī sunt, illī peccāvērunt quī ad
mīlitandum eōs ēlēgērunt; sī vicāriī datī sunt, culpa est penes eōs   5
quī dedērunt; sī ipsī, quamquam habēbant condiciōnis suae
cōnscientiam, nihilōminus vēnērunt, sevērē pūniendī erunt. neque
multum rēfert, quod nōndum in numerōs distribūtī sunt. illō enim
diē, quō prīmum probātī sunt, vēritās condiciōnis eōrum
patefacienda erat.   10

rēfert: rēferre *make a difference*
voluntāriī: voluntārius *volunteer*
vēnerint: venīre *come forward*
lēctī sint *have been chosen, have been conscripted*
vicāriī: vicārius *substitute*
datī: dare *put forward*
peccāvērunt: peccāre *do wrong, be to blame*
penes *with*
condiciōnis: condiciō *status*
cōnscientiam: cōnscientia *awareness, knowledge*
probātī sunt: probāre *examine (at time of enrolment)*
vēritās *truth*

1 What punishment are the slaves liable to suffer if they are found
   guilty?
2 Trajan refers to three possible explanations for the situation.
   What are they? What action does he think should be taken in each
   case?
3 When ought the status of the recruits to have been discovered?
4 Who seems to have the better grasp of the problem, Pliny or
   Trajan?

Language note

1 Study the following pairs of sentences:

puerī clāmōrem faciunt.   clāmor **fit**.
The boys are making a noise.   A noise is being made.

Nerō multa et dīra faciēbat.   multa et dīra **fīēbant**.
Nero was doing many terrible   Many terrible things were being
things.   done.

The words in heavy print are forms of the irregular verb 'fīō' ('I am made').

2 The verb 'faciō' ('I make, I do') has no passive forms in the present, future and imperfect tenses. Instead, the Romans used the following forms of 'fīō':

PRESENT		PRESENT INFINITIVE
fīō	I am made	fierī to be made
fis	you are made	
fit	he is made	PRESENT SUBJUNCTIVE
fiunt	they are made	fiam
		fīās *etc.*

FUTURE ('I shall be made', *etc.*)
fīam
fīēs   *etc.*

IMPERFECT	IMPERFECT SUBJUNCTIVE
('I was being made', *etc.*)	
fīēbam	fierem
fīēbās *etc.*	fierēs *etc.*

Translate the following pairs of sentences:

1a mīlitēs impetum mox facient.
1b impetus mox fīet.

2a servus nihil in culīnā faciēbat.
2b nihil in culīnā fīēbat.

3a ignōrābāmus quid senātōrēs in cūriā facerent.
3b ignōrābāmus quid in cūriā fieret.

3 Notice some of the different ways in which 'fīō' can be translated:

aliquid mīrī fīēbat.
Something strange was being done.
or Something strange was happening.

ecce! deus fīō.
Look! I'm being made into a god, *or* Look! I'm becoming a god.

Further examples:

1 crās nōs cōnsulēs fīēmus.
2 salvē, Mārce! quid in fundō tuō hodiē fit?
3 tam timidē hostēs resistēbant ut peditēs nostrī audāciōrēs fierent.

peditēs *foot soldiers, infantry*

4 The perfect, future perfect and pluperfect tenses of the passive of 'faciō' are formed in the normal way. Study the following pairs of sentences and notice some of the different ways of translating 'factus est', etc.

mīlitēs Claudium imperātōrem fēcērunt.
The soldiers made Claudius emperor.

Claudius imperātor factus est.
Claudius was made emperor, *or* Claudius became emperor.

haruspex rem rīdiculam fēcerat.
The soothsayer had done a silly thing.

rēs rīdicula facta erat.
A silly thing had been done, *or* A silly thing had happened.

incendium

I
GĀIUS PLĪNIUS TRĀIĀNŌ IMPERĀTŌRĪ

cum dīversam partem prōvinciae circumīrem, vāstissimum
incendium Nīcomēdiae coortum est. nōn modo multās cīvium
prīvātōrum domōs dēlēvit, sed etiam duo pūblica opera, Gerūsiān
et templum Īsidis. flammae autem lātius sparsae sunt, prīmum
5 violentiā ventī, deinde inertiā hominum, quī ōtiōsī et immōtī
adstābant, neque quicquam ad adiuvandum fēcērunt. praetereā,
nūllus est usquam pūblicus sīpō, nūlla hama, nūllum omnīnō
īnstrūmentum ad incendia exstinguenda. et haec quidem
īnstrūmenta, ut iam praecēpī, parābuntur; tū, domine, dispice num
10 putēs collēgium fabrōrum esse īnstituendum, dumtaxat hominum
CL. ego efficiam nē quis nisi faber in hoc collēgium admittātur, nēve
fabrī hōc iūre in aliud ūtantur; nec erit difficile custōdīre tam
paucōs.

vāstissimum: vāstus *great, large*
Nīcomēdiae *at Nicomedia*
coortum est. coorīrī *break out*
Gerūsiān: *Greek accusative of* Gerūsia *the
  Gerusia (club for wealthy elderly men)*
lātius: lātē *widely*
sparsae sunt: spargere *spread*
violentiā: violentia *violence*
inertiā: inertia *laziness, idleness*
sīpō *fire-pump*
hama *fire-bucket*

īnstrūmentum *equipment*
praecēpī: praecipere *instruct, order*
collēgium *brigade*
fabrōrum: faber *fireman*
īnstituendum: īnstituere *set up*
dumtaxat *not exceeding*
nē quis *that nobody*
nēve *and that . . . not*
iūre: iūs *right, privilege*
in aliud *for any other purpose*

A1 What has happened in Nicomedia?
  2 Where was Pliny at the time?
  3 How extensive was the damage?
  4 What was the attitude of the bystanders?
  5 In what way was the city ill-prepared for such a disaster?
  6 What preventive measure is Pliny taking?
  7 What further suggestion does he make to the emperor?

Bronze water-pump

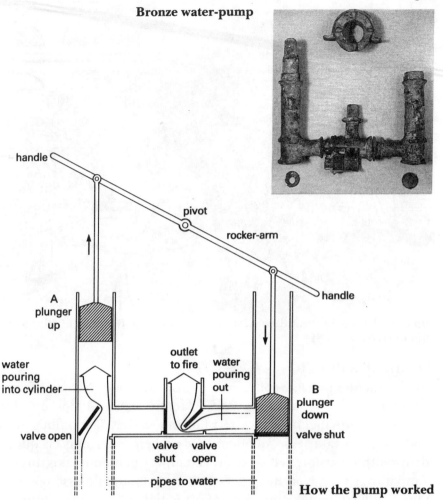

How the pump worked

B1 Why does Pliny mention his whereabouts at the time of the disaster?

2 Do the words 'ōtiōsī et immōtī adstābant' (lines 5–6) merely describe the scene, or do they also convey Pliny's attitude towards the bystanders? If so, what *is* his attitude?

3 Does Pliny's suggestion to the emperor seem to you a reasonable one? What reply would you expect to this letter?

4 Do lines 10–13 (from 'dumtaxat hominum' to the end) indicate Pliny's confidence that the emperor will agree to his suggestion, or does he think the emperor may disapprove?

admonendī quoque sunt dominī praediōrum ut ipsī flammās exstinguere cōnentur. (lines 7–8)

II

TRĀIĀNUS PLĪNIŌ

tibi in mentem vēnit collēgium fabrōrum apud Nīcomēdēnsēs
īnstituere, sīcut in aliīs prōvinciīs factum est. sed nōs oportet
meminisse prōvinciam istam et praecipuē urbēs factiōnibus eius
modī saepe vexātās esse. quodcumque nōmen dederimus eīs quī in
5 idem contractī erunt, hetaeriae brevī tempore fient. melius igitur est
comparāre ea quae ad incendia exstinguenda auxiliō esse possint;
admonendī quoque sunt dominī praediōrum ut ipsī flammās
exstinguere cōnentur; dēnique, sī opus est, auxilium ā spectantibus
est petendum.

in mentem vēnit: in mentem venīre *occur, come to mind*
praecipuē *especially*
factiōnibus: factiō *organised group*
quodcumque *whatever*
in idem *for a common purpose, for the same purpose*
contractī erunt: contrahere *bring together, assemble*
hetaeriae: hetaeria *political club*
dominī: dominus *owner*
praediōrum: praedium *property*

1 What decision does Trajan give?
2 How has the previous history of Bithynia affected Trajan's decision?
3 What three suggestions does Trajan make?
4 To what extent do you agree with the following opinion?

> 'Trajan seems more concerned with politics than with the safety of his subjects; his advice to Pliny is vague and unhelpful. He appears not to realise the seriousness of fires in large towns.'

Language note

1 Study the following examples:

tam stultus est ille puer ut ā cēterīs discipulīs semper **dērīdeātur**.
That boy is so stupid that he is always laughed at by the other pupils.

medicus ignōrat quārē hōc morbō **afflīgāris**, mī amīce.
The doctor does not know why you are stricken with this illness, my friend.

The form of the verb in heavy print is the *present subjunctive passive*.

Further examples:

1 scīre velim quot captīvī in illō carcere retineantur.
2 tot clientēs habēmus ut in viīs semper salūtēmur.
3 arma semper gerō nē ā latrōnibus interficiar.

(continued)

2 Compare the active and passive forms of the present subjunctive of 'portō':

present subjunctive active	*present subjunctive passive*
portem	porter
portēs	portēris
portet	portētur
portēmus	portēmur
portētis	portēminī
portent	portentur

Present subjunctive passive forms of 'doceō', 'trahō' and 'audiō' are given on p.193 of the Language Information section.

3 Study the following examples:

nescio quid iuvenis efficere **cōnētur**.
I do not know what the young man is trying to achieve.

crās equōs cōnscendēmus ut **proficīscāmur**.
Tomorrow we will mount our horses in order to set out.

The words in heavy print are *present subjunctive* forms of *deponent* verbs.

Further examples:

1 tam timidī sunt servī meī ut etiam umbrās vereantur.
2 dīcite mihi quārē illōs senēs sequāminī.

The present subjunctive of the deponent verbs 'cōnor', 'vereor', 'loquor' and 'mentior' is set out in full on p.196.

Exercises

1 The following list contains the 3rd person singular present and perfect forms of seven verbs, jumbled together. Sort them into pairs, writing the present form first and then the perfect, and give the meaning of each form.

For example: portat   he carries   portāvit   he carried

portat, facit, tulit, est, cōgit, fēcit, fert, ēgit, fuit, vēnit, coēgit, venit, agit, portāvit.

2 Complete each sentence with the right word and then translate.

1 ego vōs servāvī, ubi ab inimīcīs . . . .
   (accūsābāminī, fingēbāminī)
2 difficile erat nōbīs prōcēdere, quod ā turbā . . . .
   (dīcēbāmur, impediēbāmur)
3 audīte, meī amīcī! nōs ad aulam contendere . . . .
   (regimur, iubēmur)
4 rēctē nunc . . . . ., quod ā proeliō herī fūgistis.
   (culpāminī, agnōscīminī)
5 epistulam ad prīncipem hodiē mittam, mīlitēs, ut facta nostra nūntiem; sine dubiō ab illō . . . . . . (rogābimur, laudābimur)
6 iūdex 'facinus dīrum commīsistis' inquit. 'crās . . . . . .'
   (amābiminī, necābiminī)

3 This exercise is based on the letters on pp. 10–13. Refer to the letters where necessary, and complete each of the sentences below with one of the following groups of words; then translate. Use each group of words once only.

Plīnium rem dīligenter effectūrum esse
quamquam multam pecūniam impenderant
quod servī erant
num servī supplicium ultimum meruissent
ut architectum ad Bīthȳniam mitteret

1 Nīcomēdēnsēs, ..., nūllam aquam habēbant.
2 Plīnius imperātōrī persuādēre cōnābātur . . . . . .
3 Trāiānus cōnfīdēbat . . . . . .
4 Semprōnius duōs tīrōnēs ad Plīnium mīsit . . . . . .
5 Plīnius incertus erat . . . . . .

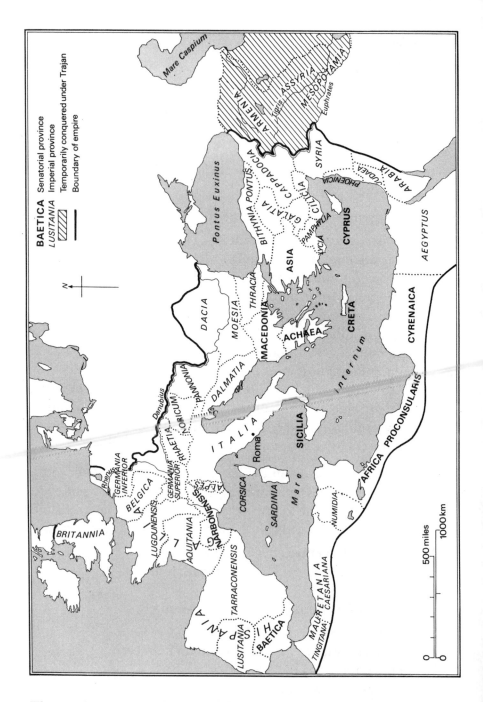

The provinces of the Roman empire during the reign of Trajan

The government of the Roman provinces

The map opposite shows the provinces of the Roman empire at the time of its greatest extent, during the reign of the Emperor Trajan. The Romans obtained these territories gradually during several centuries, starting with the island of Sicily in the third century B.C., and ending with Trajan's conquests in Dacia (modern Romania) and the east. Some provinces, such as Britain, became part of the empire as a result of a successful Roman invasion. Others were given to the Romans by their previous rulers; Bithynia, for example, was bequeathed to Rome by its king in his will.

A number of provinces (whose names are marked on the map in italics) were known as 'imperial provinces'; their governor was chosen by the emperor, and his official title was 'lēgātus Augustī' ('emperor's deputy'). The other provinces (whose names are in heavy type) were known as 'senatorial provinces'; their governor was appointed by the senate and his official title was 'prōcōnsul'. Occasionally the emperor stepped in and picked the governor of a senatorial province himself, as Trajan did when he appointed Pliny as governor of Bithynia, instead of leaving the choice to the senate.

Both the senate and the emperor took trouble to select suitable people for governorships. No senator could become the governor of a province unless he had previously held the praetorship, and some important provinces could be governed only by men who had been consul. The senate and emperor kept a lookout for men who had shown special skill or talent during the earlier part of their career. For example, both Agricola and Pliny were sent to provinces where they could put their particular qualities and experience to good use.

A small group of imperial provinces was governed by members of the equestrian class, who were known as 'praefectī'. The most important of these provinces was Egypt, whose governorship was one of the highest honours that an eques could hope for. Another province with an equestrian governor was Judaea, one of whose

Diagrammatic map of the sort used in the Roman empire. It shows travellers the road system and accommodation available using standard symbols. The places marked are roughly in the correct relationship to each other but their shapes are distorted to get the map on a narrow continuous roll for easy reference.

praefecti was the best-known of all Roman governors, Pontius Pilatus (Pilate), who offended the Jews with his harshness and tactlessness and became notorious among Christians for the crucifixion of Jesus.

A governor's first and most important duty was a military one, to protect his province against attack from outside and rebellion from inside. Under his command were one or more legions or 'auxilia'. He might, like Agricola in Scotland, use these troops to conquer further territory; he could also use them, if necessary, to deal with nuisances such as bandits or pirates. A small number of soldiers were taken away from their legions or auxilia to serve as officials on the governor's staff, but the governor was not supposed to use soldiers for jobs that could be done by civilians. (Trajan reminded Pliny firmly about this when Pliny thought of using soldiers as

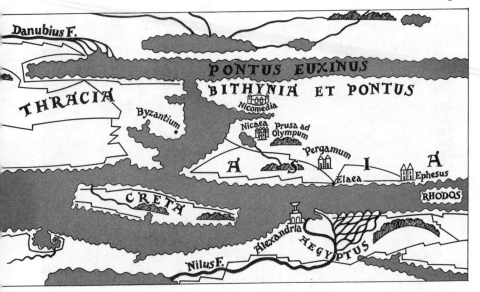

prison warders; see 'carcer' II, p.7.) Although the governor was not a professional soldier, he would not be completely inexperienced in army matters, because normally he would have served as a military tribune in the early part of his career, and in most cases he would have commanded a legion after his praetorship.

The governor's other main task was to administer the law, by travelling around his province and acting as judge in the towns' lawcourts. He had supreme power, and his decisions could not be challenged, with one exception: any Roman citizen who was sentenced to death or flogging had the right to appeal to the emperor against the governor's decision. One man who appealed in this way was Saint Paul, who was arrested in the province of Judaea. The Jews wished to try him in their own court, but Paul not only insisted on being tried in a Roman court but also appealed to the emperor. The following extract from *Acts of the Apostles* describes the confrontation between Paul and the Roman governor Festus:

'But Paul said to Festus, "Against the Jews I have committed no offence, as you very well know. If I am guilty of any capital crime, I do not ask to escape the death penalty; but if there is no truth in the charges which these men bring against me, no one has any right to hand me over to them. I appeal to Caesar!"

Relief showing official dispatch carrier

Then Festus, after consulting his council of advisers, replied, "You have appealed to Caesar; to Caesar you shall go."'

(Paul was then handed over to a centurion and put on board ship. After many adventures, including a shipwreck, he eventually reached Rome, where he may have been put to death during Nero's persecution of Christians after the great fire.)

Sometimes, especially in imperial provinces, the governor was too busy with his military tasks to carry out his other duty of administering the law. When this happened, the emperor could send out another official, known as a 'iūridicus', to take charge in the lawcourts while the governor carried on with the fighting. For example, Salvius acted as a iuridicus in the south of Britain while Agricola was busy campaigning in Scotland.

A governor appointed by the emperor was normally given 'mandāta' (instructions) about the work he was to do in the province. Pliny, for example, was instructed in his mandata to make a public announcement banning political clubs. It is likely that he was also under orders to report back to Trajan about any proposals for public building in his province. (The Bithynians had been spending large sums of money on projects of this kind, and the results had often been disastrous.) Several of Pliny's letters deal with building projects; for example, he writes to Trajan about an aqueduct in Nicomedia ('aquaeductus' I, p.10), public baths at Prusa, a theatre at Nicaea and a smelly and unhygienic sewer at Amastris.

In the first century B.C., Roman governors were often feared and hated for their greed and cruelty; the people of the provinces generally believed, with good reason, that the Romans were only interested in their empire for what they could get out of it. By the time of Trajan, there may have been some improvement. (Most of our information, however, comes from the Romans themselves, rather than the people whom they governed.) Pliny's letters often express concern for the Bithynians' well-being (e.g. in 'aquaeductus' and 'incendium', pp.10 and 16); and in one of Trajan's replies (p.4, line 4), the emperor stresses his 'benignitās' ('kindly feelings') towards the people. Tacitus, in his account of Agricola's life, claims that a deliberate attempt was made to introduce the Britons to some benefits of the Roman way of life:

'Agricola encouraged individuals and gave help to local communities for the building of temples, forums and houses. He also provided an education for the sons of the chieftains. Those who had recently refused to use the Roman language were now eager to make speeches in it. Roman clothing became a sign of status, and togas were often to be seen.'

Roman governors may have behaved in this way partly from kindness, partly from self-interest; if people are comfortable and contented, they are less likely to make trouble for their rulers. Tacitus follows his description of Agricola's policy with a cynical comment:

'The Britons were gradually led astray by the temptations of idleness and luxury – colonnades, baths and smart dinner parties. In their innocence, the Britons referred to this as "civilisation"; in fact it was part of their slavery.'

Many people, however, were bitterly hostile to the Romans and their empire. In the following extract, Tacitus imagines the speech which might have been made by a Scottish chieftain whose homeland was being invaded:

'The Romans plunder the whole world; when there is no land left for them to devastate, they search the sea as well. If their enemy is rich, they are greedy for wealth; if he is poor, they are eager for glory. They describe robbery and slaughter with the deceptive name of "empire"; they make a desert and call it "peace".'

Vocabulary checklist

dīversus, dīversa, dīversum – different
factum, factī – deed, achievement
glōria, glōriae – glory
incendium, incendiī – fire
lūdō, lūdere, lūsī – play
mereō, merēre, meruī – deserve
nōndum – not yet
opus est – there is need
peditēs, peditum – foot soldiers, infantry
perdō, perdere, perdidī, perditus – waste, lose
sī quis – if anyone
    sī quid – if anything
vīlis, vīle – cheap
vitium, vitiī – sin, fault, vice

Give the meaning of:

incendere, lūdus, vīlitās, vitiōsus

The scroll reads:

MVSA MIHI
CAVSAS MEMORA
QVO NVMINE
CAESO QVIDVE.

carmina

Phaedrus

Phaedrus, who lived in the first half of the first century A.D., was originally a slave of the emperor, and became a 'lībertus Augustī'. He composed five books of verse mainly based on the animal fables of Aesop, such as the following fable of the wolf and the lamb:

> ad rīvum eundem lupus et agnus vēnerant
> sitī compulsī; superior stābat lupus
> longēque īnferior agnus. tunc fauce improbā
> latrō incitātus iūrgiī causam intulit.
> 'quārē' inquit 'turbulentam fēcistī mihi   5
> aquam* bibentī?' lāniger contrā timēns:
> 'quī possum, quaesō, facere quod quereris, lupe?
> ā tē dēcurrit ad meōs haustūs liquor.'
> repulsus ille vēritātis vīribus:
> 'ante hōs sex mēnsēs male' ait 'dīxistī mihi.'   10
> respondit agnus: 'equidem nātus nōn eram.'
> 'pater hercle tuus' ille inquit 'male dīxit mihi';
> atque ita correptum lacerat, iniūstā nece.

rīvum: rīvus *stream*
sitī: sitis *thirst*
compulsī: compellere *drive, compel*
superior *higher, further up-stream*
īnferior *lower, further down-stream*
tunc *then*
fauce (*ablative singular*) *hunger* (*literally 'throat'*)
improbā: improbus *wicked, relentless*
latrō *the robber, i.e. the wolf*
iūrgiī: iūrgium *argument, dispute*
causam intulit: causam īnferre *make an excuse, invent an excuse*
5 turbulentam: turbulentus *disturbed, muddy*
lāniger *the woolly one, i.e. the lamb*

---

*Some noun-and-adjective phrases, in which an adjective is separated by one word or more from the noun which it describes, have been underlined.

contrā *in reply*
quī? *how?*
dēcurrit: dēcurrere *run down*
haustūs: haustus *drinking, drinking-place*
liquor *water*
repulsus *repelled, taken aback*
vīribus: vīrēs *forces, strength*
10 male . . . dīxistī: male dīcere *insult*
ait *said*
correptum: corripere *seize*
lacerat: lacerāre *tear apart*
iniūstā: iniūstus *unjust*
nece: nex *slaughter*

1 Where had the wolf and lamb come to, and why? Where did they
stand?
2 Who started the argument? What excuse did he invent?
3 What reason did the lamb give for saying that the wolf must be
wrong?
4 What accusation did the wolf then make? What was the lamb's
reply?
5 How did the wolf then change his accusation? What did he do
next?
6 Suggest a moral (or a title) for this fable. Then compare· your
moral with the one which Phaedrus wrote:
   haec propter illōs scrīpta est hominēs fābula
   quī fictīs causīs innocentēs opprimunt.

Catullus

Gaius Valerius Catullus came from Verona in the north of Italy. He was born in about 84 B.C. and died not long after 54 B.C. His poems, mostly short, vary from tender and loving to insulting and obscene. Stage 42 contains two poems by Catullus in very contrasting styles.

I

Egnātius, quod <u>candidōs</u> habet <u>dentēs,</u>
renīdet usque quāque. sī ad reī ventum est
subsellium, cum ōrātor excitat flētum,
renīdet ille; sī ad <u>piī</u> rogum <u>fīlī</u>
lūgētur, <u>orba</u> cum flet ūnicum <u>māter,</u>   5
renīdet ille. quidquid est, ubicumque est,
quodcumque agit, renīdet: hunc habet morbum,
neque ēlegantem, ut arbitror, neque urbānum
quārē monendum est tē mihi, bone Egnātī.
sī urbānus essēs aut Sabīnus aut Tīburs   10
aut pinguis Umber aut obēsus Etruscus
aut quīlibet, quī pūriter lavit dentēs,
tamen renīdēre usque quāque tē nōllem:
nam rīsū ineptō <u>rēs</u> ineptior <u>nūlla</u> est.

candidōs: candidus *bright, gleaming white*
renīdet: renīdēre *grin, smirk*
usque quāque *on every possible occasion*
reī: reus *defendant*
ventum est *people have come (literally 'there has been an arrival')*
subsellium *bench (for prisoner in court)*
ōrātor *speaker (in court), pleader*
flētum: flētus *weeping, tears*
piī: pius *good, pious*
5 lūgētur *mourning is taking place, mourning is in progress*
orba: orbus *bereaved*
flet: flēre *weep for*
ūnicum: ūnicus (fīlius) *one and only (son)*

quidquid est *whatever is happening*
ubicumque *wherever*
arbitror: arbitrārī *think*
urbānum: urbānus (*line 8*) *refined*
quārē *therefore*
10 urbānus (*line 10*) *a city-dweller, a man from Rome*
Sabīnus *a Sabine*
Tīburs *a man from Tibur*
pinguis *plump*
Umber *an Umbrian*
Etruscus *an Etruscan*
quīlibet *anyone at all*
pūriter *decently, with clean water*
nōllem *I should not want*
ineptō: ineptus *silly*

sī ad reī ventum est subsellium, cum ōrātor excitat flētum, renīdet ille.
(lines 2–4)

1 Why, according to Catullus, does Egnatius grin so continually?
2 What is happening in lines 2–5 (a) in court (b) at the funeral pyre? What does Egnatius do on each occasion? Suggest reasons why Catullus includes the words 'cum ōrātor excitat flētum' (line 3) and 'orba cum flet ūnicum māter' (line 5) in his description of the scenes.
3 Suggest a reason why the verb 'renīdet' is repeated so often (lines 2,4,6,7 and 'renīdēre' in line 13).
4 How does Catullus describe Egnatius' habit in lines 7–8?
5 What does Catullus say he must do to Egnatius in line 9?
6 Study the long sentence in lines 10–13. Does Catullus imply that Egnatius in fact comes from any of these places? Does he imply that Egnatius cleans his teeth 'pūriter'?
7 According to line 14, why would Catullus still object to Egnatius' smile, no matter where he came from?

II

multās per gentēs et multa per aequora vectus,
  adveniō <u>hās miserās</u>, frāter, ad <u>īnferiās</u>,
ut tē postrēmō dōnārem mūnere mortis
  et <u>mūtam</u> nēquīquam adloquerer <u>cinerem</u>.
quandoquidem fortūna mihī tētē abstulit ipsum,   5
  heu miser indignē frāter adēmpte mihī,
nunc tamen intereā haec*, <u>prīscō</u> quae <u>mōre</u> parentum
  trādita sunt trīstī mūnere ad īnferiās,
accipe* <u>frāternō</u> multum mānantia <u>flētū</u>,
  atque in perpetuum, frāter, avē atque valē.   10

aequora: aequor *sea*
vectus: vehī *be carried (e.g. by horse or ship), travel*
īnferiās: īnferiae *tribute to the dead*
postrēmō: postrēmus *last*
mūnere: mūnus *gift*
mūtam: mūtus *silent*
nēquīquam *in vain*
(ut) adloquerer *(so that) I might speak to*
5 quandoquidem *seeing that, since*
  mihī *from me*
  tētē = tē
  heu = ēheu
  indignē *unfairly*
  adēmpte: adēmptus *taken away*
  haec *these things, these gifts*
  prīscō . . . mōre *by the ancient custom*
  parentum: parentēs *ancestors, forefathers*
  trīstī mūnere *as a sad gift, by way of a sad gift*
  frāternō: frāternus *of a brother, fraternal*
  multum mānantia *drenched*
10 avē atque valē *hail and farewell*

*These two words go closely together.

1 How does Catullus emphasise the distance he has travelled?
2 Why has he made this journey? Why do you think he emphasises
  its length?
3 Explain 'nēquīquam' in line 4. Is your explanation supported by
  any other word in the same line?
4 Is there any indication in the poem that Catullus believes or
  disbelieves in an after-life?
5 Where in the poem does the emotion seem to be most intense?
  What, in your opinion, is the mood of the final line?

Mārtiālis

A number of Martial's epigrams were included in Stage 36. Martial (Marcus Valerius Martialis) was originally a native of Spain, and lived from about A.D.40 to about A.D.104. Pliny said of him: 'He was a talented man, sharp and shrewd, whose epigrams had plenty of salt and vinegar in them.'

I

tū Sētīna quidem semper vel Massica pōnis,
    Pāpyle, sed rūmor tam bona vīna negat:
dīceris hāc factus caelebs quater esse lagōnā.
    nec putō nec crēdō, Pāpyle, nec sitiō.

Sētīna = vīna Sētīna *Setian wine (a good wine)*
Massica = vīna Massica *Massic wine (another good wine)*
pōnis: pōnere *serve*
rūmor *rumour*
negat: negāre *deny, say that ... not*
tam bona vīna negat = negat ea esse tam bona vīna
caelebs *widower*
quater *four times*
lagōnā: lagōna *bottle*
sitiō: sitīre *be thirsty*

Relief showing slaves serving wine

II

Eutrapelus tōnsor dum circuit ōra Lupercī
expingitque genās, altera barba subit.

and he put paint on cheeks, the other beard came up.

Eutrapelus tōnsor dum = dum Eutrapelus tōnsor
circuit = circumit
expingit: expingere *paint, put paint onto*
genās: gena *cheek*
subit: subīre *come up*

III

nūbere Paula cupit nōbīs, ego dūcere Paulam
nōlō: anus est. vellem, sī magis esset anus.

nōbīs = mihi
dūcere *marry*
vellem *I should be willing*

37

Language note

1 From Unit IIB onwards, you have met sentences like these:

sī illud dīxistī, errāvistī.
If you said that, you were wrong.

sī fīlius meus mortuus est, fundum lībertīs lēgō.
If my son is dead, I leave the farm to the freedmen.

The group of words in heavy print is known as a *conditional clause*, and sentences which contain a conditional clause are known as *conditional sentences*.

2 Translate the following examples, and pick out the conditional clause in each sentence:

1 sī Mārcō crēdis, īnsānus es.
2 sī Salvius tālia facinora commīsit, pūniendus est.
3 sī illum servum magnō pretiō ēmistī, vēnālīcius tē dēcēpit.

3 From Stage 33 onwards, you have met sentences in which a conditional clause refers to the future:

sī respexeris, aliquid mīrī vidēbis.
If you look round, you will see something amazing.

sī mīlitēs bene pugnābunt, hostēs terrēbunt.
If the soldiers fight well, they will terrify the enemy.

Notice again how the verb in the Latin conditional clause is put either into the future perfect tense (as in the first example, 'respexeris') or the future tense (as in the second example, 'pugnābunt'). English, however, normally uses a present tense ('look round', 'fight').

Further examples:

1 sī pecūniam meam reppereritis, vōbīs praemium ingēns dabō.
2 sī pompam spectābis, dēlectāberis.
3 sī Virginēs Vestālēs ignem sacrum neglexerint, dī populum Rōmānum pūnient.
4 sī tū mihi nocueris, ego tibi nocēbō.

4 Notice how the word 'nisi' ('unless' or 'if . . . not') is used in conditional clauses:

nisi tacueritis, ē tabernā ēiciēminī.
Unless you are quiet, you will be thrown out of the inn.
   or, in more natural English:
If you aren't quiet, you'll be thrown out of the inn.

Further examples:

1 nisi prīnceps mē līberābit, in exiliō relīquam vītam manēbō.
2 nisi cāveris, custōdēs tē invenient.

5 In Stage 42, you have met a slightly different type of conditional sentence:

sī urbānus essēs, tamen renīdēre usque quāque tē nōllem.
If you were a city-dweller, I still shouldn't want you to be for ever grinning.

sī magis esset anus, Mārtiālis eam dūcere vellet.
If she were older, Martial would be willing to marry her.

Notice that in these sentences, Latin uses the subjunctive and English uses the words 'would' or 'should'.

Ovidius

Stage 39 included a short extract from the *Metamorphoses* of Ovid (Publius Ovidius Naso, 43 B.C. – A.D.17). The following lines are taken from Ovid's *Ars Amatoria* or *Art of Love*, of which the first two sections (or 'books') give advice to young men on how to find, win and keep a girl-friend. Here, Ovid is telling his reader what to do if a girl ignores him and sends his love-messages back without reading them:

> sī nōn accipiet scrīptum inlēctumque remittet,
>> lēctūram spērā prōpositumque tenē.
> tempore <u>difficilēs</u> veniunt ad arātra <u>iuvencī</u>,
>> tempore <u>lenta</u> patī <u>frēna</u> docentur equī.
> <u>ferreus</u> assiduō cōnsūmitur <u>ānulus</u> ūsū,   5
>> interit assiduā vōmer aduncus humō.
> quid magis est saxō dūrum, quid mollius undā?
>> <u>dūra</u> tamen mollī <u>saxa</u> cavantur aquā.
> Pēnelopēn ipsam, perstā modo, tempore vincēs:
>> <u>capta</u> vidēs sērō <u>Pergama</u>, capta tamen.   10

inlēctum: inlēctus *unread*
lēctūram spērā = spērā eam id lēctūram esse
prōpositum *intention, resolution*
tenē: tenēre *keep to, hold on to*
difficilēs: difficilis *obstinate*
arātra: arātrum *plough*
iuvencī: iuvencus *bullock, young ox*
lenta: lentus *supple*
frēna *reins*
5 ferreus *iron, made of iron*
assiduō: assiduus *continual*
interit: interīre *wear away, wear out*
vōmer *ploughshare*
cavantur: cavāre *hollow out*
Pēnelopēn: *Greek accusative of* Pēnelopē
10 sērō *late, after a long time*

Illustration from a mediaeval manuscript showing Doctor Ovid Lecturing in a Garden of Lovers

1 What is Ovid's advice to the young man? What arguments does he use to support his advice? Do these arguments actually prove Ovid's point? If not, why does he include them?
2 Using a Classical Dictionary if necessary, find out what or where Pergama (line 10) was, and how long a time is referred to by 'sērō' (line 10). Then (using the dictionary again if needed), find out who Penelope was, and suggest reasons why Ovid uses her as his example in line 9.

Vergilius

The chief work of Virgil (Publius Vergilius Maro, 70–19 B.C.) was the *Aeneid*, an epic poem in nearly ten thousand lines, which related the adventures of Aeneas, the legendary ancestor of the Romans. The following lines form a tiny but complete episode in this huge poem; Aeneas, who is describing his earlier wanderings to Dido, Queen of Carthage, tells of a storm that hit him and his Trojan companions as they sailed westwards from the island of Crete.

postquam altum tenuēre ratēs nec iam amplius ūllae
appārent terrae, caelum undique et undique pontus,
tum mihi <u>caeruleus</u> suprā caput adstitit <u>imber</u>
noctem hiememque ferēns, et inhorruit unda tenebrīs.
continuō ventī volvunt mare magnaque surgunt   5
aequora, dispersī iactāmur gurgite vāstō;
involvēre diem nimbī et nox ūmida caelum
abstulit, ingeminant abruptīs nūbibus ignēs.
excutimur cursū et <u>caecīs</u> errāmus in <u>undīs</u>.
ipse* diem noctemque negat discernere caelō   10
nec meminisse viae <u>mediā</u> Palinūrus* in <u>undā</u>.
<u>trēs adeō incertōs</u> caecā cālīgine <u>sōlēs</u>
errāmus pelagō, totidem sine sīdere noctēs.
<u>quārtō</u> terra <u>diē</u> prīmum sē attollere tandem
vīsa, aperīre procul montēs ac volvere fūmum.   15

*These two words go closely together.

altum *deep sea, open sea*
tenuēre = tenuērunt: tenēre *occupy,*
  be upon
ratēs: ratis *boat*
amplius *any more*
caeruleus *dark*
adstitit: adstāre *stand*
imber *storm-cloud*
noctem: nox *darkness*
hiemem: hiems *storm*
inhorruit: inhorrēscere *shudder*
5 continuō *immediately*
volvunt: volvere *(line 5) set rolling,*
  turn to billows
dispersī: dispergere *scatter*
gurgite: gurges *whirlpool, swirling water*
involvēre = involvērunt: involvere
  envelop, swallow up
ūmida: ūmidus *rainy, stormy*
ingeminant: ingemināre *redouble*

abruptīs: abrumpere *split, tear apart*
ignēs: ignis *lightning*
excutimur: excutere *shake off,*
  drive violently off
caecīs: caecus *(line 9) unseen*
  (literally 'blind')
10 negat = negat sē posse
discernere *distinguish*
Palinūrus *Palinurus (the Trojans'*
  helmsman)
trēs adeō *as many as three, three entire*
caecā: caecus *(line 12) impenetrable*
cālīgine: cālīgō *darkness, gloom*
sōlēs: sōl *day*
pelagō: pelagus *sea*
totidem *the same number*
prīmum *for the first time*
sē attollere *raise itself, rise up*
15 aperīre *reveal*
volvere *(line 15) send rolling upwards*

A 1 Where were the boats when the storm broke?
  2 Were they within sight of land? What were they surrounded by?
  3 What was the first sign of trouble? Where was it? What did it bring with it?
  4 What did the winds do to the ocean (line 5)? What happened to the Trojans?
  5 What was the effect of the rain-clouds (line 7)? What further detail of the storm does Virgil give in line 8?
  6 What was the next thing that happened to the Trojans?
  7 What does Palinurus say he cannot do in line 10? What other difficulty is he having?
  8 For how long did the Trojans wander? What was unusual about the 'noctēs' (line 13)?
  9 When did they finally catch sight of land?
  10 List the three stages in which the Trojans got an increasingly detailed view of land in lines 14–15.

(continued)

Ships from the Low Ham mosaic

B1 What idea is most strongly emphasised in lines 1–2? In what way is it relevant to the storm that follows?

2 What does Virgil suggest in line 4 about the appearance of the sea?

3 Compare the following three translations of 'continuō ventī volvunt mare magnaque surgunt aequora' (lines 5–6) by a seventeenth-century poet, a twentieth-century scholar and a twentieth-century poet:

(a) 'The ruffling winds the foamy billows raise.'

(John Dryden, 1697)

(b) 'The winds quickly set the sea-surface rolling and lifted it in great waves.' *(W.F. Jackson Knight, 1956)*

(c) 'Winds billowed the sea at once, the seas were running high.' *(C. Day Lewis, 1952)*

Which of the translations is most successful in conveying the feeling of Virgil's words? Which gives the most vivid picture?

4 What is the point of 'ipse' (line 10)?

5 Compare the following translations of lines 12–13:

(a) 'Three starless nights the doubtful navy strays
Without distinction, and three sunless days.' *(Dryden)*

(b) 'For three whole days, hard though they were to reckon, and as many starless nights, we wandered in the sightless murk over the ocean.' *(Jackson Knight)*

(c) 'Three days, three days befogged and unsighted by the darkness,
We wandered upon the sea, three starless nights we wandered.' *(Day Lewis)*

Language note

1 In Stage 39, you met sentences in which one noun-and-adjective phrase is placed inside another one:

cōnstitit ante *oculōs* **pulchra puella** *meōs*.
A beautiful girl stood before my eyes.

2 In Stage 42, you have met sentences like this, in which two noun-and-adjective phrases are intertwined with each other:

dura tamen **mollī** *saxa* cavantur **aquā**.
Nevertheless, hard stones are hollowed out by soft water.

Further examples:
1 **parva** necat morsū *spatiōsum* **vīpera** *taurum*. (*Ovid*)
2 *frīgidus* **ingentēs** irrigat *imber* **agrōs**.

> morsū: morsus *fangs*
> spatiōsum: spatiōsus *huge*
> vīpera *viper*
> frīgidus *cold*
> irrigat: irrigāre *to water*

3 Compare the intertwining of the noun-and-adjective phrases in paragraph 2 with the intertwining of rhymed lines in such verse as the following:

> The curfew tolls the knell of parting *day*;
> The lowing herd winds slowly o'er the **lea**;
> The ploughman homeward plods his weary *way*,
> And leaves the world to darkness and to **me**.

4 In each of the following examples, pick out the Latin adjectives and say which nouns they are describing:

1 impiaque aeternam timuērunt saecula noctem. (*Virgil*)
   The evil generations were in fear of endless night.
2 molliaque immītēs fīxit in ōra manūs. (*Propertius*)
   It fastened its cruel hands on her soft face.

5 Translate the following examples:

1 *Poets and poverty*
   Maeonidēs nūllās ipse relīquit opēs. (*Ovid*)

2 *A poet's epitaph on himself*
   hīc iacet immītī cōnsūmptus morte Tibullus. (*Tibullus*)

3 *Ovid congratulates Cupid on his forthcoming victory procession*
   haec tibi magnificus pompa triumphus erit. (*Ovid*)

   Maeonidēs = Homer, the greatest of Greek poets

Exercises

1 Notice again that there are often several different ways of translating a Latin word, and that you always have to choose the most suitable translation for the particular sentence you are working on.

For example, the vocabulary at the end of the book gives the following meanings for 'ēmittō', 'petō' and 'referō':

ēmittō – throw, send out
petō – make for, attack; seek, beg for, ask for
referō – bring back, carry, deliver, tell, report

Translate the following sentences, using suitable translations of 'ēmittō', 'petō' and 'referō' chosen from the above list:

1 dux trīgintā equitēs ēmīsit.
2 duo latrōnēs, fūstibus armātī, senem petīvērunt.
3 nūntius tōtam rem rettulit.
4 nautae, tempestāte perterritī, portum petēbant.
5 subitō mīlitēs hastās ēmittere coepērunt.
6 mercātor nihil ex Āfricā rettulit.
7 captīvus, genibus ducis haerēns, lībertātem petīvit.

2 Complete each sentence with the right word and then translate.

1 corpora mīlitum mortuōrum crās . . . . . . (sepeliētur, sepelientur)
2 nōlīte timēre, cīvēs! ā vestrīs equitibus . . . . . . (dēfendēris, dēfendēminī)
3 sī custōdēs mē cēperint, ego sine dubiō . . . . . . (interficiar, interficiēmur)
4 fābula nōtissima in theātrō . . . . . . (agētur, agentur)
5 difficile erit tibi nāvigāre; nam ventīs et tempestātibus . . . . . . (impediēris, impediēminī)
6 nisi fortiter pugnābimus, ab hostibus . . . . . . (vincar, vincēmur)

3 In each pair of sentences, translate sentence 'a', then change it from a direct statement to an indirect statement by completing sentence 'b', and translate again.

For example: a equī hodiē exercentur.
               b audiō equ. . . hodiē exerc. . . .

Translated and completed, this becomes:

a equī hodiē exercentur. The horses are being exercised today.
b audiō equōs hodiē exercērī.
   I hear that the horses are being exercised today.

In sentences 1–3, a present passive infinitive is required. For examples of the way in which this infinitive is formed, see paragraph 6 on p.195.

1a patrōnus ā clientibus cotīdiē salūtātur.
1b sciō patrōn. . . ā clientibus cotīdiē salūt. . . .
2a duae puellae in hōc carcere retinentur.
2b centuriō putat du. . . puell. . . in hōc carcere retin. . . .
3a vīlla nova prope montem aedificātur.
3b agricola dīcit . . . . prope montem . . . . . .

In sentences 4–6, a future active infinitive is required. For examples of the way in which this infinitive is formed, see paragraph 9 on page 195. Note that the first part of this infinitive (e.g. 'parātūrus' in 'parātūrus esse') changes its ending to agree with the noun it describes.

For example: a puella ad nōs scrībet.
               b spērō puell. . . ad nōs scrīp. . . . .

Translated and completed, this becomes:

a puella ad nōs scrībet. The girl will write to us.
b spērō puellam ad nōs scrīptūram esse.
   I hope that the girl will write to us.

4a gladiātor crās pugnābit.
4b exīstimō gladiāt. . . crās pugnā. . . . .
5a nostrī mīlitēs vincent.
5b dux crēdit nostr. . . mīl. . . vic. . . . .
6a discipulī crās recitābunt.
6b rhētor pollicētur . . . . . crās . . . .

Time chart

This time chart shows the dates of the five Roman poets represented in Stage 42, together with some events in Roman history.

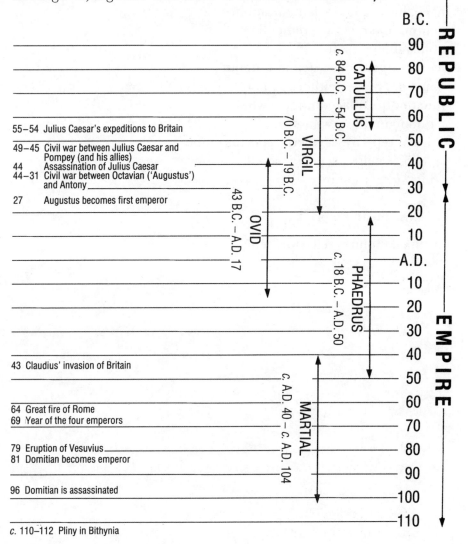

B.C.

REPUBLIC

90
80 — CATULLUS *c. 84 B.C. – 54 B.C.*
70
60
50 — VIRGIL *70 B.C. – 19 B.C.*
40
30
27   Augustus becomes first emperor
20 — OVID *43 B.C. – A.D. 17*
10
A.D.
10 — PHAEDRUS *c. 18 B.C. – A.D. 50*
20
30
40

55–54 Julius Caesar's expeditions to Britain

49–45 Civil war between Julius Caesar and
       Pompey (and his allies)
44   Assassination of Julius Caesar
44–31 Civil war between Octavian ('Augustus')
       and Antony

43 Claudius' invasion of Britain

64 Great fire of Rome
69 Year of the four emperors

79 Eruption of Vesuvius
81 Domitian becomes emperor

96 Domitian is assassinated

50 — MARTIAL *c. A.D. 40 – c. A.D. 104*
60
70
80
90
100
110

EMPIRE

c. 110–112 Pliny in Bithynia

Vocabulary checklist

adloquor, adloquī, adlocūtus sum – speak to, address
caecus, caeca, caecum – (1) blind, (2) invisible, unseen
genū, genūs – knee
longē – far, a long way
lūgeō, lūgēre, lūxī – lament, mourn
meminī, meminisse – remember
mollis, molle – soft
nec (*also spelt* neque) – and not, nor
   nec . . . nec – neither . . . nor
quīcumque, quaecumque – whoever
   quodcumque – whatever
reperiō, reperīre, repperī, repertus – find
sepeliō, sepelīre, sepelīvī, sepultus – bury
sīdus, sīderis – star

Give the meaning of:

caecitās, mollīre, repertor, sepulcrum

ūnivira

mātrōna Ephesia

Versions of the following story have been found all over the world. Its first appearance in Latin is in the fables of Phaedrus, and it was particularly popular in the Middle Ages; numerous versions exist in Latin, French, Italian, English, German, Russian, Chinese and Hebrew, and in 1946 it was turned into a stage play (*A Phoenix Too Frequent*) by Christopher Fry. The following version is based closely on the *Satyrica* by Petronius, who is probably the same man as Gaius Petronius Arbiter, Nero's 'arbiter ēlegantiae' (adviser on taste and fashion) who was eventually ordered by Nero to commit suicide in A.D. 66.

Facades of two Roman 'house' tombs

I

mātrōna quaedam, quae Ephesī habitābat, ita nōta erat propter
pudīcitiam ut ab omnibus fēminīs illīus locī laudārētur. haec ergō,
marītō mortuō, tantō dolōre affecta est ut sine eō vīvere nollet; nōn
modo fūnus eius, ut mōs erat, passīs crīnibus et veste scissā
prōsecūta est, sed etiam servīs imperāvit ut ipsa in sepulcrō eōdem   5
ūnā cum corpore marītī clauderētur. ibi corpus eius custōdīre ac
flēre tōtās noctēs diēsque coepit; neque cibum neque vīnum
accipere volēbat; precēs parentum, propinquōrum, etiam
magistrātuum, repudiāvit; cōnstituerat enim mortem inediā iuxtā
corpus marītī obīre.   10

quīntum iam diem mātrōna sine cibō agēbat, cīvibus
affirmantibus eam vērum pudīcitiae amōrisque exemplum omnibus
uxōribus praestitisse.

interim lēgātus prōvinciae trēs latrōnēs iussit crucibus affīgī
prope illud sepulcrum ubi mātrōna lūgēbat. proximā ergō nocte,   15
mīles quīdam, ad crucēs custōdiendās ēlēctus, nē corpora ad
sepultūram ā propinquīs latrōnum dētraherentur, lūmine inter
sepulcra cōnspectō et gemitū lūgentis audītō, statim contendit ad
cognōscendum quid ibi fieret. sepulcrum ingressus, vīsāque
mātrōnā pulcherrimā, attonitus cōnstitit; deinde, cum corpus   20
marītī vīdisset lacrimāsque mātrōnae, intellēxit eam dēsīderium
mortuī nōn posse patī; ad sepulcrum igitur cēnulam suam attulit,
coepitque hortārī lūgentem nē in dolōre inānī persevērāret;

Ephesī: Ephesus *Ephesus (city in Asia Minor)*
ita *so*
pudīcitiam: pudīcitia *chastity, virtue, purity*
fūnus *funeral procession*
passīs: passus *loose, dishevelled*
prōsecūta est: prōsequī *follow, escort*
propinquōrum: propinquus *relative*
repudiāvit: repudiāre *reject*
inediā: inedia *starvation*
crucibus: crux *cross*
crucibus affīgī: cruce affīgere *nail to a cross, crucify*
sepultūram: sepultūra *burial*
lūmine: lūmen *light*
dēsīderium *loss, longing*
cēnulam: cēnula *little supper*

omnibus enim mortālibus tandem pereundum esse. 'quid tibi
25 prōderit' inquit 'sī inediā perieris, sī tē vīvam sepelīveris?' et cibum
vīnumque mātrōnae obtulit. quae, inediā paene cōnfecta, tandem
passa est superārī pertināciam suam.

at mīles, quī mātrōnam esse pulcherrimam prius animadverterat,
in sepulcrō multās hōrās manēbat, et eīsdem blanditiīs pudīcitiam
30 eius aggredī coepit, quibus eam anteā incitāverat ut cibum
acciperet. multa dē pulchritūdine eius locūtus est, multa dē amōre
suō. postrēmō mīles mātrōnae persuāsit ut illam noctem ibi in
sepulcrō sēcum iacēret.

quid . . . prōderit? *what good*   pertināciam: pertinācia *obstinacy, determination*
   will it do?   aggredī *assail, make an attempt on*
passa est: patī *allow*

II

mediā autem nocte, cum mīles et fēmina in sepulcrō ūnā iacērent,
parentēs ūnīus latrōnum crucibus affīxōrum, ubi vīdērunt nēminem

mātrōnae quid accidisset exposuit. (lines 6–7)

crucēs custōdīre, corpus clam dē cruce dētractum ad rīte sepeliendum abstulērunt.

postrīdiē māne mīles, ē sepulcrō ēgressus, ubi vīdit ūnam sine 5 corpore crucem esse, supplicium ultimum sibi verēbātur. mātrōnae quid accidisset exposuit; negāvit sē iūdicis sententiam exspectātūrum esse; potius sē ipsum neglegentiam suam pūnitūrum esse. 'trāde mihi pugiōnem' inquit 'ut ego hīc in marītī tuī sepulcrō moriar atque sepeliar.' mātrōna tamen, quae nōn minus misericors 10 quam pudīca erat, 'nē illud deī sinant' inquit 'ut eōdem tempore corpora duōrum mihi cārissimōrum hominum spectem. mālō mortuum impendere quam vīvum occīdere.' quibus verbīs dictīs, imperāvit ut ex arcā corpus marītī suī tollerētur atque illī quae vacābat crucī affigerētur. itaque mīles cōnsiliō prūdentissimae 15 mātrōnae libenter ūsus est, et postrīdiē populus mīrābātur quō modō mortuus in crucem ascendisset.

rīte *properly*
neglegentiam: neglegentia *carelessness*
minus *less*
misericors *tender-hearted, full of pity*
pudīca: pudīcus *chaste, virtuous*
nē illud deī sinant! *heaven forbid! (literally 'may the gods not allow it')*
impendere *make use of*
arcā: arca *coffin*
vacābat: vacāre *be unoccupied*

1 What happened outside the tomb in the middle of the night?
2 What did the soldier see next morning when he came out of the tomb? What did he fear would happen to him? Rather than wait for this fate, what did he say he would do?
3 What did he ask the lady to do? What were his intentions?
4 What reason did the lady give for objecting violently to the soldier's request?
5 Whom did she mean by 'mortuum' and 'vīvum' (line 13)?
6 What did she tell the soldier to do?
7 Why were the people puzzled next day?
8 Do you approve of the lady's decision?
9 Why do you think this story has been so popular and been retold so often?

Language note

1 Study the following examples:

lēgātus prōvinciam tam bene regēbat ut ab omnibus **dīligerētur**.

The governor ruled the province so well that he was loved by everybody.

nesciēbāmus utrum ā sociīs nostrīs **adiuvārēmur** an **impedīrēmur**.

We did not know whether we were being helped or hindered by our companions.

The form of the verb in heavy print is the *imperfect subjunctive passive*.

Further examples:

1 intellegere nōn poteram quārē fēminae līberīque in oppidō relinquerentur.

2 tam ignāvus erat coquus ut ā cēterīs servīs contemnerētur.

3 ferōciter resistēbāmus ne ā barbarīs superārēmur.

2 Compare the active and passive forms of the imperfect subjunctive of 'portō':

imperfect subjunctive active	*imperfect subjunctive passive*
portārem	portārer
portārēs	portārēris
portāret	portārētur
portārēmus	portārēmur
portārētis	portārēminī
portārent	portārentur

Imperfect subjunctive passive forms of 'doceō', 'trahō' and 'audiō' are given on p.193.

3 Study the following examples:

tantus erat fragor ut omnēs nautae **verērentur**.
So great was the crash that all the sailors were afraid.

iūdex mē rogāvit num **mentīrer**.
The judge asked me whether I was lying.

The words in heavy print are *imperfect subjunctive* forms of *deponent* verbs.

Further examples:

1 cum ēgrederēmur, amīcus meus subitō cōnstitit.
2 pontifex cīvibus imperāvit ut deōs immortālēs precārentur.

Imperfect subjunctive forms of the deponent verbs 'cōnor', 'vereor', etc. are given on p.198.

Tūria

The funeral ceremony of a Roman noble often included a 'laudātiō' or speech in praise of the dead person, which might later be inscribed on the tomb. The following passages are based on one of these speeches, which survives (in an incomplete form) on a number of stone fragments. It is not known who the speaker was but we refer to him in this Stage as 'Vespillo', and to his wife (the subject of the inscription) as 'Turia'. As often in such speeches, the dead woman is addressed directly by her husband as 'you', as if her 'mānēs' (departed spirit) could hear the speech or read it on the inscription.

I

Vespillo and Turia lived through a time of great violence, when the Romans' system of republican government was collapsing in ruins, and Italy was torn by a series of horrific civil wars. Vespillo's laudatio in praise of Turia mentions three separate incidents which reflect the violence of the period. The first occurred on the eve of Vespillo's and Turia's wedding:

orba repente facta es ante nūptiārum diem, utrōque parente in rūsticā sōlitūdine occīsīs. per tē maximē (quod ego in Macedoniam abieram) mors parentum nōn inulta mānsit. tū officium tuum tantā dīligentiā et tantā pietāte ēgistī, efflāgitandō et investīgandō et
5 ulcīscendō, ut ego ipse, sī adfuissem, nōn amplius efficere potuissem.

orba *orphan*
sōlitūdine: sōlitūdō *lonely place*
pietāte: pietās *piety, family feeling*
efflāgitandō *by demanding justice*

investīgandō: investīgāre *investigate*
ulcīscendō: ulcīscī *take vengeance*
nōn . . . potuissem *would not have been able*

In 49 B.C., civil war broke out between Julius Caesar and Pompey the Great. Vespillo had to flee for his life, and he describes the help he received from Turia on that occasion:

mihi fugientī tū maximō auxiliō fuistī; omne aurum margarītaque
corporī tuō dētracta trādidistī quae ferrem mēcum; callidē dēceptīs
inimīcīs nostrīs, mihi absentī servōs et pecūniam et alia bona
subinde praebuistī.   10

margarīta: margarītum *pearl*   callidē *cleverly*
dētracta: dētrahere *take off*   subinde *regularly*

tanta erat virtūs tua ut mē dēfendere assiduē cōnārēris. (lines 14–15)

In 43 B.C., civil war was again raging and Vespillo was in still
greater danger; his name was published in a list of 'public enemies'
and a reward was offered for killing him. Vespillo evidently wanted
to make a bold dash for escape, but Turia persuaded him otherwise:

ubi amīcī nostrī mē ad imminentia perīcula vītanda excitābant, tuō
cōnsiliō servātus sum. tū enim mē audāciā meā efferrī nōn passa es,
sed latebrās tūtās parāvistī; mē inter cameram et tēctum cubiculī
cēlātum ab exitiō servāvistī. tanta erat virtūs tua ut mē dēfendere
assiduē cōnārēris, nōn sine magnō perīculō tuō.   15

efferrī: efferre *carry away*   cameram: camera *ceiling*

II

After the civil wars were over, Vespillo and Turia could at last enjoy
peace and prosperity. But in their private life, they had one cause of
great unhappiness:

pācātō orbe terrārum, restitūtā rēpūblicā, tandem contigit nōbīs ut
temporibus quiētīs fruerēmur. magis ac magis līberōs optābāmus,
quōs diū sors nōbīs invīderat. sī precibus nostrīs fortūna fāvisset,
quid ultrā cupīvissēmus? annīs tamen lābentibus, spēs nostrae
5 ēvānēscēbant.

diffīdēns fēcunditātī tuae et dolēns orbitāte meā, timēbās nē ego,
tenendō tē in mātrimōniō, spem habendī līberōs dēpōnerem atque
ideō fierem īnfēlīx; dīvortium igitur prōpōnere ausa es. dīxistī tē
vacuam domum nostram alicui fēminae fēcundiōrī trāditūram esse;
10 tē ipsam mihi dignam uxōrem quaesītūram, ac futūrōs līberōs prō
tuīs habitūram esse.

quibus verbīs audītīs, adeō cōnsiliō tuō incēnsus sum ut vix
redderer mihi. num mihi erat tanta cupiditās aut necessitās habendī
līberōs, ut proptereā fidem fallerem, mūtārem certa dubiīs? sed quid
15 plūra? mānsistī apud mē; nōn enim cēdere tibi sine dēdecore meō et
commūnī dolōre poteram.

pācātō: pacāre *make peaceful*	fēcundiōrī: fēcundus *fertile*
rēpūblicā: rēspūblica *'the republic' (i.e. republican government, which Augustus, the first Roman emperor, claimed to have restored)*	futūrōs: futūrus *future*
	prō *as*
	habitūram esse: habēre *regard*
contigit nōbīs ut. . . *it was our good fortune that. . . we had the good fortune to. . .*	redderer mihi: sibi reddī *be restored to one's senses, be restored to oneself*
optābāmus: optāre *pray for, long for*	cupiditās *desire*
sors *fate, one's lot*	necessitās *need*
invīderat: invīdēre *begrudge*	proptereā *for that reason*
ultrā *more, further*	fidem fallerem: fidem fallere *break one's word*
cupīvissēmus *would have wanted*	
lābentibus: lābī *pass by, slide by*	dubiīs: dubius *uncertain*
ēvānēscēbant: ēvānēscere *die away, vanish*	quid plūra? *why say more?*
fēcunditātī: fēcunditās *fertility*	dēdecore: dēdecus *disgrace*
orbitāte: orbitās *childlessness*	commūnī: commūnis *shared (by both of us)*
dēpōnerem: dēpōnere *give up, abandon*	
dīvortium *divorce*	

III

Vespillo praises Turia for being faithful, obedient and loving; he says she was conscientious in her weaving and spinning (two traditional tasks of Roman wives), elegant without being showy, and religious without being superstitious. Finally, he speaks of Turia's death and his own bereavement:

contigit nōbīs ut ad annum XXXXI sine ūllā discordiā mātrimōnium nostrum perdūcerētur. iūstius erat mihi, ut maiōrī annīs, priōrī mortem obīre. tū tamen praecucurristī; mihi dolōrem dēsīderiumque lēgāvistī. aliquandō dēspērō; sed exemplō tuō doctus, dolōrī resistere cōnor. fortūna mihi nōn omnia ēripuit; 5 adhūc enim est mihi memoria tuī.

    optō ut dī mānēs tē quiētam iacēre patiantur atque tueantur.

perdūcerētur: perdūcere *continue*
iūstius erat *it would have been fairer, more proper*
praecucurristī: praecurrere *go on ahead, run ahead*
dī mānēs *the spirits of the dead*
tueantur: tuērī *watch over, protect*

Language note

1 In Stage 41, you met the gerund used with 'ad' meaning 'for the purpose of . . .' in sentences like these:

ego et frāter meus ad **certandum** missī sumus.
My brother and I were sent for the purpose of competing.
  or, in more natural English:
My brother and I were sent to compete.

In these examples, the gerund is in the *accusative* case, because it is being used with the preposition 'ad'.

2 In Stage 43, you have met the *genitive* and *ablative* cases of the gerund, used in sentences like these:

genitive nūlla spēs **habendī** līberōs iam manet.
  No hope of having children remains now.

in omnibus āthlētīs ingēns cupīdō **vincendī** inest.
  In all athletes, there is an immense love of winning.

ablative **investīgandō**, Tūria cognōvit quid accidisset.
  By investigating, Turia found out what had happened.

nūntius, celerrimē **currendō**, Rōmam prīmā lūce pervēnit.
  The messenger, by running very fast, reached Rome at dawn.

The cases of the gerund are listed in full on p.195.

3 Further examples of the gerund used in the accusative, genitive and ablative cases:

1 cōnsul ōs ad respondendum aperuit; nihil tamen dīcere poterat.
2 optimam occāsiōnem effugiendī nunc habēmus.
3 ad bene vīvendum, necesse est magnās opēs possidēre.
4 cantandō et saltandō, puellae hospitēs dēlectāvērunt.
5 poētae nihil dē arte nāvigandī sciunt.
6 et Agricola et mīlitēs magnam glōriam adeptī sunt, ille imperandō, hī pārendō.

Exercises

1 Match each word in the left-hand column with a word of similar meaning taken from the right-hand column.

For example: aedificāre exstruere

aedificāre	ergō
epistula	supplicium
festīnāre	autem
fīdus	colloquium
igitur	interficere
metus	litterae
nihilōminus	exstruere
occīdere	iterum
poena	contendere
rūrsus	coniūnx
sermō	timor
uxor	fidēlis

2 Complete each sentence with the most suitable word from the list below, and then translate.

erit, reperiēmus, necābunt, gaudēbit, poteritis, dabit

1 sī mēcum domum revēneris, frāter meus . . . . . .
2 sī dīligenter quaesīverimus, equum āmissum mox . . . . . .
3 sī mea fīlia huic senī nūpserit, semper miserrima . . . . . .
4 mīlitēs sī urbem oppugnāverint, multōs cīvēs . . . . . .
5 sī patrōnus meus tē ad cēnam invītāverit, vīnum optimum tibi
   . . . . . .
6 sī ad forum hodiē ieritis, pompam spectāre . . . . . .

3 Translate each sentence into Latin by selecting correctly from the list of Latin words.

1 We were being hindered by shortage of water.

    inopiae   aquae   impediēmur

    inopiā   aquā   impediēbāmur

2 They were afraid that the robbers would return next day.

    timēbant   nōn   latrōnī   postrīdiē   revenīrent

    timēbunt   nē   latrōnēs   cotīdiē   reveniēbant

3 As the enemy approached, I heard strange noises.

    hostibus   appropinquantibus   sonitum   mīrōs   audītī

    hostēs   appropinquantēs   sonitūs   mīrum   audīvī

4 We tried to set out at first light.

    prīmam   lūcem   proficīscī   cōnātus   erāmus

    prīmā   lūce   proficīscimur   cōnātī   sumus

5 Why do you promise what you cannot carry out?

    cūr   pollicēmur   id quod   suscipere   nōn   vultis

    ubi   pollicēminī   is quī   efficere   nusquam   potestis

Language note

1 Study the following examples:

dīcō testem mentīrī.

I say that the witness is lying.

rogāvimus quis cibum relīquum cōnsūmpsisset.

We asked who had eaten the rest of the food.

dux **nūntiāvit** sociōs nōbīs mox subventūrōs esse.

The leader announced that our companions would soon come to our help.

Each sentence contains

1 a *verb of speaking, asking, etc.*, e.g. 'dīcō', 'rogāvimus',

2 an indirect statement or indirect question.

Notice that in each example, the verb of speaking, asking, etc. is placed at the *beginning* of the sentence.

2 Compare the examples in paragraph 1 with the following sentences:

multōs barbarōs **dīcimus** in proeliō cecidisse.
We say that many barbarians fell in the battle.

quid prīnceps cupiat, numquam **sciō**.
I never know what the emperor wants.

haruspex deōs nōbīs favēre **affirmāvit**.
The soothsayer declared that the gods favoured us.

In these examples, the verb of speaking, asking, knowing, etc. is placed in the *middle* or at the *end* of the sentence.

3 Read through each of the following sentences, noticing the position of the verb of speaking, asking, etc.; then translate the sentence.

1 nūntius hostēs in eōdem locō manēre dīcit.
2 quārē familiam convocāverīs, omnīnō ignōrō.
3 togam tuam vīdī scissam esse.
4 fabrōs opus iam perfēcisse audīvimus.
5 ubi rēx exercitum suum collocāvisset, incertum erat.
6 ego vērō et gaudeō et gaudēre mē dīcō. (*Pliny*)

    convocāverīs: convocāre *call together*

Divorce and remarriage

The Romans believed that the first divorce in Rome took place in about 230 B.C., when the senator Spurius Carvilius, although he loved his wife deeply, divorced her because she was unable to have children.

The story of Carvilius' divorce may be partly or entirely fiction; it certainly cannot have happened in 230 B.C., because by that date laws about divorce had already been in existence for two hundred years. But the reason for Carvilius' divorce is a very typical one; it is the same reason as the one put forward by 'Turia' on p.60. Roman marriage was supposed to produce children; and when a marriage ended in divorce, childlessness was the reason in many cases.

There were, of course, many other reasons why a husband or wife, or both, might decide to end a marriage. Continual quarrelling and disagreement, or objectionable behaviour such as unfaithfulness or brutality, could all lead to divorce. Divorces were sometimes arranged for political reasons, especially in the first century D.C.; for example, an ambitious man might divorce his wife in order to remarry into a wealthier or more powerful family.

If a wife was under the legal control ('manus') of her husband, he could divorce her but she could not divorce him. But if the marriage had taken place 'sine manū' and the wife was free from her husband's legal control, both husband and wife had the power to divorce the other.

The only thing necessary for divorce, in the eyes of the law, was that the husband or wife, or both, had to demonstrate that they regarded the marriage as finished and intended to live separately in future; if one partner moved out of the marital house and began to live somewhere else, nothing else was legally required. But the husband and wife could also follow certain procedures, in action or in writing, to emphasise that they intended their separation to be permanent. In the early years of Rome's history, a husband could divorce his wife by addressing her, in front of witnesses, with the phrase 'tuās rēs tibi agitō' ('take your things and go'), or by

Part of the inscription on which the story of Vespillo and Turia is based

demanding the return of the keys of the house. By the first century A.D., these picturesque customs were no longer in common use; instead, one partner might send the other a written notification of divorce, or the husband and wife might make a joint declaration, either spoken before witnesses or put in writing, as in the following agreement, which was discovered on an Egyptian papyrus:

'Zois daughter of Heraclides and Antipater son of Zeno agree that they have separated from each other, ending the marriage which they made in the seventeenth year of Augustus Caesar, and Zois acknowledges that she has received from Antipater by hand the goods which he was previously given as dowry, namely clothes to the value of 120 drachmas and a pair of gold earrings. Hereafter it shall be lawful both for Zois to marry another man and for Antipater to marry another woman without either of them being answerable.'

It is difficult to discover how common divorce was in Rome. Among the richer classes, it may perhaps have reached a peak in the first century B.C., and then declined during the following century.

(Nothing is known about the divorce rate of Rome's poor.) Some Roman writers speak as if divorce was rare in early Roman history but common in their own times. Juvenal says of one woman that she 'wears out her wedding veil as she flits from husband to husband, getting through eight men in five years'. But it is impossible to tell how much truth there is in Juvenal's description, and how much is exaggeration; nor do we know how typical such women were. Any husband who was thinking of divorcing his wife had to bear in mind that he would have to return all or part of her 'dōs' or dowry (payment of money or property made by the bride's family to the husband at the time of marriage), as in the papyrus document quoted above; this may have made some husbands have second thoughts about going ahead with the divorce.

Remarriage after divorce was frequent. 'They marry in order to divorce; they divorce in order to marry,' said one Roman writer. Remarriage was also common after the death of a husband or wife, especially if the surviving partner was still young. For example, a twelve-year-old girl who married an elderly husband might find herself widowed in her late teens, and if a wife died in childbirth, a man might become a widower within a year or two of the marriage, perhaps while he himself was still in his early twenties; in this situation, the idea of remarriage was often attractive and sensible for the surviving partner.

Nevertheless, the Romans had a special respect for women who married only once. They were known as 'ūnivirae' and had certain religious privileges; for a long time, they were the only people allowed to worship at the temple of Pudicitia (Chastity), and it was a Roman tradition for a bride to be undressed by 'ūnivirae' on her wedding night. Some women took great pride in the idea that they were remaining faithful to a dead husband, and the description 'ūnivira' is often found on tombstones.

The idea of being a 'ūnivira' is sometimes used by Roman authors for the purposes of a story or poem. For example, the lady in the story on pp. 52–5 is so determined to remain loyal to her dead husband that she refuses to go on living after his death, until a twist in the story persuades her to change her mind. A similar idea provides the starting-point of Book Four of Virgil's poem, the

Aeneid. In an earlier part of the poem, the Trojan prince Aeneas has landed in Africa and been hospitably received by Dido, Queen of Carthage. The two are strongly attracted to each other, and Dido is very much moved by Aeneas' account of his adventures (a short extract from his story appeared in Stage 42, p.42). Aeneas, however, is under orders from the gods to seek a new home in Italy, while Dido has sworn an oath of loyalty to her dead husband, binding herself like a Roman 'ūnivira' never to marry again; and so, although a love affair quickly develops between Dido and Aeneas, it ends in disaster and death.

Vocabulary checklist

aggredior, aggredī, aggressus sum – attack, make an attempt on
bona, bonōrum – goods, property
contemnō, contemnere, contempsī, contemptus – despise, disregard
efferō, efferre, extulī, ēlātus – carry out, carry away
   ēlātus – carried away, excited
fīdus, fīda, fīdum – loyal, trustworthy
inopia, inopiae – shortage, scarcity, poverty
iuxtā – next to
magistrātus, magistrātūs – elected government official
negō, negāre, negāvī – deny, say . . . not
possideō, possidēre, possēdī, possessus – possess
propter – because of
repente – suddenly
ulcīscor, ulcīscī, ultus sum – avenge, take revenge on

Give the meaning of:

opēs, repentīnus, ultiō, ultor

Daedalus et Īcarus

The following story is taken from Ovid's poem, the *Metamorphoses*, an immense collection of myths, legends and folk-tales which begins with the creation of the world and ends in Ovid's own day.

I

Daedalus, who was famous as a craftsman and inventor, came from Athens to the island of Crete at the invitation of King Minos. The king, however, quarrelled with him and refused to allow him and his son Icarus to leave the island.

Daedalus intereā Crētēn longumque perōsus
exilium, tāctusque locī nātālis amōre,
clausus erat pelagō. 'terrās licet' inquit 'et undās
obstruat, at caelum certē patet; ībimus illāc!
omnia possideat, nōn possidet āera Mīnōs.'   5
dīxit et <u>ignōtās</u> animum dīmittit in <u>artēs,</u>
nātūramque novat. nam pōnit in ōrdine pennās,
ut clīvō crēvisse putēs; sīc <u>rūstica</u> quondam
<u>fistula</u> disparibus paulātim surgit avēnīs.

Crētēn: *accusative of* Crētē *Crete*
perōsus *hating*
tāctus: tangere *touch, move*
locī nātālis: locus nātālis *place of birth, native land*
clausus erat: claudere *cut off*
licet *although*
obstruat *he (i.e. Minos) may block my way through*
at *yet*
certē *at least*
patet: patēre *lie open*
illāc *by that way*
5 omnia possideat *he may possess everything (else)*
āera: *accusative of* āēr *air*
dīmittit: dīmittere *turn, direct*
novat: novāre *change, revolutionise*
pennās: penna *feather*
clīvō: clīvus *slope*
crēvisse: crēscere *grow*
crēvisse = pennās crēvisse
putēs *you would think*
sīc *in the same way*
rūstica: rūsticus *of a countryman*

quondam *sometimes*
fistula *pipe*
disparibus: dispār *of different length*
surgit: surgere *grow up, be built up*
avēnīs: avēna *reed*

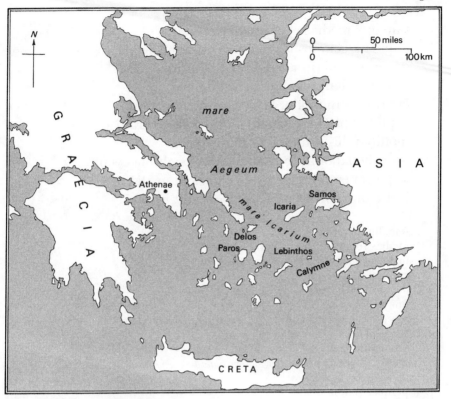

Crete and the Greek islands

1 Why was Daedalus eager to leave Crete?
2 Why was it difficult for him to get away?
3 What method of escape did he choose?
4 How did he set about preparing his escape?
5 What did the arrangement of feathers resemble?

II

tum līnō mediās et cērīs adligat īmās,
atque ita compositās parvō curvāmine flectit,
ut vērās imitētur avēs. puer Īcarus ūnā
stābat et, ignārus sua sē tractāre perīcla,
ōre renīdentī modo, quās vaga mōverat aura,   5
captābat plūmās, flāvam modo pollice cēram
mollībat, lūsūque suō mīrābile patris
impediēbat opus. postquam manus ultima coeptō
imposita est, geminās opifex lībrāvit in ālās
ipse suum corpus mōtāque pependit in aurā.   10

līnō: līnum *thread*
mediās (pennās) *the middle (of the feathers)*
īmās (pennās) *the bottom (of the feathers)*
curvāmine: curvāmen *curve*
flectit: flectere *bend*
ūnā *with him*
sua ... perīcla *cause of danger for himself (literally 'his own danger')*
tractāre *handle, touch*
5 ōre renīdentī *with smiling face*
modo ... modo *now ... now, sometimes ... sometimes*
aura *breeze*
plūmās: plūma *feather*
flāvam: flāvus *yellow, golden*
mollībat = molliēbat: mollīre *soften*
lūsū: lūsus *play, games*
manus ultima *final touch*
coeptō: coeptum *work, undertaking*
geminās ... ālās *the two wings*
opifex *inventor, craftsman*
lībrāvit: lībrāre *balance*
10 mōtā: mōtus *moving (literally 'moved', i.e. by the wings)*

1 What materials did Daedalus use to fasten the feathers together? Where did he fasten them? What did he then do to the wings?
2 In line 4, what was Icarus failing to realise?
3 How did Icarus amuse himself while his father was working? Judging from lines 5–8, what age would you imagine Icarus to be?
4 What actions of Daedalus are described in lines 9–10? Has the journey begun at this point?

Daedalus winged: bronze by Michael Ayrton

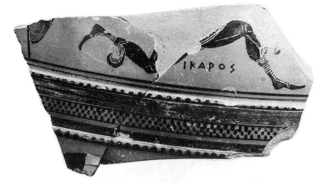

Fragment of Greek painted vase

III

īnstruit et nātum, 'mediō'que 'ut līmite currās,
Īcare', ait 'moneō, nē, sī dēmissior ībis,
unda gravet pennās, sī celsior, ignis adūrat.
inter utrumque volā! nec tē spectāre Boōtēn
aut Helicēn iubeō strictumque Ōrīonis ēnsem: 5
mē duce carpe viam!' pariter praecepta volandī
trādit et ignōtās umerīs accommodat ālas.

īnstruit: īnstruere *equip, fit (with wings)*
nātum: nātus *son*
īnstruit et nātum = et īnstruit nātum
mediō . . . līmite *middle course*
currās: currere *go, fly*
ait *says*
dēmissior *lower (than you should), i.e. too low*
pennās: penna *wing*
celsior *higher (than you should), i.e. too high*
ignis *fire, heat of sun*
adūrat: adūrere *burn*
volā: volāre *fly*
Boōtēn: *accusative of* Boōtēs *Bear-keeper (constellation; also known as the Herdsman)*
5 Helicēn: *accusative of* Helicē *Great Bear, Big Bear (constellation)*
strictum: stringere *draw, unsheathe*
Ōrīonis: Ōrīōn *Orion, the hunter (constellation)*
ēnsem: ēnsis *sword*
carpe: carpere *hasten upon*
pariter *at the same time*
praecepta: praeceptum *instruction*
accommodat: accommodāre *fasten*

Language note

1   Study the following example:

fūr per fenestram intrāvit. circumspexit; sed omnia tacita erant. subitō sonitum **audit**; ē tablīnō canis **sē praecipitat**. fūr effugere **cōnātur**; **lātrat** canis; **irrumpunt** servī et fūrem **comprehendunt**.

A thief entered through the window. He looked round; but all was silent. Suddenly he **hears** a noise; a dog **hurtles** out of the study. The thief **tries** to escape; the dog **barks**; the slaves **rush in** and **seize** the thief.

2   Notice that all the verbs in the above example, after the first two sentences, are in the *present* tense, even through the event obviously happened in the past. This is known as the *historic* use of the present tense (*'historic present'* for short); it is often used by Roman writers to make the narration rather more lively and vivid, as if the action were happening before the reader's (or listener's) eyes.

3   A historic present in Latin can be translated *either* by an English present tense (as in the example in paragraph 1), *or* by a past tense.

4   Look again at lines 6–7 of Part I on p.72. Which verbs in these two lines are in the historic present tense, and which in the perfect tense?

5   You have already met examples of the historic present in sentences containing the word 'dum' (meaning 'while'):

dum equitēs **morantur**, nūntius prīncipia irrūpit.
While the cavalry were delaying, a messenger burst into headquarters.

IV

inter opus monitūsque genae maduēre senīlēs,
et patriae tremuēre manūs. dedit ōscula nātō
nōn iterum repetenda suō pennīsque levātus
ante volat, comitīque timet, velut āles, ab <u>altō</u>
quae teneram prōlem prōdūxit in āera <u>nīdō</u>;   5
hortāturque sequī, damnōsāsque ērudit artēs,
et movet ipse <u>suās</u> et nātī respicit <u>ālās</u>.
hōs* aliquis, <u>tremulā</u> dum captat <u>harundine</u> piscēs,
aut pāstor baculō stīvāve innīxus arātor
vīdit* et obstipuit, quīque aethera carpere possent   10
crēdidit esse deōs.

inter *during*
monitūs: monitus *warning, advice*
maduēre = maduērunt: madēscere *become wet*
senīlēs: senīlis *old*
patriae: patrius *of the father*
tremuēre = tremuērunt
nōn iterum repetenda *never to be repeated, never to be sought again*
levātus: levāre *raise, lift up*
ante *in front*
velut *like*
āles *bird*
5 teneram: tener *tender, helpless*
prolem: prōlēs *offspring, brood*
prōdūxit: prōdūcere *bring forward, bring out*
damnōsās: damnōsus *ruinous, fatal*
ērudit: ērudīre *teach*
tremulā: tremulus *quivering*
harundine: harundō *rod*
baculō: baculum *stick, staff*
stīvā: stīva *plough-handle*
-ve *or*
innīxus: innītī *lean on*
10 obstipuit: obstipēscere *gape in amazement*
carpere *hasten through, fly through*

*These two words go closely together.

A 1 What signs of emotion did Daedalus show while speaking to Icarus?

2 What was his last action before the journey began?

3 What is Daedalus compared to as he sets out on his flight?

4 Who witnessed the flight? What did they think of Daedalus and Icarus, and why?

B 1 What do you think caused Daedalus' agitation in lines 1–2?

2 In what ways is the comparison in lines 4–5 appropriate?

3 Does Ovid suggest in any way that the journey will end in disaster?

Wall-painting from Pompeii

V

et iam Iūnōnia laevā
parte Samos (fuerant Dēlosque Parosque **relictae**),
dextra Lebinthos erat fēcundaque melle **Calymne**,
cum puer audācī coepit gaudēre **volātū**
dēseruitque ducem, caelīque cupīdine **tractus**   5

The Fall of Icarus, by Allegrini

altius ēgit iter. rapidī vīcīnia sōlis
mollit <u>odōrātās</u>, pennārum vincula, <u>cērās</u>.
tābuerant cērae; nūdōs quatit ille lacertōs,
rēmigiōque carēns nōn ūllās percipit aurās.
ōraque <u>caeruleā</u> patrium clāmantia nōmen   10
excipiuntur <u>aquā</u>, quae nōmen trāxit ab illō.
at pater īnfēlīx nec iam pater 'Īcare' dīxit,
'Īcare', dīxit, 'ubi es? quā tē regiōne requīram?
Īcare', dīcēbat; pennās aspexit in undīs,
dēvōvitque suās artēs corpusque sepulcrō   15
condidit, et tellūs ā nōmine dicta sepultī.

Iūnōnia: Iūnōnius *sacred to Juno*
laevā parte *on the left hand*
-que . . . -que *both . . . and*
dextra: dexter *on the right*
fēcunda . . . melle *rich in honey*
gaudēre *be delighted*
volātū: volātus *flying, flight*
5 tractus: trahere *draw on, urge on*
altius *higher (than he should), i.e. too high*
ēgit iter: iter agere *make one's way, travel*
rapidī: rapidus *blazing, consuming*
vīcīnia *nearness*
odōrātās: odōrātus *sweet-smelling*
vincula *fastenings*
tābuerant: tābēscere *melt*

nūdōs: nūdus *bare*
quatit: quatere *shake, flap*
lacertōs: lacertus *arm*
rēmigiō: rēmigium *wings (literally 'oars')*
carēns: carēre *lack, be without*
percipit: percipere *take hold of, get a grip on*
10 ōra *mouth*
caeruleā: caeruleus *dark blue, dark green*
trāxit: trahere *draw, derive*
nec iam *no longer*
requīram: requīrere *search for*
aspexit: aspicere *catch sight of*
15 dēvōvit: dēvovēre *curse*
condidit: condere *bury*
dicta =dicta est: dīcere *call, name*
sepultī: sepultus *the one who was buried*

A1 On the map on p.73, find the point reached by Daedalus and Icarus in lines 1–3.

2 What mistake did Icarus make?

3 What effect did this have on his wings?

4 Where did he fall? What was he doing as he fell?

5 How did Daedalus learn of his son's fate? What did he do then?

B1 Why did Icarus not obey his father's instructions?

2 Why is Daedalus described as 'pater . . . nec iam pater' in line 12?

3 After reading this story, what impression do you have of the different personalities of Daedalus and Icarus?

Language note

1   From Unit IIA onwards, you have met sentences like this:

Britannī cibum laudāvērunt, Rōmānī vīnum.
The Britons praised the food, the Romans (praised) the wine.

2   In Unit IIB, you met a slightly different type of sentence:

Britannī cibum, Rōmānī vīnum laudāvērunt.

3   Compare the examples in paragraphs 1 and 2 with a longer way
of expressing the same idea:

Britannī cibum laudāvērunt, Rōmānī vīnum laudāvērunt.

This kind of sentence is grammatically correct, but is not often
used in Latin; the Romans would normally prefer the shorter
versions in paragraphs 1 and 2, to avoid repeating the word
'laudāvērunt'.

4   Sentences similar to the ones in paragraphs 1 and 2 are very
common in Latin. Study the following examples, which you
have met in Stages 36 and 44:

Thāis habet nigrōs, niveōs Laecānia dentēs.
Thais has black teeth, Laecania has white ones.
(Compare this with a longer way of expressing the same idea:
Thāis dentēs nigrōs habet, Laecānia dentēs niveōs habet.)

et movet ipse suās et nātī respicit ālās.
He both moves his own wings himself and looks back at the
wings of his son.
(Compare: et ipse suās ālās movet et ālās nātī respicit.)

5 Further examples:

1 centuriō gladium, mīles hastam gerēbat.
   (Compare: centuriō gladium gerēbat, mīles hastam gerēbat.)
2 hic caupō vēndit optimum, ille vīnum pessimum.
   (Compare: hic caupō vīnum optimum vēndit, ille caupō vīnum pessimum vēndit.)
3 nōs in urbe, vōs prope mare habitātis.
4 altera fēmina quīnque līberōs habēbat, altera nūllōs.
5 dīvitiās quaerit senex, spernit iuvenis.
6 ēnumerat mīles vulnera, pāstor ovēs. (*Propertius*)
7 culpāvit dominus, laudāvit domina vīlicum.
8 nōn semper viātōrēs ā latrōnibus, aliquandō latrōnēs ā viātōribus occīduntur.

ēnumerat: ēnumerāre *count*   viātōrēs: viātor *traveller*

Exercises

1 In Stage 42, the different ways of translating 'ēmittere', 'petere' and 'referre' were practised. Another verb with a wide variety of translations is 'solvere', which you have often met with the meaning 'untie' but which can be translated in many other ways as well. Match each of the phrases in the left-hand column with the correct English translation from the right-hand column.

nāvem solvere	relaxed by the wine
catēnās ex aliquō solvere	to discharge a promise made to the gods
vīnō solūtus	to set out on a voyage
aenigma solvere	to settle a debt
margarītam in acētō solvere	to free somebody from chains
pecūniam solvere	to solve a puzzle
vōtum solvere	to dissolve a pearl in vinegar

Suggest reasons why the Romans used 'solvere' in all these phrases: is there any connection in meaning between them?

2 Complete each sentence by describing the word in heavy print with a suitable adjective chosen from the list below, using paragraphs 1 and 2 on pages 180–1 to help you put your chosen adjective into the correct form. Do not use any adjective more than once. The gender of the word in heavy print is given after each sentence. (An adjective which indicates size or quantity is usually placed *before* the noun it describes; other adjectives *after*. But the Romans did not observe this as a strict rule.)

īrātus, ingēns, fortis, pulcher, magnus, fēlīx, longus, audāx, gravis

1 dominus **ancillās** arcessīvit. (f.)
2 iuvenis pecūniam **senī** reddidit. (m.)
3 sacerdōtēs **templum** intrāvērunt. (n.)
4 dux virtūtem **mīlitum** laudāvit. (m.)
5 cīvēs **spectāculō** dēlectātī sunt. (n.)
6 centuriō, **hastā** armātus, extrā carcerem stābat. (f.)

3 In each pair of sentences, translate sentence 'a'; then with the help of pages 190–1 express the same idea in a passive form by completing the noun and verb in sentence 'b' in the correct way, and translate again.

For example: a hostēs nōs circumveniēbant.
                     b ab host. . . circumveni. . . .
Translated and completed, this becomes:
  a hostēs nōs circumveniēbant.
     The enemy were surrounding us.
  b ab hostibus circumveniēbāmur.
     We were being surrounded by the enemy.

1a cūr centuriō tē culpābat?
1b cūr ā centuriō. . . culp. . . ?
2a optimē labōrāvistis, puerī; vīlicus vōs certē laudābit.
2b optimē labōrāvistis, puerī; ā vīlic. . . certē laud. . . .
3a moritūrus sum; amīcī mē in hōc locō sepelient.
3b moritūrus sum; ab amīc. . . in hōc locō sepel. . . .
4a medicus mē cotīdiē vīsitat.
4b ā med. . . cotīdiē vīsit. . . .
5a barbarī nōs interficient.
5b ā barbar. . . interfici. . . .

4 Complete each sentence with the right infinitive or group of words from the list below, and then translate.

nūllam pecūniam habēre
per hortum suum flūxisse
scrīptam esse
aedificārī
equum occīsūrōs esse

1 nūntius sciēbat epistulam ab Imperātōre . . . . . .
2 senex affirmāvit sē . . . . . .
3 rēx crēdēbat leōnēs . . . . . .
4 agricola querēbātur multam aquam . . . . . .
5 puer dīxit novum templum . . . . . .

Language note

1   In Stage 6, you met the 3rd person plural of the perfect tense:

cīvēs gladiātōrem **incitāvērunt**.
The citizens urged the gladiator on.

2   From Stage 36 onwards, you have met examples like this:

centum mē **tetigēre** manūs.   clientēs patrōnum **salūtāvēre**.
A hundred hands touched me.   The clients greeted their
                                 patron.

In these examples, the 3rd person plural of the perfect tense ends
in '-ēre' instead of '-ērunt'. The meaning is unchanged. This
way of forming the 3rd person plural of the perfect is especially
common in verse.

3   Translate the following:

1 servī contrā dominum coniūrāvēre.
2 in illō proeliō multī barbarī periēre.
3 coniūnxēre; ēripuēre; perdidēre; respexēre; studuēre.

Icarus in art

The tale of Daedalus and Icarus has attracted many artists. The oldest surviving version of the story in picture form comes from Greece; a small fragment of a painted vase (see p.76) shows the lower edge of a tunic, two legs wearing winged boots, and the inscription I K A P O Σ (Icarus). The vase was made in the middle of the sixth century B.C., more than five hundred years earlier than Ovid's version of the story.

Daedalus and Icarus also appear in wall-paintings excavated at Pompeii. One of these paintings is shown on p.79. The figure of Daedalus flying in the centre has been almost entirely lost, because of the hole in the painting, and only the wing tips are visible. Icarus, however, appears twice, once at the top near the sun, and again at the bottom. The bystanders gaze skywards in wonder, as in Ovid's account (p.78, lines 10–11). The sun is shown not as a ball of fire but as a god driving his chariot and horses across the sky.

The work reproduced on p.75 is by the twentieth-century artist Michael Ayrton. Ayrton was fascinated by the story of Daedalus and Icarus, and came back to it again and again during a period of several years. He created a large number of drawings, reliefs and sculptures dealing not only with the making of the wings and the fall of Icarus, but also with other details of the Daedalus story, such as the maze which Daedalus built in Crete, and the monstrous half-man, half-bull known as the Minotaur, who lived at the centre of the maze. Ayrton also retold the Daedalus story in his own words in two short novels.

In about 1555, Pieter Bruegel painted the picture which is reproduced on p.88. Some of the details of his painting are very close to Ovid's account; the ploughman leaning on his plough, the shepherd with his staff, and the fisherman (p.78, lines 8–9) are all there. In other ways, however, Bruegel's treatment of the story is unusual and at first sight surprising; for example the bystanders in Bruegel's picture are behaving very differently from those in the painting by Allegrini, reproduced on p.80.

The Fall of Icarus, by Pieter Bruegel

In this way, the story of Daedalus and Icarus, as told by Ovid and other writers, became a subject for Bruegel and other artists. Bruegel's painting, in turn, became the subject of the following poem by W.H. Auden. Auden's title, *Musée des Beaux Arts*, refers to the gallery in Brussels where *Icarus* and other paintings by Bruegel are hung.

Musée des Beaux Arts

About suffering they were never wrong,
The Old Masters: how well they understood
Its human position; how it takes place
While someone else is eating or opening a window or just
    walking dully along;
How, when the aged are reverently, passionately waiting
For the miraculous birth, there always must be
Children who did not specially want it to happen, skating
On a pond at the edge of the wood:
They never forgot
That even the dreadful martyrdom must run its course
Anyhow in a corner, some untidy spot
Where the dogs go on with their doggy life and the torturer's
    horse
Scratches its innocent behind on a tree.

In Bruegel's *Icarus*, for instance: how everything turns away
Quite leisurely from the disaster; the ploughman may
Have heard the splash, the forsaken cry,
But for him it was not an important failure; the sun shone
As it had to on the white legs disappearing into the green
Water; and the expensive delicate ship that must have seen
Something amazing, a boy falling out of the sky,
Had somewhere to get to and sailed calmly on.

Vocabulary checklist

aspiciō, aspicere, aspexī, aspectus – look towards, catch sight of
coniungō, coniungere, coniūnxī, coniūnctus – join
coniūrō, coniūrāre, coniūrāvī – conspire, plot
crēscō, crēscere, crēvī – grow
cupīdō, cupīdinis – desire
fēlīx, *gen.* fēlīcis – lucky, happy
licet, licēre – be allowed
   mihi licet – I am allowed
paulātim – gradually
studeō, studēre, studuī – study
tellūs, tellūris – land, earth
ūnā cum – together with
uterque, utraque, utrumque – both, each of two
vinculum, vinculī – fastening, chain

Give the meaning of:

coniūrātiō, cupere, fēlīcitās, vincīre

Lesbia

Some of Catullus' most famous poems are concerned with a woman to whom he gave the name 'Lesbia'. Stage 45 contains eight of the Lesbia poems.

I

ille mī pār esse deō vidētur,
ille, sī fās est, superāre dīvōs,
quī sedēns adversus identidem tē
    spectat et audit

dulce rīdentem, <u>miserō</u> quod omnēs   5
ēripit sēnsūs <u>mihi</u>: nam simul tē,
Lesbia, aspexī, nihil est super mī
    vōcis in ōre,

lingua sed torpet, tenuis sub artūs
flamma dēmānat, sonitū suōpte   10
tintinant aurēs, <u>geminā</u> teguntur
    lūmina <u>nocte</u>.

ōtium, Catulle, tibi molestum est:
ōtiō exsultās nimiumque gestīs:
ōtium et rēgēs prius et beātas   15
    perdidit urbēs.

mī = mihi	sub *to the depths of*
fās *right*	artūs: artus *limb*
superāre *surpass*	10 dēmānat: dēmānāre *flow down*
adversus *opposite*	suōpte = suō
5 dulce *sweetly*	tintinant: tintināre *ring*
quod *(a thing) which*	geminā: geminus *twofold, double*
sēnsūs: sēnsus *sense*	teguntur: tegere *cover*
simul = simulac	lūmina *eyes*
nihil . . . vōcis *no voice*	exsultās: exsultāre *get excited*
est super = superest: superesse	gestīs: gestīre *become restless*
remain, be left	15 prius *before now*
torpet: torpēre *be paralysed*	beātās: beātus *prosperous, wealthy*
tenuis *thin, subtle*	

1 Why does Catullus regard 'ille' (lines 1 and 2) as fortunate? Why does he regard himself as 'miserō' (line 5)?
2 'omnēs ēripit sēnsūs' (lines 5–6): give an example of this from lines 7–12.
3 What warning does Catullus give himself in lines 13–16? Do you think these lines follow on naturally from lines 1–12, or are they a separate poem?

II

vīvāmus, mea Lesbia, atque amēmus,
rūmōrēsque senum sevēriōrum
omnēs ūnius aestimēmus assis!
sōlēs occidere et redīre possunt;
nōbīs, cum semel occidit brevis lux,   5
nox est perpetua ūna dormienda.
dā mī bāsia mīlle, deinde centum,
dein mīlle altera, dein secunda centum,
deinde usque altera mīlle, deinde centum,
dein, cum mīlia multa fēcerimus,   10
conturbābimus illa, nē sciāmus,
aut nē quis malus invidēre possit,
cum tantum sciat esse bāsiōrum.

vīvāmus *let us live*
rūmōrēs *gossip*
sevēriōrum: sevērior *over-strict*
ūnius . . . assis *at a single 'as' (smallest Roman coin)*
aestimēmus: aestimāre *value*
5 semel *once*
est . . . dormienda *must be slept through*
bāsia: bāsium *kiss*
dein = deinde
usque altera *yet another*
11 conturbābimus: conturbāre *mix up, lose count of*
nē quis *in case anyone*
invidēre *cast an evil eye*
tantum *so much, such a large number*

(continued)

vīvāmus, mea Lesbia, atque amēmus! (line 1, page 93)

1 Who, according to Catullus, might be making comments about him and Lesbia? What does he think he and Lesbia should do about these comments?

2 What contrast does Catullus draw between 'sōlēs' (line 4) and 'nōs' ('nōbīs', line 5)?

3 What have lines 7–9 got to do with lines 4–6?

4 Why does Catullus suggest in line 11 that he and Lesbia should deliberately lose count?

Language note

1 Study the following examples:

vīvāmus atque amēmus!   Let us live and let us love!
nē dēspērēmus!   Let us not despair!
aut vincāmus aut vincāmur! Let us either conquer or be
                             conquered!

In these sentences, the speaker is ordering or encouraging himself and one or more other people to do something. The 1st-person plural form ('we') is used, and the verb is in the present tense of the subjunctive. This is known as the *jussive* use of the subjunctive. Further examples:

1 in mediam pugnam ruāmus!   *let us rush into the midst of the battle*
3 sociōs nostrōs adiuvēmus.   *Let us help our allies.*
2 nē haesitēmus!   *lets not hesitate*
4 opus perficiāmus.   *let us finish the work.*
5 gaudeāmus igitur, iuvenēs dum sumus.   *let us be glad, therefor while we are young.*
6 flammās exstinguere cōnēmur!   *Let us try to exstinguish the fire*

2 The jussive subjunctive can also be used in a 3rd-person form of the verb ('he', 'she', 'it' or 'they'):

omnēs captīvī interficiantur!   Let all the prisoners be killed!
                         or, All the prisoners are to be killed.

nē respiciat!   Let him not look back!
                         or, He is not to look back.

Further examples:
1 statim redeat!   *Let him return immediately*
2 sit amīcitia inter nōs et vōs.   *let there be friendship between us and you*
3 prīmum taurus sacrificētur; deinde precēs Iovī adhibeantur.

3 Occasionally, the jussive subjunctive is used in a 2nd-person form ('you'):

dēsinās querī.   You should stop complaining.

But it is far more common for Latin to use the imperative:

dēsine querī!   Stop complaining!

III

lūgēte, ō Venerēs Cupīdinēsque,
et quantum est hominum venustiōrum!
passer mortuus est meae puellae,
passer, dēliciae meae puellae,
quem plūs illa oculīs suīs amābat.   5
nam mellītus erat suamque nōrat
ipsam tam bene quam puella mātrem,
nec sēsē ā gremiō illius movēbat,
sed circumsiliēns modo hūc modo illūc
ad sōlam dominam usque pīpiābat;   10
quī nunc it per iter tenebricōsum
illūc, unde negant redīre quemquam.
at vōbīs male sit, malae tenebrae
Orcī, quae omnia bella dēvorātis:
tam bellum mihi passerem abstulistis.   15
ō factum male! ō miselle passer!
tuā nunc operā, meae puellae
flendō turgidulī rubent ocellī.

Wall-painting from Herculaneum showing cupids at play

Venerēs Cupīdinēsque *gods and goddesses of love, Venuses and Cupids*
quantum est *all the company, (literally 'as much as there is')*
venustiōrum: venustus *tender, loving*
passer *sparrow*
6 mellītus *sweet as honey*
nōrat = nōverat
ipsam: ipsa *mistress*
tam . . . quam *as . . . as*
sēsē = sē
gremiō: gremium *lap*
circumsiliēns: circumsilīre *hop around*
10 usque *continually*
tenebricōsum: tenebricōsus *dark, shadowy*
quemquam: quisquam *anyone*
vōbīs male sit *curses on you*
Orcī: Orcus *the Underworld, Hell*
16 ō factum male! *O dreadful deed! (literally 'O dreadfully done!')*
miselle: misellus *wretched little*
tuā . . . operā *by your doing, because of you*
turgidulī: turgidulus *swollen*
rubent: rubēre *be red*
ocellī: ocellus *poor eye, little eye*

1 What has happened?
2 Who are asked to mourn in line 1? Why are they appropriate mourners on this occasion?
3 Is Catullus chiefly concerned about the death, or about something else?
4 Why does he speak as if *he* had been bereaved ('mihi', line 15)?
5 Compare the two descriptions of the sparrow in (*a*) lines 8–10, (*b*) lines 11–12. Do they sound equally serious, or is one of the descriptions slightly comic? How serious is the poem as a whole?

IV

nūllī sē dīcit mulier mea nūbere mālle
　quam mihi, nōn sī sē Iuppiter ipse petat.
dīcit: sed mulier cupidō quod dīcit amantī,
　in ventō et rapidā scrībere oportet aquā.

nūllī: *used as dative of* nēmō
mulier *woman*
nōn sī *not even if*
sed mulier . . . quod dīcit = sed quod mulier . . . dīcit
cupidō: cupidus *eager, passionate*
amantī: amāns *lover*
rapidā: rapidus *rushing, racing*

Wall-painting from Herculaneum showing lovers on a couch

1 What does Lesbia say in lines 1–2? Why does the mention of Jupiter imply a compliment to Catullus?

2 What would be the best translation for the first 'dīcit' in line 3?
   (a) 'She says'
   (b) 'She says so'
   (c) 'That's what she *says*'
   (d) '*That's* what she says'
   or none of these?

3 What comment does Catullus then make about Lesbia's remark?

4 What does he mean? Does he mean, for example, that women can't be trusted? Or is he suggesting something more precise than that? Is Catullus being cynical or fair-minded?

V

dīcēbās quondam sōlum tē nōsse Catullum,
    Lesbia, nec prae mē velle tenēre Iovem.
dīlēxī tum tē non tantum ut vulgus amīcam,
    sed pater ut gnātōs dīligit et generōs.
nunc tē cognōvī: quārē etsī impēnsius ūror,   5
    multō mī tamen es vīlior et levior.
quī potis est, inquis? quod amantem iniūria tālis
    cōgit amāre magis, sed bene velle minus.

nōsse = nōvisse	etsī *although, even if*
prae *instead of, rather than*	impēnsius: impēnsē *strongly, violently*
tenēre *possess*	ūror: ūrere *burn*
vulgus *the ordinary man, common man*	levior: levis *worthless*
amīcam: amīca *mistress, girl-friend*	quī potis est? *how is that possible?*
gnātōs = nātōs	*how can that be?*
5 quārē *and so, wherefore*	bene velle *like, be friendly*

1 What statement by Lesbia does Catullus recall in lines 1–2? What were his feelings about her at that time, according to lines 3–4?

2 What is the point of the comparison in line 4?

3 Explain what Catullus means by 'nunc tē cognōvī' (line 5). In what way has his discovery affected his feelings for Lesbia? Why has it had this effect?

Language note

1 From Unit IIIA onwards, you have met sentences in which forms of the pronoun 'is' are used as antecedents of the relative pronoun 'quī':

is *quī nūper servus erat* nunc dīvitissimus est.
He who was recently a slave is now extremely rich.

id *quod mihi nārrāvistī* numquam patefaciam.
That which you have told me I shall never reveal.
   or, in more natural English:
I shall never reveal what you have told me.

dominus **eōs** pūniet *quī pecūniam āmīsērunt*.
The master will punish those who lost the money.

Notice that in these sentences the antecedent (in heavy print) comes *before* the relative clause (italicised).

Further examples:

1 id quod dīcis vērum est.
2 is quī rēgem vulnerāvit celeriter fūgit.
3 nūllum praemium dabitur eīs quī officium neglegunt.

2 You have also met sentences like these, in which the antecedent comes *after* the relative clause:

quī auxilium mihi prōmīsērunt, **eī** mē iam dēserunt.
Those who promised me help are now deserting me.

quod potuimus, **id** fēcimus.
That which we could do, we did.
   or, in more natural English:
We did what we could.

Further examples:

1 quod saepe rogāvistī, ecce! id tibi dō.
2 quōs per tōtum orbem terrārum quaerēbam, eī in hāc urbe inventī sunt.

3 In Unit IVB, you have met sentences in which the antecedent is omitted altogether:

quod mulier dīcit amantī, in ventō scrībere oportet.
What a woman says to her lover should be written on the wind.

quī numquam timet stultus est.
He who is never frightened is a fool.

quī speciem amīcitiae praebent nōn semper fidēlēs sunt.
Those who put on an appearance of friendship are not always faithful.

Further examples:

1 quod suscēpī, effēcī.
2 quae tū mihi heri dedistī, tibi crās reddam.
3 quī multum habet plūs cupit.
4 quod sentīmus loquāmur.
5 quī rēs adversās fortiter patiuntur, maximam laudem merent.

    laudem: laus *praise, fame*

VI
ōdī et amō. quārē id faciam, fortasse requīris.
   nescio, sed fierī sentiō et excrucior.

   requīris: requīrere *ask*

Do the first three words of this poem make sense? Does Catullus mean that he hates at some times and loves at others, or that he hates and loves simultaneously?

VII

miser Catulle, dēsinās ineptīre,
et quod vidēs perīsse perditum dūcās.
fulsēre quondam candidī tibi sōlēs,
cum ventitābās quō puella dūcēbat
amāta nōbīs quantum amābitur nūlla.   5
ibi illa multa cum iocōsa fīēbant,
quae tū volēbās nec puella nōlēbat,
fulsēre vērē candidī tibi sōlēs.

nunc iam illa nōn volt: tū quoque impotēns nōlī,
nec quae fugit sectāre, nec miser vīve,   10
sed obstinātā mente perfer, obdūrā.

valē, puella. iam Catullus obdūrat,
nec tē requīret nec rogābit invītam.
at tū dolēbis, cum rogāberis nūlla.
scelesta, vae tē, quae tibi manet vīta?   15
quis nunc tē adībit? cui vidēberis bella?
quem nunc amābis? cuius esse dīcēris?
quem bāsiābis? cui labella mordēbis?
at tū, Catulle, dēstinātus obdūrā.

ineptīre *be a fool*
perditum: perditus *completely lost, gone for ever*
dūcās: dūcere *consider*
candidī: candidus *bright*
ventitābās: ventitāre *often go, go repeatedly*
5 nōbīs = mihi *by me*
quantum *as, as much as*
ibi *then, in those days*
illa multa cum . . . fīēbant = cum illa multa . . . fīēbant
iocōsa *moments of fun, moments of pleasure*
vērē *truly*
nunc iam *now however, as things are now*
volt = vult
impotēns *being helpless, being powerless*
10 sectāre: *imperative of* sectārī *chase after*
perfer: perferre *endure*
obdūrā: obdūrāre *be firm*
requīret: requīrere *go looking for*
nūlla: nūllus *not at all*
15 scelesta: scelestus *wretched*
vae tē! *alas for you!*
bāsiābis: bāsiāre *kiss*
labella: labellum *lip*
mordēbis: mordēre *bite*
dēstinātus *determined*

1 Explain the advice which Catullus gives himself in lines 1–2. What English proverb corresponds to the idea expressed in line 2?
2 Does line 3 simply mean that it was fine weather?
3 Which word in line 9 contrasts with 'quondam' (line 3)?
4 What future does Catullus foresee in lines 14–15?
5 On the evidence of lines 12–19, does Catullus seem capable of following his own advice? Give reasons for your view.
6 What is the mood of the poem? Sad, angry, bitter, determined, resigned? Does the mood change during the course of the poem? If so, where and in what way?

VIII

In the first four verses of this poem, given here in translation, Catullus describes the loyalty and friendship of Furius and Aurelius:

Furius and Aurelius, comrades of Catullus,
whether he journeys to furthest India,
whose shores are pounded by far-resounding
    Eastern waves,

or whether he travels to soft Arabia,   5
to Persia, Scythia, or the arrow-bearing Parthians,
or the plains which are darkened by the seven mouths
    of the river Nile,

or whether he crosses the lofty Alps,
visiting the scene of great Caesar's triumphs,   10
over the Rhine and the ocean, to Britain on the
    edge of the world,

ready to join in any adventure,
whatever the will of the gods may bring,
carry a few bitter words   15
    to my girl.

The poem's last two verses are Catullus' message:

cum <u>suīs</u> vīvat valeatque <u>moechīs,</u>
quōs simul complexa tenet trecentōs,
nūllum amāns vērē, sed identidem omnium
    īlia rumpēns;   20

nec meum respectet, ut ante, amōrem,
quī illius culpā cecidit velut prātī
ultimī flōs, <u>praetereunte</u> postquam
    tāctus <u>arātrō</u> est.

valeat: valēre *thrive, prosper*
moechīs: moechus *lover, adulterer*
complexa: complectī *embrace*
trecentōs: trecentī *three hundred*
20 īlia *groin*
rumpēns: rumpere *burst, rupture*
respectet: respectāre *look towards, count on*
illius culpā *through her fault, thanks to her*
cecidit: cadere *die*
prātī: prātum *meadow*
ultimī: ultimus *furthest, at the edge*

1 Why does Catullus spend so much of this poem describing Furius' and Aurelius' loyalty?
2 What is the gist of the message which he asks them to deliver?
3 Do any phrases or words in lines 17 and 19 remind you of other poems by Catullus that you have read?
4 'His final goodbye to Lesbia'. Do you think this is an accurate description of the last two verses?

Exercises

1 Match each word in the left-hand column with a word of the opposite meaning, taken from the right-hand column.

amor	tollere
celeriter	adiuvāre
dare	gaudēre
dēmittere	paulō
hiems	odium
impedīre	perīculum
incipere	lūx
lūgēre	dēsinere
multō	aestās
poena	accipere
salūs	lentē
tenebrae	praemium

2 In each pair of sentences, translate sentence 'a'; then change it from a direct question to an indirect question by completing sentence 'b' with the correct form of the present subjunctive active or passive, and translate again.

For example: a cūr semper errātis?

b dīcite nōbīs cūr semper . . . . . .

Completed and translated, sentence 'b' becomes:

dīcite nōbīs cūr semper errētis.

Tell us why you are always wandering about.

The active and passive forms of the present subjunctive are given on pp.192–3. You may also need to consult the vocabulary at the end to find which conjugation a verb belongs to.

1a ubi habitās?
1b dīc mihi ubi . . . . . .
2a quō captīvī illī dūcuntur?
2b scīre volō quō captīvī illī . . . . . .
3a quot fundōs possideō?
3b oblītus sum quot fundōs . . . . . .

4a quid quaerimus?
4b tibi dīcere nōlumus quid . . . . . .
5a novumne templum aedificātur?
5b incertus sum num novum templum . . . . . .
6a cūr in hōc locō sedētis?
6b explicāte nōbīs cūr in hōc locō . . . . . .

3 Complete each sentence with the right word or phrase and then translate.

1 dēnique poēta . . . . . surrēxit. (ad recitandum, ad dormiendum)
2 nūntius, celeriter . . . . ., mox ad castra pervēnit. (scrībendō, equitandō)
3 captīvī, quī nūllam spem . . . . . habēbant, dēspērābant. (coquendī, effugiendī)
4 omnēs hospitēs in triclīnium . . . . . contendērunt. (ad cēnandum, ad pugnandum)
5 senex, quī procul ā marī habitābat, artem . . . . . numquam didicerat. (nāvigandī, spectandī)
6 pater meus, dīligenter . . . . ., tandem magnās dīvitiās adeptus est. (labōrandō, bibendō)

Language note

1 In Stage 9, you met the dative used in sentences like this:

   pater **nōbīs** dōnum ēmit.   Father bought a present **for us**.

   This use of the dative is sometimes described as the *dative of advantage*.

2 In Unit IVB, you have met the dative used in sentences like these:

   Fortūna **mihi** frātrem ēripuit. Fortune has snatched my brother away **from me**.

   tenebrae Orcī **eī** passerem abstulērunt. The shades of Hell stole the sparrow **from her**.

   This use of the dative is sometimes described as the *dative of disadvantage*.

   Further examples:

   1 fūr mihi multam pecūniam abstulit.
   2 barbarī eīs cibum ēripuērunt.
   3 Rōmānī nōbīs lībertātem auferre cōnantur.

Dancing-girls on a mosaic from Sicily

Clodia

The real identity of 'Lesbia' is uncertain, but there are reasons for thinking that she was a woman named Clodia. Clodia came from the aristocratic family of the Claudii, and was married to Metellus, a wealthy and distinguished noble. She was an attractive, highly educated woman, whose colourful life-style caused continual interest and gossip at Rome. Among the other rumours that regularly circulated around her, she was said to have murdered her husband and commited incest with her brother.

One of Clodia's lovers was the lively and talented Marcus Caelius Rufus. Their relationship lasted for about two years, before being broken off by Caelius. There was a violent quarrel; and Clodia, furious and humiliated, was determined to revenge herself. She launched a prosecution against Caelius, alleging (among other things) that he had robbed her and attempted to poison her.

Clodia, in spite of her doubtful reputation, was a powerful and dangerous enemy, with many influential friends, and the prosecution was a serious threat to Caelius. To defend himself against her charges, he turned to various friends, including Rome's leading orator, Cicero. Not only was Cicero a close friend of Caelius, but he had a bitter and long-running feud with Clodia's brother Clodius.

Some of the charges were dealt with by other speakers for the defence; Cicero's job was to deal with Clodia's allegations of theft and poisoning. It would not be enough to produce arguments and witnesses; Clodia herself had to be discredited and (if possible) made to look ridiculous, if a verdict of 'not guilty' was to be achieved.

The following paragraphs are from Cicero's speech in defence of Caelius:

> Two charges in particular have been made: theft and attempted murder, and both charges involve the same individual. It is alleged that the gold was stolen from Clodia, and that the poison was obtained for administering to Clodia. The rest of the chief prosecutor's speech was not a list of charges, but a string of insults, more suitable to a vulgar slanging-match than a court of law. When the prosecutor calls my client 'adulterer, fornicator, swindler', these are not accusations, but mere abuse. Such charges have no foundation; they are wild mud-slinging, by an accuser who has lost his temper and has no one to back him up.
>
> But when we come to the charges of theft and attempted murder, we have to deal not with the prosecutor but with the person behind him. In speaking of these charges, gentlemen of the jury, my concern is wholly with Clodia, a lady who possesses not only nobility of birth but also a certain notoriety. However, I shall say nothing about her except in connection with the charges against my client. I should be more energetic and forceful in speaking about Clodia, but I do not wish to seem influenced by my political quarrel with her husband – I mean her *brother*, of course (I'm always making that mistake). I

shall speak in moderate language, and will go no further than I am obliged by my duty to my client and the facts of the case: for I have never felt it right to quarrel with a woman, especially with one who has always been regarded not as any man's enemy but as *every* man's friend . . .

I shall name no names, but suppose there were a woman, unmarried, blatantly living the life of a harlot both here in the city and in the public gaze of the crowded resort of Baiae, flaunting her behaviour not only by her attitude and her appearance, not only by her passionate glances and her saucy tongue, but by lustful embraces, drinking-sessions and beach-parties, so that she seemed to be not merely a harlot, but a harlot of the lewdest and most lascivious description – suppose that a young man, like my client, were to associate with such a woman; do you seriously claim that he would be seducing an innocent victim? . . .

I was present, gentlemen, and indeed it was perhaps the saddest and bitterest occasion of my whole life, when Quintus Metellus, who only two days previously had been playing a leading part in the political life of our city, a man in the prime of his years, in the best of health and at the peak of his physical strength, was violently, suddenly, shockingly taken from us. How can the woman, who comes from that house of crime, now dare to speak in court about the rapid effects of poison?

Caelius was acquitted. Nothing is known of Clodia's later fate.

Vocabulary checklist

aestās, aestātis – summer
candidus, candida, candidum – bright, shining
culpa, culpae – blame
fleō, flēre, flēvī – weep
modo . . . modo – now . . . now, sometimes . . . sometimes
mulier, mulieris – woman
orbis, orbis – circle, globe
    orbis terrārum – world
ōtium, ōtiī – leisure
quisquam, quicquam – anyone, anything
rumpō, rumpere, rūpī, ruptus – break, split
speciēs, speciēī – appearance
tegō, tegere, tēxī, tēctus – cover
tenuis, tenue – thin

Give the meaning of:

candor, culpāre, ērumpere, flētus, irrumpere

clādēs

Pliny wrote two letters to the historian Tacitus giving an eye-witness account of the eruption of Mount Vesuvius, which had taken place in August A.D. 79 when Pliny was seventeen. In the first letter, he described the death of his uncle (Pliny the Elder), who went too near the danger zone on a rescue mission, and was choked to death by the fumes. In the second letter, on which the passages in this Stage are based, Pliny describes the adventures which he and his mother had at Misenum after Pliny the Elder had departed on his mission.

tremōrēs

profectō avunculō, ipse reliquum tempus studiīs impendī (ideō
enim remānseram); deinde balneum, cēna, somnus inquiētus et
brevis. per multōs diēs priōrēs, tremor terrae sentiēbātur, minus
formīdolōsus quia Campāniae solitus; sed illā nocte ita invaluit, ut
non movērī omnia sed ēvertī vidērentur. irrūpit cubiculum meum 5
māter; surgēbam ipse, ad eam excitandam sī dormīret. cōnsēdimus
in āreā domūs, quae mare ā tēctīs modicō spatiō dīvidēbat; ego, ut
timōrem mātris meā sēcūritāte lēnīrem, popōscī librum et quasi per
ōtium legere coepī. subitō advenit amīcus quīdam avunculī, quī ubi
mē et mātrem sedentēs, mē vērō etiam legentem videt, vituperat 10
illīus patientiam, sēcūritātem meam. ego nihilōminus intentus in
librum manēbam.
    iam hōra diēī prīma; sed adhūc dubia lūx. iam quassātīs proximīs
tēctīs, magnus et certus ruīnae metus. tum dēmum fugere
cōnstituimus; nam sī diūtius morātī essēmus, sine dubiō 15
periissēmus. ultrā tēcta prōgressī, ad respīrandum cōnsistimus.
multa ibi mīrābilia vidēmus, multās fōrmīdinēs patimur.

avunculō: avunculus *uncle*
remānseram: remanēre *stay behind*
somnus *sleep*
fōrmīdolōsus *alarming*
Campāniae *in Campania*
solitus *common, usual*
invaluit: invalēscere *become strong*
tēctīs: tēctum *building*
spatiō: spatium *space, distance*
dīvidēbat: dīvidere *separate*
sēcūritāte: sēcūritās *unconcern, lack of anxiety*
per ōtium *at leisure, free from care*
quassātīs: quassāre *shake violently*
ruīnae: ruīna *collapse*
ultrā *beyond*
respīrandum: respīrāre *recover one's breath, get one's breath back*
fōrmīdinēs: fōrmīdō *fear, terror*

II

nam vehicula, quae prōdūcī iusserāmus, quamquam in plānissimō
campō, in contrāriās partēs agēbantur, ac nē lapidibus quidem fulta
in eōdem locō manēbant. praetereā mare in sē resorbērī vidēbāmus,
quasi tremōre terrae repulsum esset. certē prōcesserat lītus,
5 multaque maris animālia siccīs arēnīs dētinēbantur. ab alterō latere
nūbēs ātra et horrenda in longās flammārum figūrās dēhīscēbat,
quae et similēs et maiōrēs fulguribus erant. tum vērō ille amīcus
avunculī vehementius nōs hortātus est ut effugere cōnārēmur: 'sī
frāter' inquit, 'tuus, tuus avunculus, vīvit, salūtem vestram cupit; sī
10 periit, superstitēs vōs esse voluit; cūr igitur cūnctāminī?'
respondimus nōs salūtī nostrae cōnsulere nōn posse, dum dē illō
incertī essēmus. nōn morātus ultrā, sē convertit et quam celerrimē ē
perīculō fūgit.
    nec multō post, illa nūbēs ātra dēscendit in terrās, operuit maria;
15 cēlāverat Capreās, Mīsēnī prōmunturium ē cōnspectū abstulerat.
tum māter mē ōrāre hortārī iubēre, ut quōquō modō fugerem;
affirmāvit mē, quod iuvenis essem, ad salūtem pervenīre posse; sē,
quae et annīs et corpore gravārētur, libenter moritūram esse, sī mihi
causa mortis nōn fuisset. ego respondī mē nōlle incolumem esse nisi
20 illa quoque effūgisset; deinde manum eius amplexus, addere
gradum cōgō. pāret invīta, castīgatque sē, quod mē morētur.

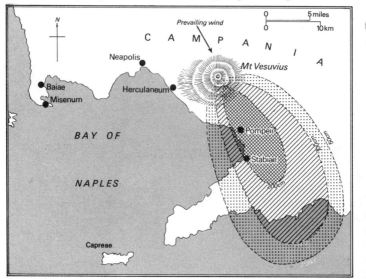

The area
affected by
ashfall after
the eruption
of Vesuvius
in A.D.79

Relief from House of Caecilius showing effects of earthquake at Pompeii, A.D.62.

plānissimō: plānus *level, flat*
campō: campus *ground*
partēs: pars *direction*
agēbantur: agī *move, roll*
fulta: fulcīre *prop up, wedge*
resorbērī: resorbēre *suck back*
siccīs: siccus *dry*
arēnīs: arēna *sand*
dētinēbantur: dētinēre *hold back, strand*
latere: latus *side*
dēhīscēbat: dēhīscere *gape open*
fulguribus: fulgur *lightning*
cūnctāminī: cūnctārī *delay, hesitate*

cōnsulere *take thought for, give consideration to*
operuit: operīre *cover*
Capreās: Capreae *Capri*
Mīsēnī: Mīsēnum *Misenum*
prōmunturium *promontory*
ōrāre hortārī iubēre = ōrābat hortābātur iubēbat
quōquō: quisquis *whatever (i.e. whatever possible)*
incolumem: incolumis *safe*
amplexus: amplectī *grasp, clasp*
addere gradum *go forward step by step (literally 'add one step (to another)')*

1 What strange things were happening to (*a*) Pliny's carriages, (*b*) the sea and shore, (*c*) the sea-creatures?

2 Describe what Pliny saw in the sky (lines 5–7).

3 What did the friend of Pliny's uncle urge Pliny and his mother to do? What reason did they give for refusing? What did the friend then do?

4 What were the effects of the black cloud, as described in lines 14–15?

5 Why did Pliny's mother think they should separate? What action did Pliny take in response to her entreaties?

6 What impression do you have of the character of (*a*) the friend of Pliny's uncle, (*b*) Pliny and his mother, as shown by their behaviour during the eruption?

Language note

1   In Stage 30, you met the pluperfect indicative passive:

omnēs servī dīmissī erant.
All the slaves had been sent away.

2   In Stage 46, you have met sentences like these:

cum omnēs servī **dīmissī essent**, ad āream rediimus.
When all the slaves had been sent away, we returned to the courtyard.

Plīnius scīre voluit num avunculus **servātus esset**.
Pliny wanted to know whether his uncle had been saved.

The form of the verb in heavy print is the *pluperfect subjunctive passive*.

Further examples:

1 ancilla cognōvit quid in testāmentō dominī scrīptum esset.
2 cum victimae sacrificātae essent, pontifex pauca verba dīxit.
3 amīcī vestrī ignōrābant quāle comprehēnsī essētis.

3   Compare the indicative and subjunctive forms of the pluperfect passive of 'portō':

pluperfect indicative passive	*pluperfect subjunctive passive*
portātus eram	portātus essem
portātus erās	portātus essēs
portātus erat	portātus esset
portātī erāmus	portātī essēmus
portātī erātis	portātī essētis
portātī erant	portātī essent

Pluperfect subjunctive passive forms of 'doceō', 'trahō' and 'audiō' are given on p.193.

4 Study the following examples:

iūdex rogāvit quantam pecūniam mercātor mihi **pollicitus esset**.
The judge asked how much money the merchant had promised me.

cum Rōmam **regressus essem**, prīnceps mē arcessīvit.
When I had returned to Rome, the emperor sent for me.

The words in heavy print are *pluperfect subjunctive* forms of *deponent* verbs.

Further examples:

1 cum multās gemmās adeptī essēmus, domum revēnimus.
2 memineram quid māter mea locūta esset.

Pluperfect subjunctive forms of 'cōnor', 'vereor' etc. are given on p.198.

tenebrae

iam dēcidēbat cinis, adhūc tamen rārus. respiciō; dēnsa cālīgō,
tergīs nostrīs imminēns, nōs sequēbātur quasi ingēns flūmen ātrum
in terram effūsum esset. 'dēflectāmus' inquam, 'dum vidēmus, nē in
viā sternāmur et in tenebrīs ā multitūdine fugientium obterāmur.'

5 vix cōnsēderāmus, cum dēscendit nox dēnsissima, quasi omnia
lūmina in conclāvī clausō exstincta essent. sī adfuissēs, audīvissēs
ululātūs fēminārum, infantum vāgitūs, clāmōrēs virōrum; aliī
vōcibus parentēs requirēbant, vōcibusque nōscitābant, aliī līberōs,
aliī coniugēs; hī suum cāsum, aliī suōrum lūgēbant; nōnnūllī metū
10 mortis mortem precābantur; multī ad deōs manūs tollēbant, plūrēs
nusquam iam deōs ūllōs esse affirmābant.

paulum relūxit, quod nōn diēs nōbīs, sed appropinquantis ignis
indicium vidēbātur. ignis tamen procul substitit; deinde tenebrae
rūrsus, cinis rūrsus, multus et gravis. nisi identidem surrēxissēmus
15 et cinerem excussissēmus, sine dubiō opertī atque etiam oblīsī
pondere essēmus.

tandem cālīgō tenuāta nō dissolūta est, sīcut fūmus vel nebula.
mox diēs rediit; sōl etiam fulgēbat, pallidus tamen. attonitī vidimus
omnia mūtāta altōque cinere tamquam nive operta. regressī
20 Mīsēnum, noctem spē ac metū exēgimus. metus praevalēbat; nam
tremor terrae persevērābat. nōbīs tamen nūllum cōnsilium abeundī
erat, dōnec cognōscerēmus num avunculus servātus esset.

rārus *occasional*
dēflectāmus: dēflectere *turn aside,*
  turn off the road
sternāmur: sternere *knock over*
obterāmur: obterere *trample to death*
ululātūs: ululātus *shriek*
vāgītūs: vāgītus *wailing, crying*
nōscitābant: nōscitāre *recognise*
paulum *a little, to a slight extent*
relūxit: relūcēscere *become light again*
opertī = opertī essēmus: operīre *bury*

oblīsī . . . essēmus: oblīdere *crush*
pondere: pondus *weight*
tenuāta: tenuāre *thin out*
dissolūta est; dissolvere *disperse, dissolve*
nebula *mist*
nive: nix *snow*
Mīsēnum *to Misenum*
exēgimus: exigere *spend*
praevalēbat: praevalēre *prevail,*
  be uppermost
dōnec *until*

Language note

1 Study the following conditional sentences:

sī iuvenis respexisset, latrōnem vīdisset.
If the young man had looked round, he would have seen the robber.

sī mē vocāvissēs, statim vēnissem.
If you had called me, I should have come at once.

nisi canis lātrāvisset, servī effūgissent.
If the dog had not barked, the slaves would have escaped.

sī imperātor ipse hanc rem iūdicāvisset, damnātī essētis.
If the emperor himself had judged this case, you would have been condemned.

Notice that:

1 the Latin verbs are in the *pluperfect* tense of the *subjunctive*;
2 the English translations contain the words 'had . . .', followed by 'would have . . .' or 'should have . . .'.

2 Further examples:

1 sī nautae in portū mānsissent, tempestātem vītāvissent.
2 sī satis pecūniae obtulissētis, agricola vōbīs equum vēndidisset.
3 sī centuriō tergum vertisset, minus graviter vulnerātus esset.
4 sī fīlia tua illī senī nūpsisset, miserrima fuisset.
5 sī exercitus noster superātus esset, prīnceps novās cōpiās ēmīsisset.
6 nisi pater mē prohibuisset, tibi subvēnissem.

Exercises

1 Translate each sentence; then, referring if necessary to the table of nouns on pages 178–9 and to the vocabulary at the end of the book, change the *number* of the words in heavy print (i.e. change singular words to plural, and plural words to singular) and translate again.

   1 centuriō barbarōs **catēnīs** vīnxit.
   2 fūr vestēs **amīcī tuī** abstulit.
   3 sacerdōs ad **templa** ambulābat.
   4 multitūdō artem **gladiātōris** mīrābātur.
   5 pāstōrēs strepitum **canum** audīvērunt.
   6 puer cum **ancillīs** et **iuvenibus** stābat.
   7 **mercātōrī** pecūniam trādidit.
   8 ego callidior **meīs inimīcīs** sum.

2 This exercise is based on lines 1–12 of 'tremōrēs', Part I on page 115. Read the lines again, then translate the following sentences into Latin. All necessary vocabulary can be found on page 115 in lines 1–12, but you will need to make various alterations to the word-endings, e.g. by changing a verb form from 1st person to 3rd person, or a noun from the nominative to the genitive; refer to the appropriate pages of the Language Information section where necessary.

   1 Plinius spent the remaining time *on dinner*[1] and *sleep*[1].
   2 Throughout those days, tremors were being felt.
   3 Plinius began to read a book, in order that he might calm *his*[2] mother's fear.
   4 They *saw*[3] uncle's friend arriving.
   5 Plinius, having been scolded *by the friend*[4], was nevertheless remaining in the courtyard.

    [1]dative   [2]omit   [3]use either perfect or historic present
    [4]'ab' + ablative

3 Translate each pair of sentences; then replace the word in heavy print with the correct form of the relative pronoun 'quī', using the table in paragraph 8 on page 186 and adjusting the word order if necessary so that the relative pronoun comes at the beginning of the second sentence; then translate again. Do NOT join the two sentences together, but translate the relative pronoun as a 'connecting relative', i.e. as 'he', 'she', 'it', 'this', etc.

For example: in mediā urbe stābat templum. simulatque **templum** intrāvī, attonitus cōnstitī.

In the middle of the city stood a temple. As soon as I entered the **temple**, I halted in amazement.

This becomes: in mediā urbe stābat templum. **quod** simulatque intrāvī, attonitus cōnstitī.

In the middle of the city stood a temple. As soon as I entered **it**, I halted in amazement.

The gender of the word in heavy print is given after each sentence. For ways of translating the connecting relative, see paragraph 8 on p.186.

1 subitō appāruērunt duo lupī. cum **lupōs** vīdissent, pāstōrēs clāmōrem sustulērunt. (m.)

2 agricola uxōrem monuit ut fugeret. **uxor** tamen obstinātē recūsāvit. (f.)

3 rēx epistulam celeriter dictāvit. cum servus **epistulam** scrīpsisset, nūntius ad Imperātōrem tulit. (f.)

4 fūr ātrium tacitē intrāvit. **fūre** vīsō, canis lātrāvit. (m.)

5 Quīntus 'Salvium perfidiae accūsō', inquit. **verbīs** audītīs, Salvius tacuit. (n.)

6 'ubi est pecūnia mea?' rogāvit mercātor. nēmō **mercātōrī** respondēre audēbat. (m.)

7 hominēs clāmāre coepērunt. clāmōribus **hominum** excitātus, surrēxī. (m.)

8 crās pontifex sacrificium faciet. ut **sacrificium** videās, tē ad templum dūcam. (n.)

Language note

1   From Unit I onwards, you have met sentences like these, containing various forms of the verb 'esse' ('to be'):

nihil tam ferōx est quam leō.
Nothing is as ferocious as a lion.

postrīdiē discessimus; sed iter longum et difficile erat.
We left next day; but the journey was long and difficult.

2   Sometimes, however, the various forms of 'esse' are omitted, especially in verse or fast-moving narrative. In Unit IVB you have met sentences like these:

nihil tam terribile quam incendium.
Nothing is as frightening as a fire.

caelum undique et pontus.
On every side was sky and sea.

subitō fragōrem audīvimus; deinde longum silentium.
Suddenly we heard a crash; then there was a long silence.

3   Translate again lines 13–14 of 'tremōrēs', Part I (p.115), from 'iam' to 'metus'. How many times does the Latin omit the word 'erat' where the English translation contains the word 'was'?

Time chart of Roman authors

The chart opposite shows the dates of eight Roman authors who appear in Unit IVB (in Latin or in translation), together with a brief indication of their work.

B.C.		B.C.
110		110
100	M. Tullius CICERO (106 B.C.-43 B.C.)	100
90	Speeches (including	90
80	speech in defence of Caelius), letters and	C. Valerius CATULLUS (c.84 B.C.-54 B.C.)	80
70	other work		70
60		poetry, including the 'Lesbia' poems	P. Vergilius Maro (VIRGIL) (70 B.C.-19 B.C.)	60
50		50
40	P. Ovidius Naso (OVID) (43 B.C.-A.D.17)	poetry, including *Aeneid*	40
30		30
20	poetry, including *Metamorphoses* and *Ars Amatoria*	20
10		10

A.D.		A.D.
10	C. PETRONIUS Arbiter (?? - A.D.66)	10
20	*Satyrica* (novel)	20
30		30
40		40
50	M. Valerius Martialis (MARTIAL) (c. A.D.40- c. A.D.104)	50
60		Cornelius TACITUS (c. A.D.55- c. A.D.116)	60
70	epigrams	C. Plinius Caecilius Secundus (PLINY) (c. A.D.61- c. A.D.112)	70
80		history, including biography of his father-in-law Agricola	80
90		letters to his friends, and official correspondence with the Emperor Trajan	90
100		100
110		110
120		120

Vocabulary checklist

clādēs, clādis – disaster
iūdicō, iūdicāre, iūdicāvī, iūdicātus – judge
lapis, lapidis – stone
lūmen, lūminis – light
minus – less
paulum – a little, slightly
quisquis – whoever
    quidquid (*also spelt* quicquid) – whatever
reliquus, reliqua, reliquum – remaining, the rest
requīrō, requīrere, requīsīvī – ask, seek
somnus, somnī – sleep
sternō, sternere, strāvī, strātus – lay low, knock over
tēctum, tēctī – building
ultrā – further

Give the meaning of:

iūdex, iūdicium, lapillus

lūdī

The following narrative, told partly in Latin and partly in translation, comes from Book Five of Virgil's *Aeneid*.

certāmen

During their wanderings after the destruction of Troy, Aeneas and his Trojan followers have arrived at the island of Sicily, where Aeneas' father Anchises is buried. They decide to mark the anniversary of Anchises' death by holding a festival of games in his honour.

I

First is a race between four ships,
Picked from the whole fleet, well-matched with heavy oars:
The speedy *Pristis*, with a keen crew led by Mnestheus;
Massive *Chimaera*, huge as a city, commanded by Gyas;
The large *Centaur*, which carries Sergestus,   5
And sea-blue *Scylla*, with Cloanthus as captain.

immōtā ... attollitur undā. (II, line 4)

II

est procul in pelagō saxum spūmantia contrā
lītora, quod <u>tumidīs</u> summersum tunditur ōlim
<u>flūctibus,</u> hībernī condunt ubi sīdera Cōrī;
tranquillō silet immōtāque attollitur undā.
hīc viridem <u>Aenēās</u> frondentī ex īlice mētam   5
cōnstituit signum nautīs <u>pater,</u> unde revertī
scīrent et longōs ubi circumflectere cursūs.

spūmantia: spūmāre *foam*
contrā *opposite*
tumidīs: tumidus *swollen*
tunditur: tundere *beat, buffet*
ōlim *sometimes*
flūctibus: flūctus *wave*
hībernī: hībernus *wintry, of winter*
condunt: condere *hide*
hībernī condunt ubi = ubi hībernī . . . condunt
Cōrī: Cōrus *north-west wind*
tranquillō: tranquillum *calm weather*
attollitur: attollī *rise*
5 viridem: viridis *green*
frondentī: frondēns *leafy*
īlice: īlex *oak tree*
cōnstituit: cōnstituere *set up, place*
circumflectere cursūs: circumflectere cursum *turn one's course round*

1 Where is the rock? What happens to it when the weather is
  stormy? What happens in calm weather?
2 What does Aeneas place on the rock? Why? Which noun in lines
  5–7 emphasises Aeneas' position of responsibility?

inde ubi clāra dedit sonitum tuba, f̲ī̲n̲i̲b̲u̲s̲ omnēs
(haud mora) prōsiluēre s̲u̲ī̲s̲; ferit aethera clāmor
nauticus, adductīs spūmant freta versa lacertīs.   10
    effugit ante aliōs prīmīsque ēlābitur undīs
turbam inter fremitumque Gyās; quem deinde Cloanthus
cōnsequitur, melior rēmīs, sed pondere pīnus
tarda tenet. post hōs aequō discrīmine Pristis
Centaurusque locum tendunt superāre priōrem;   15
et nunc Pristis habet, nunc victam praeterit ingēns
Centaurus, nunc ūnā ambae iūnctīsque feruntur
frontibus et longā sulcant vada salsa carīnā.

clāra: clārus *loud (literally 'clear')*
fīnibus: fīnis *starting-place*
ferit: ferīre *strike*
10 nauticus *made by the sailors*
adductīs: addūcere *pull, draw up (to the chest)*
freta: fretum *water, sea*
versa: vertere *churn up*
fremitum: fremitus *noise, din*
cōnsequitur: cōnsequī *follow, chase*
pīnus *pine tree, i.e. boat (made of pine wood)*
tarda: tardus *slow*
tenet: tenēre *hold back*
aequō discrīmine *at an equal distance (from the leaders)*
15 tendunt: tendere *strain, strive*
superāre *achieve, win*
iūnctīs: iūnctus *side by side*
frontibus: frōns *prow*
sulcant: sulcāre *plough through*
vada: vadum *water*
salsa: salsus *salty*
carīnā: carīna *keel*

3 What is the starting-signal? What do the words 'haud mora' and 'prōsiluēre' (line 9) indicate about the manner in which the competitors move off?
4 What does Virgil say in lines 9–10 about (*a*) the shouting of the sailors? (*b*) the appearance of the sea? (*c*) the movements of the oarsmen?
5 Who takes the lead?
6 Who comes next? What advantage does he have, and what disadvantage?
7 Which two ships are struggling for third place? What is happening at each of the three stages of the struggle, introduced by 'nunc . . . nunc . . . nunc' (lines 16–17)?
8 The verb 'sulcāre' ('sulcant', line 18) literally means 'to drive a furrow'. In what way is it appropriate to the description of the ships' course?

Gyās et Cloanthus

I

They were nearing the rock, close to the turning-point,
When Gyas, leading at the halfway mark,
Cried out to his helmsman Menoetes: 'What are you doing?
Don't wander so far to the right! Keep over this way!
Run close to the rock, let the oars on the port side graze it!   5
The rest can stay out at sea, if they want.' But Menoetes,
Fearing a hidden reef, turned the prow to the open water.
'Where are you off to?' cried Gyas again. 'Make for the rock!'
And looking round as he shouted, he saw Cloanthus,
Hard on his tail, cutting in between him and the rock.   10
Cloanthus, scraping through on the inside, took the lead
And reached safe water, leaving the turning-post far behind.

II

tum vērō exarsit iuvenī dolor ossibus ingēns
nec lacrimīs caruēre genae, sēgnemque Menoetēn
in mare praecipitem puppī dēturbat ab altā;
ipse gubernāclō rēctor subit, ipse magister
hortāturque virōs clāvumque ad lītora torquet.   5
at <u>gravis</u> ut fundō vix tandem redditus īmō est
iam senior madidāque fluēns in veste <u>Menoetēs</u>
summa petit scopulī siccāque in rūpe resēdit.
illum et lābentem Teucrī et rīsēre natantem
et salsōs rīdent revomentem pectore flūctūs.   10

exarsit: exardēre *blaze up*
ossibus: os *bone*
sēgnem: sēgnis *timid, unenterprising*
Menoetēn: *Greek accusative of* Menoetēs
puppī: puppis *poop, stern*
dēturbat: dēturbāre *push, send flying*
gubernāclō: gubernāclum *helm, steering-oar*
rēctor *helmsman*
subit: subīre *take over*
magister *pilot*
5 clāvum: clāvus *tiller, helm*
torquet: torquēre *turn*
ut *when*
fundō: fundus *depth*
vix tandem *at long last*
īmō: īmus *lowest*
senior *elderly*
fluēns *dripping, streaming*
scopulī: scopulus *rock*
resēdit: resīdere *sit down, sink down*
Teucrī *Trojans*
10 revomentem: revomere *vomit up*
pectore: pectus *chest*

1 Who is the 'iuvenis' (line 1)? What does he do to Menoetes in lines 2–3?
2 Who replaces Menoetes as helmsman? What are his first actions on taking over?
3 Which words and phrases in line 6 indicate that Menoetes (*a*) went a long way down, (*b*) did not resurface for some time, (*c*) could do nothing about getting to the surface himself but could only wait for the sea to disgorge him?
4 Why do you think Virgil includes the phrase 'iam senior' (line 7) in his description of Menoetes? Which word in line 6 is partly explained by the phrase 'madidāque fluēns in veste' in line 7?
5 What did Menoetes do as soon as he had resurfaced?
6 What three actions of Menoetes are described in lines 9–10? Do the Trojans show any sympathy for him? Does Virgil?

Sergestus et Mnēstheus

I

And now the two tail-enders, Mnestheus and Sergestus,
Are fired with a joyful hope of catching Gyas.
As they reach the rock, Sergestus is in the lead,
Though not by as much as a boat-length; his bows are in front,
But his stern is overlapped by the eager *Pristis*.   5
And Mnestheus, pacing between his lines of rowers,
Is driving them on: 'Now pull with your oars;
Once you were comrades of Hector, and when Troy fell
You became my chosen companions; now summon your strength,
Now summon the courage you showed on the African sandbanks, 10
The Ionian sea, the racing waves of Greece.
I can hope no longer now to finish first
(Though perhaps . . . but victory lies in the hands of Neptune) –
Yet to come in last, my friends, would be shameful;
Prevent the disgrace!' And his men, with a mighty heave,   15
Pulled hard on their oars; the whole ship shook with their efforts;
The sea raced by beneath them, their throats and limbs
Were gripped by breathless exertion, they streamed with sweat.

II

attulit ipse virīs optātum cāsus honōrem.
namque <u>furēns animī</u> dum prōram ad saxa suburget
interior spatiōque subit <u>Sergestus</u> inīquō,
īnfēlīx saxīs in prōcurrentibus haesit.
cōnsurgunt nautae et magnō clāmōre morantur   5
ferrātāsque trudēs et acūtā cuspide contōs
expediunt frāctōsque legunt in gurgite rēmōs.

Relief from Athens, A.D.165, showing competitors in a boat-race

cāsus *chance*
furēns animī *furiously determined, with furious eagerness*
prōram: prōra *prow*
suburget: suburgēre *drive . . . up close*
interior *on the inside*
subit: subīre *approach*
inīquō: inīquus *narrow, dangerous*
prōcurrentibus: prōcurrere *project*
5 cōnsurgunt: cōnsurgere *jump up*
morantur: morārī *hold (the ship) steady*
ferrātās: ferrātus *tipped with iron*
trudēs: trudis *pole*
acūtā: acūtus *sharp*
cuspide: cuspis *point*
contōs: contus *pole, rod*
expediunt: expedīre *bring out, get out*
legunt: legere *gather up*

Language note

1 From Unit I onwards, you have met sentences like these:

sacerdōs **ā templō** discessit.
The priest departed from the temple.

servī **in agrīs** labōrābant.
The slaves were working in the fields.

In these sentences, 'from' is expressed by one of the prepositions 'ā', 'ab', 'ē' or 'ex', while 'in' is expressed by the preposition 'in'. Each preposition is followed by a noun in the ablative case.

2 In verse, however, the idea of 'in' or 'from' is often expressed by the ablative case alone, without any preposition:

ipse diem noctemque negat discernere **caelō** . . . Palinūrus.
Palinurus himself says he cannot distinguish day and night in the sky.

fīnibus omnēs . . . prōsiluēre **suīs**.
They all leapt forward from their starting-places.

. . . **immōtāque** attollitur **undā**.
. . . and it rises up from the still water.

Further examples:

1 nōbīs tempus erat patriā discēdere cārā.
2 flūmine nant piscēs, arbore cantat avis.
3 iamque senex laetus nostrā proficīscitur urbe.
4 dīcitur immēnsā Cyclōps habitāre cavernā.

victor

I

at laetus Mnēstheus successūque ācrior ipsō
prōna petit maria et pelagō dēcurrit apertō.
et prīmum in scopulō <u>lūctantem</u> dēserit altō
<u>Sergestum</u> brevibusque vadīs frūstrāque vocantem
auxilia et frāctīs discentem currere rēmīs.   5
inde Gyān ipsamque ingentī mōle Chimaeram
cōnsequitur; cēdit, quoniam spoliāta magistrō est.

successū: successus *success*
ācrior: ācer *eager, excited*
prōna: prōnus *easy*
dēcurrit: dēcurrere *speed, race*
dēserit: dēserere *leave behind*
brevibus: brevis *shallow*
5 currere *race, row*
Gyān: *Greek accusative of* Gyās
mōle: mōlēs *bulk*
quoniam *since*
spoliāta . . . est: spoliāre *deprive*

1 Why does Mnestheus feel encouraged at this point?
2 Who is the first competitor to be overtaken by Mnestheus? What
   is he doing, and trying to do?
3 Whom does Mnestheus overtake next? Why is he able to do so?

II

solus iamque ipsō superest in fīne Cloanthus:
quem petit et summīs adnīxus vīribus urget.
tum vērō ingeminat clāmor cūnctīque sequentem
īnstīgant studiīs, resonatque fragōribus aethēr.
hī proprium decus et partum indignantur honōrem   5
nī teneant, vītamque volunt prō laude pacīscī;
hōs successus alit: possunt, quia posse videntur.
et fors aequātīs cēpissent praemia rōstrīs,
nī palmās pontō tendēns utrāsque Cloanthus
fūdissetque precēs dīvōsque in vōta vocāsset: 10
'dī, quibus imperium est pelagī, quōrum aequora currō,
vōbīs laetus ego hōc candentem in lītore taurum
cōnstituam ante ārās vōtī reus, extaque salsōs
prōiciam in flūctūs et vīna liquentia fundam.'
dīxit, eumque īmīs sub flūctibus audiit omnis   15
Nēreidum Phorcīque chorus Panopēaque virgō,
et pater ipse manū magnā Portūnus euntem
impulit: illa Notō citius volucrīque sagittā
ad terram fugit et portū sē condidit altō.

adnīxus: adnītī *strain, exert oneself*	rōstrīs: rōstrum *prow*
urget: urgēre *pursue, press upon*	palmās: palma *hand (literally 'palm')*
cūnctī: cūnctus *all*	tendēns: tendere *stretch out*
īnstīgant: īnstīgāre *urge on*	10 fūdisset: fundere *pour out*
studiīs: studium *shout of support, cheer*	in vōta *to (hear) his vow*
resonat: resonāre *resound*	vocāsset = vocāvisset
fragōribus: fragor *shout*	candentem: candēns *gleaming white*
5 proprium: proprius *one's own, that belongs to one*	vōtī reus *bound by one's vow, in payment of one's vow*
decus *glory*	prōiciam: prōicere *cast (as an offering)*
partum: parere *gain, win*	liquentia: liquēre *flow*
indignantur: indignārī *feel shame, think it shameful*	16 Nēreidum: Nēreis *sea-nymph*
nī = nisi	Phorcī: Phorcus *Phorcus (a sea-god)*
indignantur . . . nī teneant *think it shameful if they do not hold on to*	Panopēa *Panopea (one of the sea-nymphs)*
pacīscī *exchange, bargain*	Portūnus *Portunus (god of harbours)*
alit: alere *encourage*	citius: citō *quickly*
fors *perhaps*	volucrī: volucer *winged, swift*
aequātīs: aequātus *level, side by side*	sagittā: sagitta *arrow*
	sē condidit: sē condere *bring oneself to rest*

A1 Which two captains are involved in the final dash for victory? Which of them has the better chance, and which phrase in line 1 emphasises this?

  2 What happens in line 3 to the noise-level? Suggest a reason for this. Which contestant do the spectators support?

  3 Why are Cloanthus' men especially anxious not to be beaten? How deeply (according to Virgil) do they care about winning?

  4 What psychological advantages do Mnestheus and his men have?

  5 What would the result have been, but for Cloanthus' prayer?

  6 Which gods does Cloanthus address? What three promises does he make? Does his prayer imply a request as well as a promise?

  7 Who heard the prayer? What help did Cloanthus receive?

  8 Which word in lines 17–18 has Virgil placed in an especially emphatic position, and why?

  9 What is the speed of Cloanthus' boat compared to? What is the result of Portunus' action?

(continued)

B1 To what extent (if any) do the *personalities* of the four captains influence the action and result of the race?

2 Consider how Part II of 'victor' should be read aloud. At which point or points should the reading be liveliest? How should Cloanthus' prayer be read? Are there any points where the reading should be calm or quiet?

Language note

1 Study the following quotations from Latin verse:

ōraque caeruleā patrium clāmantia nōmen
excipiuntur aquā. (*Ovid*)

And his mouth, shouting the name of his father, was received by the dark blue water.

per amīca **silentia** lūnae (*Virgil*)
through the friendly silence of the moonlight

cōnscendit furibunda **rogōs**. (*Virgil*)
She climbed the funeral pyre in a mad frenzy.

In each of these phrases or sentences, the poet uses a *plural* noun ('ōra', 'silentia', 'rogōs') with a singular meaning ('mouth', 'silence', 'pyre'). A similar use of the plural is sometimes found in English verse:

Breaking the silence of the **seas**
Among the furthest Hebrides.

Then felt I like some watcher of the **skies**
When a new planet swims into his ken.

2 From each of the following lines in Stage 47, pick out one example of a plural noun used with a singular meaning:

1 'victor' Part I (p.137), line 5.
2 'victor' Part II (p.138), line 14.

Exercises

1 Match each word in the left-hand column with a word of similar meaning taken from the right-hand column.

castīgāre	suāvis
dēcipere	quod
dīvitiae	culpāre
dulcis	laedere
ignis	quidem
nocēre	vincere
nōn	fallere
ōlim	contemnere
quia	haud
scelus	opēs
spernere	verērī
superāre	incolumis
timēre	facinus
tūtus	quondam
vērō	incendium

2 Complete each sentence with the right word and then translate.

1 sī mē rogāvissēs, ... (dūxissem, respondissem)
2 sī Īcarus mandātīs patris pāruisset, nōn in mare . . . . . . (cecidisset, crēdidisset)
3 sī exercituī nostrō subvēnissētis, vōbīs magnum praemium . . . . . . (dedissēmus, exstrūxissēmus)
4 sī in Circō herī adfuissēs, spectāculō . . . . . . (dēlectātus essēs, dēpositus essēs)
5 nisi senex ā lībertīs dēfēnsus esset, latrōnēs eum . . . . . . (exiissent, occīdissent)

3 Translate each sentence, then replace the verb in heavy print with the correct form of the verb in brackets, keeping the same person, tense, etc. Refer if necessary to the vocabulary at the end of the book, and to the tables of deponent verbs on pp.196–8.

For example: cōnsul pauca verba **dīxit**. (loquī)
This becomes: cōnsul pauca verba locūtus est.
                        The consul said a few words.

1 dux nautās **incitābat**. (hortārī)
2 captīvus quidem sum; sed effugere **temptābō**. (cōnārī)
3 crās ab hōc oppidō **discēdēmus**. (proficīscī)
4 **prōmīsī** mē pecūniam mox redditūrum esse. (pollicērī)
5 mīlitēs arma nova **comparāvērunt**. (adipīscī)
6 cognōscere volēbam num omnēs nūntiī **revēnissent**. (regredī)

4 Complete each sentence with the most suitable word from the list below, and then translate. Refer to the story on pages 129–38 where necessary.

ēiceret, taurum, tuba, relictō, parum

1 simulatque . . . sonuit, omnēs nāvēs prōsiluērunt.
2 iuvenis adeō īrātus erat ut senem ē nāve . . . .
3 Sergestus, quī . . . . . caute nāvigābat, in scopulum incurrit.
4 saxō . . . . ., nautae cursum ad lītus dīrigēbant.
5 Cloanthus pollicitus est sē . . . . . deīs sacrificātūrum esse.

The chariot-race in Homer's *Iliad*

When Virgil wrote the *Aeneid*, part of his inspiration came from two famous epic poems of ancient Greece, the *Iliad* and *Odyssey* of Homer. Throughout his poem, Virgil uses ideas, incidents and phrases from Homer, but reshapes them, combines them with his own subject-matter, and handles them in his own style, to produce a poem which in some ways is very similar to the *Iliad* and *Odyssey*, but in other ways is utterly different.

The following extracts from Book Twenty-three of Homer's *Iliad* describe the chariot-race which took place during the funeral games held by the Achaians (Greeks) outside the walls of Troy during the Trojan War. Homer's account provided Virgil with some of the raw material for his description of the boat-race. The chief characters involved are:

ACHILLEUS (often known as Achilles), who has organised the games in honour of his dead friend Patroklos;

ANTILOCHOS son of Nestor and grandson of Neleus;

DIOMEDES son of Tydeus, hated by the god Phoibos Apollo but befriended and supported by the goddess Athene; he drives a team of horses which he has captured from the Trojans, and his companion is named Sthenelos;

EUMELOS son of Admetos (sometimes described as son of Pheres);

MENELAOS son of Atreus (Atreides), brother of the great king Agamemnon, whose mare Aithe he has borrowed for the chariot-race.

The winner of the race is to receive as his prize a skilled slave-woman and a huge tripod with ear-shaped handles.

They stood in line for the start, and Achilleus showed them the turn-post
far away on the level plain, and beside it he stationed
a judge, Phoinix the godlike, the follower of his father . . .

Then all held their whips high-lifted above their horses,
then struck with the whip thongs and in words urged their horses
          onward   5
into speed. Rapidly they made their way over the flat land
and presently were far away from the ships. The dust lifting
clung beneath the horses' chests like cloud or a stormwhirl.
Their manes streamed along the blast of the wind, . . .
              . . . the drivers 10
stood in the chariots, with the spirit beating in each man
with the strain to win, and each was calling aloud upon his own
horses, and the horses flew through the dust of the flat land.
But as the rapid horses were running the last of the race-course
back, and toward the grey sea, then the mettle of each began to 15
show itself, and the field of horses strung out, and before long
out in front was the swift-stepping team of the son of Pheres,
Eumelos, and after him the stallions of Diomedes,
the Trojan horses, not far behind at all, but close on him,
for they seemed forever on the point of climbing his chariot 20
and the wind of them was hot on the back and on the broad shoulders
of Eumelos. They lowered their heads and flew close after him.

A Greek two-horse chariot

And now he might have passed him or run to a doubtful decision,
had not Phoibos Apollo been angry with Diomedes,
Tydeus' son, and dashed the shining whip from his hands, so   25
that the tears began to stream from his eyes, for his anger
as he watched how the mares of Eumelos drew far ahead of him
while his own horses ran without the whip and were slowed. Yet
Athene did not fail to see the foul play of Apollo
on Tydeus' son. She swept in speed to the shepherd of the people   30
and gave him back his whip, and inspired strength into his horses.
Then in her wrath she went on after the son of Admetos
and she, a goddess, smashed his chariot yoke, and his horses
ran on either side of the way, the pole dragged and Eumelos
himself was sent spinning out beside the wheel of the chariot   35
so that his elbows were all torn, and his mouth, and his nostrils,
and his forehead was lacerated about the brows, and his eyes
filled with tears, and the springing voice was held fast within him.

Then the son of Tydeus, turning his single-foot horses to pass him,
went far out in front of the others, seeing that Athene   40
had inspired strength in his horses and to himself gave the glory.
After him came the son of Atreus, fair-haired Menelaos.
But Antilochos cried out aloud to his father's horses:
'Come on, you two. Pull, as fast as you can! I am not
trying to make you match your speed with the speed of those others,   45
the horses of Tydeus' valiant son, to whom now Athene
has granted speed and to their rider has given the glory.
But make your burst to catch the horses of the son of Atreus
nor let them leave you behind, for fear Aithe who is female
may shower you in mockery. Are you falling back, my brave horses?   50
For I will tell you this, and it will be a thing accomplished.
There will be no more care for you from the shepherd of the people,
Nestor, but he will slaughter you out of hand with the edge
of bronze, if we win the meaner prize because you are unwilling.
Keep on close after him and make all the speed you are able.   55
I myself shall know what to do and contrive it, so that
we get by in the narrow place of the way. He will not escape me.'

So he spoke, and they fearing the angry voice of their master
ran harder for a little while, and presently after this
battle-stubborn Antilochos saw where the hollow way narrowed.   60
There was a break in the ground where winter water had gathered
and broken out of the road, and made a sunken place all about.
Menelaos shrinking from a collision of chariots steered there,
but Antilochos also turned out his single-foot horses
from the road, and bore a little way aside, and went after him;   65

Fragment of Greek painted vase showing spectators watching a chariot-race

and the son of Atreus was frightened and called out aloud to Antilochos:
'Antilochos, this is reckless horsemanship. Hold in your horses.
The way is narrow here, it will soon be wider for passing.
Be careful not to crash your chariot and wreck both of us.'
   So he spoke, but Antilochos drove on all the harder   70
with a whiplash for greater speed, as if he had never heard him.
As far as is the range of a discus swung from the shoulder
and thrown by a stripling who tries out the strength of his young
     manhood,
so far they ran even, but then the mares of Atreides gave way
and fell back, for he of his own will slackened his driving   75
for fear that in the road the single-foot horses might crash
and overturn the strong-fabricated chariots, and the men
themselves go down in the dust through their hard striving for victory.
But Menelaos of the fair hair called to him in anger:
'Antilochos, there is no other man more cursed than you are.   80
Damn you. We Achaians lied when we said you had good sense.
Even so, you will not get this prize without having to take oath.'

(*The finish:*)
   . . . and now Tydeus' son in his rapid course was close on them
and he lashed them always with the whipstroke from the shoulder. His
    horses
still lifted their feet light and high as they made their swift passage.   85
Dust flying splashed always the charioteer, and the chariot
that was overlaid with gold and tin still rolled hard after
the flying feet of the horses, and in their wake there was not much
trace from the running rims of the wheels left in the thin dust.
The horses came in running hard. Diomedes stopped them   90
in the middle of where the men were assembled, with the dense sweat
    starting
and dripping to the ground from neck and chest of his horses.
He himself vaulted down to the ground from his shining chariot
and leaned his whip against the yoke. Nor did strong Sthenelos
delay, but made haste to take up the prizes, and gave the woman   95
to his high-hearted companions to lead away and the tripod
with ears to carry, while Diomedes set free the horses.

   After him Neleian Antilochos drove in his horses,
having passed Menelaos, not by speed but by taking advantage.
But even so Menelaos held his fast horses close on him . . .   100
. . . At first he was left behind the length of a discus
thrown, but was overhauling him fast, with Aithe
of the fair mane, Agamemnon's mare, putting on a strong burst.
If both of them had had to run the course any further,
Menelaos would have passed him, and there could have been no
    argument . . .   105

   Last and behind them all came in the son of Admetos
dragging his fine chariot and driving his horses before him.
                         (translation by Richmond Lattimore)

1 What part do the gods play in Homer's chariot-race? In what way
    does it differ from the part they play in Virgil's boat-race?
2 Compare the incident at the 'narrow place' (lines 43–82) with the
    incident at the rock in 'Sergestus et Mnēstheus', Parts I and II,
    p.134, and 'victor', Part I, p.137. What are the similarities and
    differences between the two incidents?
3 What other points of similarity do you notice between Virgil's
    account of the boat-race and Homer's account of the chariot-
    race?

Vocabulary checklist

aequor, aequoris – sea
careō, carēre, caruī – lack, be without
flūctus, flūctūs – wave
lābor, lābī, lāpsus sum – (1) fall, glide, (2) pass by
laus, laudis – praise
mora, morae – delay
optō, optāre, optāvī, optātus – pray for, long for
parum – too little
pondus, ponderis – weight
quoniam – since
sagitta, sagittae – arrow
spatium, spatiī – space, distance
vīrēs, vīrium – strength

Give the meaning of:

fluere, morārī, ponderōsus, sagittārius

Nerō et
Agrippīna

The two chief characters in this Stage are the Emperor Nero, who ruled from A.D.54 to A.D.68, and his mother Agrippina. The Latin text is based on the account written by Tacitus in his *Annals* (a history of Rome from the accession of the Emperor Tiberius to the death of Nero).

Agrippina was an able, ambitious and unscrupulous woman. In A.D.54 she arranged the murder of her husband, the Emperor Claudius, by poison. Then with the help of Burrus, the commander of the praetorian guard, she had Nero proclaimed Emperor, although he was still only a youth of sixteen.

At first Agrippina enjoyed not only great prestige as the emperor's mother but also considerable power. Possible rivals to the young emperor were removed quickly, efficiently and ruthlessly. But before long, Agrippina's power and influence were considerably weakened by Burrus and by Nero's tutor Seneca, who established themselves as Nero's chief advisers. They handled Nero skilfully, mixing their advice with flattery, and in this way they controlled most of the major decisions about the government of Rome and the empire.

As time went on, however, Nero became more and more interested in getting his own way. He also increasingly hated his mother, partly because he had fallen violently in love with the beautiful Poppaea Sabina, and was determined to marry her, while his mother was equally determined that he should not. In the following pages, the outcome of their struggle is described.

īnsidiae

ministrōs convocātōs cōnsuluit utrum venēnō an ferrō vel quā aliā vī
ūterētur. (lines 3–4)

I

at Nerō, quī vetustāte imperiī fīēbat iam audācior, amōre Poppaeae
magis magisque accēnsus, postrēmō mātrem interficere cōnstituit;
ministrōs convocātōs cōnsuluit utrum venēnō an ferrō vel quā aliā vī
ūterētur. placuit prīmō venēnum. sī tamen inter epulās prīncipis
5 venēnum darētur, mors cāsuī assignārī nōn poterat, nam similī
exitiō Britannicus anteā perierat; atque Agrippīna ipsa
praesūmendō remēdia mūnierat corpus. quō modō vīs et caedēs
cēlārentur nēmō excōgitāre poterat; et metuēbat Nerō nē quis tantō
facinorī dēlēctus iussa sperneret.

tandem Anicētus lībertus, cui Agrippīna odiō erat, cōnsilium 10
callidum prōposuit: nāvem posse compōnī cuius pars, in ipsō marī
per artem solūta, Agrippīnam ēiceret ignāram. subrīdēns Anicētus
'nihil' inquit, 'tam capāx fortuitōrum quam mare; et sī naufragiō
Agrippīna perierit, quis adeō suspīciōsus erit ut scelerī id assignet
quod ventī et flūctūs fēcerint? mātre dēfūnctā, facile erit prīncipī 15
pietātem ostendere templō exstruendō vel ad ārās sacrificandō.'

vetustāte: vetustās *length, duration*
imperiī: imperium *rule, reign*
accēnsus *inflamed, on fire*
quā: quī *some*
epulās: epulae *feast, banquet*
assignārī: assignāre *attribute, put down to*
Britannicus *Britannicus (the Emperor Claudius' son, poisoned on Nero's orders)*
praesūmendō: praesūmere *take in advance*
caedēs *murder*
metuēbat: metuere *be afraid, fear*
nē quis *lest anyone, that anyone*
dēlēctus: dēligere *choose, select*
sperneret: spernere *disobey, disregard*
compōnī: compōnere *construct*
per artem *deliberately, by design*
ignāram: ignārus *unsuspecting*
subrīdēns: subrīdēre *smile, smirk*
capāx *liable to, full of*
fortuitōrum: fortuita *accidents*
dēfūnctā: dēfūnctus *dead*

1 What two reasons, according to Tacitus, led Nero to make up his
   mind to kill his mother?
2 Whose advice did Nero seek? What question did he put to them?
3 What were the two disadvantages of poison? What were the two
   disadvantages of violence?
4 Who offered a solution to the problem? What plan did he suggest?
5 Why (according to Anicetus) would his plan be unlikely to arouse
   suspicion? What further steps did he suggest to convince people of
   Nero's innocence?

II

placuit Nerōnī calliditās Anicētī; praetereā occāsiō optima reī
temptandae aderat, nam Nerō illō tempore Bāiās ad diem fēstum
celebrandum vīsitābat. illūc mātrem ēlicuit; advenientī in itinere
obviam iit; excēpit manū et complexū; ad vīllam eius maritīmam,
5 Baulōs nōmine, dūxit. stābat prope vīllam nāvis ōrnātissima, quasi
ad mātrem prīncipis honōrandam; invītāta est Agrippīna ad epulās
Bāiīs parātās, ut facinus nocte ac tenebrīs cēlārētur. rūmōre tamen
īnsidiārum per aliquem prōditōrem audītō, Agrippīna incerta
prīmō num crēderet, tandem Bāiās lectīcā vecta est. ibi blanditiae
10 sublevāvēre metum: cōmiter excepta, iuxtā Nerōnem ipsum ad
cēnam collocāta est. Nerō modo familiāritāte iuvenīlī sē gerēbat,
modo graviter loquēbātur. tandem, cēnā multīs sermōnibus diū
prōductā, prōsequitur Agrippīnam abeuntem, artius oculīs et
pectorī haerēns, vel ad simulātiōnem explendam vel quod peritūrae
15 mātris suprēmus aspectus saevum animum eius retinēbat.

Bāiās: Bāiae *Baiae (seaside resort)*
complexū: complexus *embrace*
maritīmam: maritīmus *seaside, by the sea*
Baulōs: Baulī *Bauli (villa owned by*
  Agrippina)
Bāiīs *at Baiae*
prōditōrem: prōditor *betrayer, informer*
Bāiās (*line 9*) *to Baiae*
sublevāvēre: sublevāre *remove, relieve*
familiāritāte: familiāritās *friendliness*
iuvenīlī: iuvenīlis *youthful*

prōductā: prōdūcere *prolong, continue*
artius *particularly closely*
haerēns: haerēre *linger, cling*
simulātiōnem: simulātiō *pretence,*
  play-acting
implendam: explēre *complete, put*
  final touch to
suprēmus *last*
aspectus *sight*
retinēbat: retinēre *restrain, check*

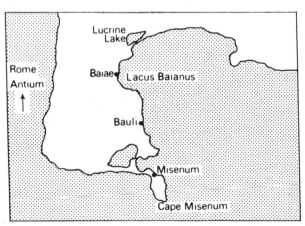

The coast near Baiae

Wall-painting from Pompeii

1 What did Nero think of Anicetus' suggestion? Why did he have a good opportunity to put the plan into operation?
2 What did Nero do when Agrippina arrived? Suggest a reason for his behaviour.
3 What method of travel was available to Agrippina at Bauli? What did Nero invite her to do? Why was it important to Nero that his mother's journey to Baiae should take place in the evening?
4 What happened at this point to upset Nero's plan? What was Agrippina's first reaction to the information? How did she eventually travel to Baiae?
5 In what way did her feelings change at Baiae? How was she treated there? How did Nero vary his manner during the feast?
6 How did Nero behave on his mother's departure? What two explanations does Tacitus give for this?

Language note

1 From Unit IVA onwards, you have met sentences like these:

quid faciam?   quā tē regiōne requīram?
What am I to do?   In what region am I to search for you?

utrum captīvōs līberēmus an interficiāmus?
Should we free the prisoners or kill them?

Questions like these are usually known as *deliberative questions* (or sometimes as *direct deliberative* questions), because the speaker is 'deliberating', or wondering what to do.

Further examples:

1 quid dīcam?   3 quō mē vertam?
2 unde auxilium petāmus?   4 utrum abeāmus an maneāmus?

2 You have also met sentences like these:

prīnceps amīcōs rogāvit quid faceret.
The emperor asked his friends what he should do.

pater nesciēbat quā regiōne fīlium requīreret.
The father did not know in what region he was to search for his son.

incertus eram utrum vī an venēnō ūterer.
I was uncertain whether to use violence or poison.

In each of these examples, a deliberative question is being *reported* or *mentioned*. Examples like these are known as *indirect deliberative questions*.

Further examples of indirect deliberative questions:

1 difficile erat Nerōnī scīre quid respondēret.
2 lībertum rogābō quō modō rem administrem.
3 mīlitēs incertī erant utrum cēderent an resisterent.
4 in animō volvēbāmus quāle dōnum rēgī darēmus.

3 Notice that the verb in a deliberative question, whether direct or indirect, is always subjunctive.

naufragium

I

deī noctem sīderibus illūstrem et placidō marī quiētam praebuēre,
quasi ad scelus patefaciendum. nec multum erat prōgressa nāvis,
duōbus amīcīs Agrippīnam comitantibus ex quibus Crepereius
Gallus haud procul gubernāculō adstābat, Acerrōnia ad pedēs
Agrippīnae cubitantis recumbēns paenitentiam fīliī per gaudium 5
commemorābat, cum datō signō ruere tēctum multō plumbō grave.
pressus Crepereius statim periit; Agrippīna et Acerrōnia
ēminentibus lectī parietibus prōtēctae sunt. nec dissolūtiō nāvis
sequēbātur, turbātīs omnibus et quod plērīque nautae, sceleris
ignārī, eōs impediēbant quī cōnsciī erant. hī igitur cōnātī sunt ūnum 10
in latus inclīnāre atque ita nāvem summergere; nōn tamen eīs erat
prōmptus in rem subitam cōnsēnsus, et aliī contrā nītentēs dedēre
Agrippīnae facultātem lēniter in mare dēscendendī.

illūstrem: illūstris *bright*	prōtēctae sunt: prōtegere *protect*
cubitantis: cubitāre *lie down, rest*	dissolūtiō *disintegration, break-up*
paenitentiam: paenitentia *repentance,*	turbātīs: turbātus *confused*
change of heart	inclīnāre *lean*
per gaudium *joyfully*	prōmptus *quick*
ruere = ruit: ruere *collapse*	in rem subitam *to meet the sudden crisis*
plumbō: plumbum *lead*	cōnsēnsus *agreement*
pressus: premere *crush*	contrā *in the opposite direction*
ēminentibus: ēminēre *project*	nītentēs: nītī *lean*
parietibus: pariēs *side*	facultātem: facultās *opportunity*

1 In what way, according to Tacitus, did the gods take sides (or
seem to take sides) in the murder attempt?

2 What was Acerronia doing when the roof fell in? Why does
Tacitus mention this?

3 What did the conspirators try to do after the original plan
misfired? Why were they again unsuccessful?

Acerrōnia autem, dum sē Agrippīnam esse imprūdenter clāmat
15 utque subvenīrētur mātrī prīncipis, contīs et rēmīs cōnficitur.
Agrippīna silēns eōque minus agnita (ūnum tamen vulnus umerō
excēpit) ad lēnunculōs quōsdam nandō pervenit quī haud procul
erant; deinde in Lucrīnum lacum vecta, ad vīllam suam dūcitur.

ibi cōgitābat quid faceret; animadverterat enim nāvem neque
20 ventīs ad lītus āctam, neque saxīs impulsam esse, sed summā suī
parte velut terrestre māchināmentum concidisse. observāns etiam
Acerrōniae caedem, simul suum vulnus aspiciēns, sōlum
īnsidiārum remēdium esse putāvit, sī nōn intellegere vidērētur.

mīsit igitur lībertum quī nūntiāret fīliō sē benignitāte deōrum et
25 fortūnā eius ēvāsisse gravem cāsum; ōrāre ut Nerō, quamvīs
perīculō mātris perterritus, vīsendī cūram differret; sibi ad praesēns
quiēte opus esse. atque interim medicāmenta vulnerī adhibet;
imperat quoque ut testāmentum Acerrōniae requīrātur – hoc sōlum
nōn per simulātiōnem.

imprūdenter *stupidly, foolishly*
subvenīrētur *help should be brought*
cōnficitur: cōnficere *finish off, murder*
eō *therefore, for this reason*
agnita: agnōscere *recognise*
lēnunculōs: lēnunculus *small boat*
Lucrīnum lacum: Lucrīnus lacus *the Lucrine lake (a lagoon near Baiae)*
āctam: agere *drive*
summā suī parte *from the top downwards (literally 'from its highest part')*
terrestre: terrestris *on land*
māchināmentum *machine, contraption*
concidisse: concidere *collapse*
observāns: observāre *notice, observe*
ēvāsisse: ēvādere *escape*
quamvīs *although*
vīsendī: vīsere *come to visit*
cūram: cūra *trouble, bother*
ad praesēns *for the present, for the moment*

4 Why do you think Acerronia shouted out that she was Agrippina?
  Is there more than one possible explanation for her action?
5 What reasons led Agrippina to realise that the shipwreck had
  been a deliberate attempt on her life? What did she decide was her
  only hope of safety?

6 In her message, Agrippina described Nero as 'perīculō mātris perterritus'. Is this likely to be true? If not, why did Agrippina describe him in this way?
7 What order did Agrippina give? What do you think her reason was?
8 What impression do you gain from this passage of Agrippina's ability and character?

II

at Nerōnī, nūntiōs patrātī facinoris exspectantī, affertur Agrippīnam ēvāsisse ictū levī vulnerātam. tum pavōre exanimis et affirmāns iam iamque adfore mātrem ultiōnis avidam, Burrum et Senecam statim arcessīvit. longum utrīusque silentium; tandem Seneca respexit Burrum ac rogāvit num mīlitēs caedem Agrippīnae 5 exsequī iubērentur. ille praetōriānōs tōtī Caesarum domuī obstrictōs esse respondit: 'mīlitēs' inquit, 'nihil ātrōx adversus fīliam Germānicī facere audēbunt; efficiat Anicētus prōmissa.' quī haudquāquam haesitat; poscit summam sceleris. ad haec verba Nerō profitētur illō diē sibi tandem darī imperium auctōremque 10 tantī mūneris esse lībertum; Anicētō imperāvit ut ad vīllam statim proficīscerētur dūceretque sēcum hominēs fidēlissimōs.

patrātī: patrāre *accomplish, commit*
affertur: afferre *bring news, report*
ictū: ictus *blow*
exanimis *out of one's mind*
iam iamque *at any moment now*
adfore: *future infinitive of* adesse *be present, arrive*
exsequī *carry out*
Caesarum: Caesarēs *the Caesars (family of the first Roman emperors)*
domuī: domus *family*
obstrictōs esse: obstringere *bind (with oath of loyalty)*
ātrōx *violent, dreadful*
Germānicī: Germānicus *Germanicus (Agrippina's father, a popular general and member of the imperial family)*
prōmissa: prōmissum *promise*
summam: summa *full responsibility, supreme command*
profitētur: profitērī *declare*

(continued)

**Members of the praetorian guard, the emperor's personal bodyguard
(see pp. 170–1)**

1 Describe Nero's reaction to the news of Agrippina's escape. Compare it with Agrippina's own reaction to the attempt on her life.

2 Why do you think Seneca and Burrus are so silent and unhelpful (lines 4–8)? Why do you think Anicetus is so eager to carry out the deed (lines 8–9)?

3 How does Nero's mood change after Anicetus has taken charge? Explain his comment 'illō diē . . . esse lībertum' (lines 10–11).

Language note

1 From Unit I onwards, you have met sentences like this:

Pompēiānī rīdēbant, clāmābant, plaudēbant.
The Pompeians were laughing, shouting and applauding.

2 In Unit IVB, you have met a different way of expressing the same idea:

Pompēiānī rīdēre clāmāre plaudere.

Further examples:

māter ōrāre hortārī iubēre ut fugerem.
My mother begged, urged and ordered me to flee.

spectāculum horribile in campīs patentibus – sequī fugere occīdī capī.
There was a ghastly sight on the open plains – men were chasing, were fleeing, were being killed and being captured.

Notice how the *infinitive* of the verb is used in these examples, instead of an indicative tense such as an imperfect, to describe events happening in the past. This is known as the *historic* use of the infinitive (*'historic infinitive'* for short). It occurs most often in descriptions of lively and rapid action.

3 Further examples:

1 omnēs amīcī bibere cantāre saltāre.
2 in urbe maximus pavor; aliī ad portās fugere; aliī bona sua in plaustra impōnere; aliī uxōrēs līberōsque quaerere; omnēs viae multitūdine complērī. (*from the historian Sallust*)

percussōrēs

interim vulgātō Agrippīnae perīculō, omnēs, ut quisque audīverat,
dēcurrere ad lītus. hī mōlēs, hī proximās scaphās cōnscendere; aliī,
quantum corpus sinēbat, prōcēdere in mare; nōnnūllī manūs
extendere; omnis ōra complērī questibus, precibus, clāmōre
5 hominum dīversa rogantium aut incerta respondentium; affluere
ingēns multitūdō cum lūminibus, atque ubi incolumem esse
Agrippīnam vulgātum est, ad grātulandum sēsē expedīre, dōnec
aspectū agminis hominum armātōrum et minantium disiectī sunt.
Anicētus vīllam mīlitibus circumvenit, effrāctāque iānuā servōs eōs
10 abripit quī obstant, dōnec ad forēs cubiculī venīret; ibi paucī
adstābant, cēterīs terrōre irrumpentium exterritīs. cubiculō
modicum lūmen inerat et ancillārum ūna; magis ac magis anxia

'dīcite mihi quārē hūc missī sītis.' (line 16)

fīēbat Agrippīna quod nēmō ā fīliō vēnisset. abeunte dēnique
ancillā, Agrippīna 'tū quoque mē dēseris' inquit; tum respicit
Anicētum triērarchō et centuriōne comitātum. 'quī estis?' inquit. 15
'dīcite mihi quārē hūc missī sītis.' nūllum respōnsum; circumsistunt
lectum percussōrēs et prior triērarchus fūstī caput eius afflīxit.
deinde centuriōnī gladium ad occīdendum dēstringentī Agrippīna
prōtendēns uterum 'ventrem ferī' exclāmāvit multīsque vulneribus
cōnfecta est. 20

    cremāta est eādem nocte convīvālī lectō et exequiīs vīlibus; num
īnspexerit mātrem mortuam Nerō (ut multī affirmant) et fōrmam
corporis eius admīrātus sit, incertum est. hunc fore suī fīnem multōs
ante annōs crēdiderat Agrippīna contempseratque. nam eī rogantī
dē fortūnā Nerōnis respondērunt astrologī illum imperātūrum 25
mātremque occīsūrum; atque Agrippīna 'occīdat' inquit, 'dum
imperet.'

percussōrēs: percussor *assassin*	exterritīs: exterrēre *frighten away*
vulgātō: vulgāre *make known*	triērarchō: triērarchus *naval captain*
ut quisque *as soon as each one*	circumsistunt: circumsistere *take up*
hī . . . hī *some . . . others*	*position around*
mōlēs: mōlēs *embankment, sea-wall*	fūstī: *ablative of* fūstis
quantum *as far as*	afflīxit: afflīgere *strike*
sinēbat: sinere *allow*	prōtendēns: prōtendere *thrust forward*
questibus: questus *lamentation,*	uterum: uterus *womb*
cry of grief	convīvālī: convīvālis *dining*
affluere *flock to the spot*	exequiīs: exequiae *funeral rites*
sēsē expedīre *prepare oneself, get ready*	fore = futūrum esse
disiectī sunt: disicere *scatter, disperse*	contempserat: contemnere *disregard*
abripit: abripere *remove by force*	imperātūrum (esse): imperāre *be emperor*
forēs *door*	dum *provided that*

Language note

1   In Stage 30, you met the perfect indicative passive:

duo cōnsulēs creātī sunt.   Two consuls have been appointed.

2   In Stage 48 you have met sentences like these:

puer stultus nescit quot cōnsulēs **creātī sint**.
The stupid boy does not know how many consuls have been
appointed.

dominus cognōscere vult quanta pecūnia **impēnsa sit**.
The master wants to find out how much money has been spent.

The form of the verb in heavy print is the *perfect subjunctive passive*.

Further examples:

1   incertī sumus utrum Agrippīna servāta an necāta sit.
2   dīcite mihi quot hostēs captī sint.
3   ignōrō quārē ā centuriōne ēlēctus sim.

3   Compare the indicative and subjunctive forms of the perfect
passive of 'portō':

perfect indicative passive	*perfect subjunctive passive*
portātus sum	portātus sim
portātus es	portātus sīs
portātus est	portātus sit
portātī sumus	portātī sīmus
portātī estis	portātī sītis
portātī sunt	portātī sint

Perfect subjunctive passive forms of 'doceō', 'trahō' and 'audiō'
are given on page 193.

4   Study the following examples:

tam callidus est mercātor ut magnās opēs **adeptus sit**.
The merchant is so clever that he has obtained great wealth.

iūdex scīre vult num senī umquam **minātī sīmus**.

The judge wants to know whether we have ever threatened the old man.

The words in heavy print are *perfect subjunctive* forms of *deponent* verbs.

Further examples:

1 dīc mihi quid patrōnus tibi pollicitus sit.
2 scīre volō quārē nūntiī nōndum profectī sint.

Perfect subjunctive forms of 'cōnor', 'vereor', etc. are given on p. 198.

Exercises

1 Translate each sentence into Latin by selecting correctly from the list of Latin words.

1 I gave money to the boy (who was) carrying the books.
    puerī   librōs   portantī   pecūnia   dedī
    puerō   līberōs   portātī   pecūniam   dederam

2 The same women are here again, master.
    eadem   fēminae   simul   adsunt   dominus
    eaedem   fēminam   rūrsus   absunt   domine

3 By running, he arrived at the prison more quickly.
    currendō   ad carcerem   celeriter   advēnit
    currentī   ā carcere   celerius   advēnī

4 If you do not obey the laws, you will be punished.
    sī   lēgibus   pārueritis   pūnīminī
    nisi   lēgī   pārēbātis   pūniēminī

5 Let us force the chiefs of the barbarians to turn back.
    prīncipēs   barbarīs   revertor   cōgimus
    prīncipem   barbarōrum   revertī   cōgāmus

6 Men of this kind ought not to be made consuls.
    hominibus   huius   generis   cōnsulem   facere   nōnne   dēbet
    hominēs   huic   generī   cōnsulēs   fierī   nōn   dēbent

2 In each pair of sentences, translate sentence 'a'; then, with the help of pages 178–9 and 193, express the same idea in a passive form by correctly completing the nouns and verbs in sentence 'b', and translate again. For example:

a timēbam nē mīlitēs mē caperent.
b timēbam nē ā mīl. . . caper. . . .
Translated and completed, this becomes:
a timēbam nē mīlitēs mē caperent.
  I was afraid that the soldiers would catch me.
b timēbam nē ā mīlitibus caperer.
  I was afraid that I would be caught by the soldiers.

a dīc mihi quārē domina numquam ancillās laudet.
b dīc mihi quārē ancill. . . numquam ā domin. . . laud. . . .
Translated and completed, this becomes:
a dīc mihi quārē domina numquam ancillās laudet.
  Tell me why the mistress never praises the slave-girls.
b dīc mihi quārē ancillae numquam ā dominā laudentur.
  Tell me why the slave-girls are never praised by the mistress.

1a dominus cognōscere vult num servī cēnam parent.
1b dominus cognōscere vult num cēn. . . ā serv. . . par. . . .
2a tantum erat incendium ut flammae aulam dēlērent.
2b tantum erat incendium ut aul. . . flamm. . . dēlēr. . . .
3a barbarī frūmentum incendērunt ut inopia cibī nōs impedīret.
3b barbarī frūmentum incendērunt ut inop. . . cibī imped. . . .
4a in silvā tibi latendum est nē hostēs tē videant.
4b in silvā tibi latendum est nē ab host. . . vid. . . .
5a nisi vōs adiūvissem, barbarī vōs circumvēnissent.
5b nisi vōs adiūvissem, ā barbar. . . circumven. . . . .
6a nescio quārē prīnceps mē relēgāverit.
6b nescio quārē ā prīncip. . . relēg. . . . .

The emperor

By A.D.59, when the events described in Stage 48 took place, Rome had been ruled by emperors for nearly a century. The Republican system of government (in which two consuls were elected annually as joint heads of state, assisted by other magistrates and the senate) had collapsed in violence and bloodshed at the end of the first century B.C. Supreme power in the Roman world was in the hands of a single ruler: the emperor.

To the senate and people of Rome, the emperor was often known as the 'prīnceps' (chief citizen); to the soldiers, he was 'imperātor' (commander). But the word 'rēx' (king), which might seem a very appropriate title in view of the emperor's great personal power, was deliberately avoided, because the Romans had a long tradition of hatred towards the idea of kings. Kings had ruled Rome in the distant past, and the last one had been so unpopular that he was driven out; four-and-a-half centuries later, when Julius Caesar was suspected of intending to make himself a king, he was assassinated.

The first emperor (Augustus) and most of his successors tried to encourage the belief that in many ways the business of government was being carried on much as before. For example, consuls and other magistrates continued to be appointed, and the senate continued to meet, just as in the days of the Republic. However, the senate, consuls and magistrates were now much less powerful than before; and they were no longer elected by the people of Rome, but were in many cases appointed directly by the emperor.

The lives and reigns of the emperors in the first century A.D. are narrated by Tacitus in his *Annals* and *Histories*, and by Suetonius in his *Lives of the Emperors*. They give a vivid and sometimes appalling description of the emperors' immense personal power, the stupidity, greed, lust, extravagance and cruelty of individual emperors, the frequent plottings and struggles for power that went on among the emperors' advisers and associates, and the savagery and ruthlessness with which emperors treated possible rivals or conspirators.

But even when the emperor was vicious, eccentric or tyrannical, government of the empire still carried on, and the emperor himself had a crucial part to play; otherwise he risked losing popularity and power. Some emperors behaved sadistically or arrogantly to individuals and still carried out humane and efficient policies in government. For example, Domitian treated the senate with insolence and contempt, and put several of its members to death with little or no excuse, but Suetonius says of him that 'he took such great care in supervising the city magistrates and provincial governors that they were more honest and just during his reign than at any other time'.

If an emperor was conscientious, his work-load was heavy. He took an important and ever-increasing part in administering the law; he chose men for provincial governorships, legionary commands, consulships, the senate and numerous other posts and privileges; he acted as the commander-in-chief of the Roman army, determining the soldiers' pay, selecting the officers, allocating the legions and auxiliaries to particular parts of the empire, and (in the case of some emperors) leading troops on military campaigns; he received ambassadors from provinces and foreign states who

Roman bridge built by Trajan at Alcantara, Spain

brought him greetings, petitions, complaints or accusations, to which he would be expected to make an eloquent speech in reply (one of the causes of Nero's quarrel with his mother was her attempt to sit at his side, as if she were joint ruler with him, when foreign ambassadors came to see him); he dealt with the problems referred to him by provincial governors (the Bithynia correspondence of Pliny and Trajan provides a good example of this); he often had to care for the 'plēbs' or ordinary people of Rome, by providing regular distributions of corn or money to the citizens, putting on splendid and costly shows in the circus and amphitheatre, and undertaking large programmes of public building to beautify the city and relieve unemployment; he had the power to make law by bringing proposals before the senate; and by holding the post of Pontifex Maximus he was the official head of the state religion.

The emperor at work

For much of his time, the emperor carried out his responsibilities by receiving and replying to requests, and by hearing and judging disputes. The following examples (based on actual situations and incidents) give some indication of the variety of pleas and problems which he dealt with:

'The inhabitants of a neighbouring town have made a violent attack on us, killing and injuring many innocent people.'

'Please will you give Roman citizenship to a doctor who cured me of a dangerous illness.'

'Several towns in this province have been badly damaged by an earthquake; please can troops and money be sent.'

'My husband has been in exile for many years and is now old and ill; I appeal to you to allow him to come back.'

'There is a serious danger of revolt by the local tribes, and our soldiers urgently need reinforcements.'

'Please grant our city the privilege of building a temple in honour of your late father.'

'My neighbour claims this slave is his, but he's a liar; the slave is mine.'

'Please will you grant me the honour of the "lātus clāvus" (broad purple stripe on tunic and toga, indicating membership of the senate).'

'The governor of our province has illegally tortured and executed Roman citizens; we ask that he be tried and punished.'

Some of these requests and disputes were handled in writing; a constant stream of letters, petitions, appeals, accusations and other documents poured onto the emperor's desk. He was expected to deal with each one personally, deciding the substance of the reply and in many cases dictating its actual words, occasionally adding a sentence or two in his own handwriting. This correspondence was sometimes carried on in Latin, but often in Greek, especially when dealing with the eastern part of the empire. Other requests and disputes were presented verbally to the emperor in person by the people concerned, some of whom travelled vast distances to do so. An anecdote told by the Greek writer Dio about the Emperor Hadrian illustrates the way in which a Roman emperor was expected to make himself available to his subjects:

'When Hadrian was on a journey, he was stopped by a woman who wished to put a request to him. Being in a hurry, he moved on, saying "I'm too busy", whereupon the woman shouted after him "Then stop being emperor!" On hearing this, Hadrian turned round, came back and listened to her request.'

The emperor's helpers

It was impossible, of course, for one man to govern an empire of fifty million inhabitants single-handed, and although the emperors were reluctant to share power with other people, they needed reliable assistants of various sorts. For military tasks, the emperor could turn to the praetorian guard, who acted as his personal bodyguard and could be immensely important at times of crisis. In Tacitus' account of Nero's attempt to murder Agrippina, one of the first

The Emperor Marcus Aurelius as Pontifex Maximus presiding at a sacrifice

people the emperor sends for when the plot goes wrong is Burrus, the praetorian guard's commander (see p.159, line 3). When the emperor was administering the law or taking a decision on which he wanted advice, he could summon his 'cōnsilium' (council) and ask for the opinions of his 'amīcī' (friends). For assistance in the day-to-day running of government, the emperor could make use of his slaves and (more particularly) his freedmen. These were not official employees of the state, but were members of the emperor's personal household. Some of the freedmen possessed great power and influence; for instance, in the events related in Stage 48, a crucial part was played by the freedman Anicetus, who not only invented a method for carrying out Agrippina's murder (p.153, lines 10–16), but also took control of the situation when the plot misfired (p.159, lines 8–12).

The succession

One of the most important questions facing an emperor was to decide who should succeed him. Sometimes the position of emperor was inherited by a son from his father; sometimes an emperor with no sons of his own adopted another member of the family as his heir and successor. Some emperors deliberately looked outside their family in an effort to find the most suitable person; the Emperor Nerva chose an experienced and popular general (Trajan) to succeed him, and adopted him as his heir in preference to any of his own relatives. But on many occasions, the question was settled by force and violence. For example, in A.D. 41 the soldiers of the praetorian guard, having murdered the Emperor Caligula, found Caligula's uncle Claudius hiding in the palace and proclaimed him as the new emperor; nobody was in a position to stop them, because they could get their way by physical force. And in A.D.69, which became known as the 'year of the four emperors', there was a savage civil war, in which several rival candidates, supported by different sections of the Roman army, each tried to make himself emperor.

Emperor-worship

At his death, an emperor was normally deified. He received the title 'dīvus' (god) and was honoured with prayers and sacrifices; altars and (sometimes) temples were dedicated to him. Some emperors were worshipped as gods even during their lifetime, especially in the eastern provinces, which had long been accustomed to paying divine honours to their own rulers. For many inhabitants of the empire, worship of this kind was a natural response to the immense power possessed by a Roman emperor.

Carved gem showing the deification of the Emperor Augustus

Vocabulary checklist

caedēs, caedis – murder, slaughter
dōnec – until
ēvādō, ēvādere, ēvāsī – escape
incolumis, incolume – safe
latus, lateris – side
metuō, metuere, metuī – be afraid, fear
mūnus, mūneris – gift
nē quis – in case anyone
    nē quid – in case anything
pectus, pectoris – breast, heart
pietās, pietātis – duty, piety (respect for (1) the gods, (2) homeland,
    (3) family)
premō, premere, pressī, pressus – press, crush
quisque – each
vel. . . vel – either. . . or
velut – as if, like
vīs – force, violence

Give the meaning of:

caedere, incolumitās, invādere, metus, pius   (continued)

Numbers

ūnus – one	prīmus – first
duo – two	secundus – second
trēs – three	tertius – third
quattuor – four	quārtus – fourth
quīnque – five	quīntus – fifth
sex – six	sextus – sixth
septem – seven	septimus – seventh
octō – eight	octāvus – eighth
novem – nine	nōnus – ninth
decem – ten	decimus – tenth

ūndecim – eleven
duodecim – twelve
trēdecim – thirteen
quattuordecim – fourteen
quīndecim – fifteen
sēdecim – sixteen
septendecim – seventeen
duodēvīgintī – eighteen
ūndēvīgintī – nineteen
vīgintī – twenty

trīgintā – thirty
quadrāgintā – forty
quīnquāgintā – fifty
sexāgintā – sixty
septuāgintā – seventy
octōgintā – eighty
nōnāgintā – ninety
centum – a hundred

ducentī – two hundred
trecentī – three hundred
quadringentī – four hundred
quīngentī – five hundred
sescentī – six hundred
septingentī – seven hundred
octingentī – eight hundred
nōngentī – nine hundred
mīlle – a thousand
duo mīlia – two thousand

Language
Information

Contents

PART ONE: ACCIDENCE

Nouns

1

	first declension	second declension			third declension	
	f.	*m.*	*m.*	*n.*	*m.*	*m.*
SINGULAR						
nominative and vocative	puella	servus (*voc.* serve)	puer	templum	mercātor	leō
accusative	puellam	servum	puerum	templum	mercātōrem	leōnem
genitive	puellae	servī	puerī	templī	mercātōris	leōnis
dative	puellae	servō	puerō	templō	mercātōrī	leōnī
ablative	puellā	servō	puerō	templō	mercātōre	leōne
PLURAL						
nominative and vocative	puellae	servī	puerī	templa	mercātōrēs	leōnēs
accusative	puellās	servōs	puerōs	templa	mercātōrēs	leōnēs
genitive	puellārum	servōrum	puerōrum	templōrum	mercātōrum	leōnum
dative	puellīs	servīs	puerīs	templīs	mercātōribus	leōnibus
ablative	puellīs	servīs	puerīs	templīs	mercātōribus	leōnibus

	fourth declension		fifth declension
	f.	*n.*	*m.*
SINGULAR			
nominative and vocative	manus	genū	diēs
accusative	manum	genū	diem
genitive	manūs	genūs	diēī
dative	manuī	genū	diēī
ablative	manū	genū	diē
PLURAL			
nominative and vocative	manūs	genua	diēs
accusative	manūs	genua	diēs
genitive	manuum	genuum	diērum
dative	manibus	genibus	diēbus
ablative	manibus	genibus	diēbus

m.	m.	f.	n.	n.	n.	
						SINGULAR
cīvis	rēx	urbs	nōmen	tempus	mare	*nominative and vocative*
cīvem	rēgem	urbem	nōmen	tempus	mare	*accusative*
cīvis	rēgis	urbis	nōminis	temporis	maris	*genitive*
cīvī	rēgī	urbī	nōminī	temporī	marī	*dative*
cīve	rēge	urbe	nōmine	tempore	marī	*ablative*
						PLURAL
cīvēs	rēgēs	urbēs	nōmina	tempora	maria	*nominative and vocative*
cīvēs	rēgēs	urbēs	nōmina	tempora	maria	*accusative*
cīvium	rēgum	urbium	nōminum	temporum	marium	*genitive*
cīvibus	rēgibus	urbibus	nōminibus	temporibus	maribus	*dative*
cīvibus	rēgibus	urbibus	nōminibus	temporibus	maribus	*ablative*

2 For examples of the locative case, see p.206.

3 For the ways in which the different cases are used, see pp. 204–6.

4 In some of the Latin verse in Unit IVB, you have met phrases and sentences in which the plural of a noun is used with a singular meaning:

ignārus sua sē tractāre **perīcla**
unaware that he was handling **a cause of danger** to himself

Adjectives

1   first and second declension:

	masculine	*feminine*	*neuter*
SINGULAR			
nominative and vocative	bonus (*voc.* bone)	bona	bonum
accusative	bonum	bonam	bonum
genitive	bonī	bonae	bonī
dative	bonō	bonae	bonō
ablative	bonō	bonā	bonō
PLURAL			
nominative and vocative	bonī	bonae	bona
accusative	bonōs	bonās	bona
genitive	bonōrum	bonārum	bonōrum
dative		bonīs	
ablative		bonīs	

	masculine	*feminine*	*neuter*
SINGULAR			
nominative and vocative	pulcher	pulchra	pulchrum
accusative	pulchrum	pulchram	pulchrum
genitive	pulchrī	pulchrae	pulchrī
dative	pulchrō	pulchrae	pulchrō
ablative	pulchrō	pulchrā	pulchrō
PLURAL			
nominative and vocative	pulchrī	pulchrae	pulchra
accusative	pulchrōs	pulchrās	pulchra
genitive	pulchrōrum	pulchrārum	pulchrōrum
dative		pulchrīs	
ablative		pulchrīs	

2   third declension:

	masc. and fem.	neuter	masc. and fem.	neuter
SINGULAR				
nominative and vocative	fortis	forte	fēlīx	fēlīx
accusative	fortem	forte	fēlīcem	fēlīx
genitive	fortis		fēlīcis	
dative	fortī		fēlīcī	
ablative	fortī		fēlīcī	
PLURAL				
nominative and vocative	fortēs	fortia	fēlīcēs	fēlīcia
accusative	fortēs	fortia	fēlīcēs	fēlīcia
genitive	fortium		fēlīcium	
dative	fortibus		fēlīcibus	
ablative	fortibus		fēlīcibus	

	masc. and fem.	neuter	masc. and fem.	neuter
SINGULAR				
nominative and vocative	ingēns	ingēns	longior	longius
accusative	ingentem	ingēns	longiōrem	longius
genitive	ingentis		longiōris	
dative	ingentī		longiōrī	
ablative	ingentī		longiōre	
PLURAL				
nominative and vocative	ingentēs	ingentia	longiōrēs	longiōra
accusative	ingentēs	ingentia	longiōrēs	longiōra
genitive	ingentium		longiōrum	
dative	ingentibus		longiōribus	
ablative	ingentibus		longiōribus	

Comparison of adjectives and adverbs

1 Adjectives:

	comparative	superlative
longus	longior	longissimus
long	*longer*	*longest, very long*
pulcher	pulchrior	pulcherrimus
beautiful	*more beautiful*	*most beautiful, very beautiful*
fortis	fortior	fortissimus
brave	*braver*	*bravest, very brave*
fēlīx	fēlīcior	fēlīcissimus
lucky	*luckier*	*luckiest, very lucky*
prūdēns	prūdentior	prūdentissimus
shrewd	*shrewder*	*shrewdest, very shrewd*
facilis	facilior	facillimus
easy	*easier*	*easiest, very easy*

Irregular forms:

bonus	melior	optimus
good	*better*	*best, very good*
malus	peior	pessimus
bad	*worse*	*worst, very bad*
magnus	maior	maximus
big	*bigger*	*biggest, very big*
parvus	minor	minimus
small	*smaller*	*smallest, very small*
multus	plūs	plūrimus
much	*more*	*most, very much*
multī	plūrēs	plūrimī
many	*more*	*most, very many*

The forms of the comparative adjective 'longior' are shown on p.181.

Superlative adjectives such as 'longissimus' change their endings in the same way as 'bonus' (shown on p.180).

2 Adverbs:

	comparative	superlative
lātē	lātius	lātissimē
widely	*more widely*	*most widely, very widely*
pulchrē	pulchrius	pulcherrimē
beautifully	*more beautifully*	*most beautifully, very beautifully*
fortiter	fortius	fortissimē
bravely	*more bravely*	*most bravely, very bravely*
fēlīciter	fēlīcius	fēlīcissimē
luckily	*more luckily*	*most luckily, very luckily*
prūdenter	prūdentius	prūdentissimē
shrewdly	*more shrewdly*	*most shrewdly, very shrewdly*
facile	facilius	facillimē
easily	*more easily*	*most easily, very easily*

Irregular forms:

bene	melius	optimē
well	*better*	*best, very well*
male	peius	pessimē
badly	*worse*	*worst, very badly*
magnopere	magis	maximē
greatly	*more*	*most, very greatly*
paulum	minus	minimē
little	*less*	*least, very little*
multum	plūs	plūrimum
much	*more*	*most, very much*

Pronouns

1 ego and tū ('I', 'you', etc.)

	singular		plural	
nominative	ego	tū	nōs	vōs
accusative	mē	tē	nōs	vōs
genitive	meī	tuī	nostrum	vestrum
dative	mihi	tibi	nōbīs	vōbīs
ablative	mē	tē	nōbīs	vōbīs

2 sē ('himself', 'herself', 'themselves', etc.)

	singular	plural
accusative	sē	sē
genitive	suī	suī
dative	sibi	sibi
ablative	sē	sē

3 hic ('this', 'these', etc.; also used with the meaning 'he', 'she', 'they', etc.)

	singular			plural		
	masculine	feminine	neuter	masculine	feminine	neuter
nominative	hic	haec	hoc	hī	hae	haec
accusative	hunc	hanc	hoc	hōs	hās	haec
genitive		huius		hōrum	hārum	hōrum
dative		huic			hīs	
ablative	hōc	hāc	hōc		hīs	

4 ille ('that', 'those', etc.; also used with the meaning 'he', 'she', 'they', etc.)

	singular			plural		
	masculine	feminine	neuter	masculine	feminine	neuter
nominative	ille	illa	illud	illī	illae	illa
accusative	illum	illam	illud	illōs	illās	illa
genitive		illīus		illōrum	illārum	illōrum
dative		illī			illīs	
ablative	illō	illā	illō		illīs	

5 ipse ('myself', 'yourself', 'himself', etc.)

	singular			plural		
	masculine	feminine	neuter	masculine	feminine	neuter
nominative	ipse	ipsa	ipsum	ipsī	ipsae	ipsa
accusative	ipsum	ipsam	ipsum	ipsōs	ipsās	ipsa
genitive		ipsīus		ipsōrum	ipsārum	ipsōrum
dative		ipsī			ipsīs	
ablative	ipsō	ipsā	ipsō		ipsīs	

6 is ('he', 'she', 'it', etc.; also used with the meaning 'that', 'those', etc.)

	singular			plural		
	masculine	feminine	neuter	masculine	feminine	neuter
nominative	is	ea	id	eī	eae	ea
accusative	eum	eam	id	eōs	eās	ea
genitive		eius		eōrum	eārum	eōrum
dative		eī			eīs	
ablative	eō	eā	eō		eīs	

For examples in which forms of 'is' are used with the relative pronoun 'quī', see paragraph 9 on p.187.

7 īdem ('the same')

	singular			plural		
	masculine	feminine	neuter	masculine	feminine	neuter
nominative	īdem	eadem	idem	eīdem	eaedem	eadem
accusative	eundem	eandem	idem	eōsdem	eāsdem	eadem
genitive		eiusdem		eōrundem	eārundem	eōrundem
dative		eīdem			eīsdem	
ablative	eōdem	eādem	eōdem		eīsdem	

8 quī ('who', 'which', etc.; also used at the start of sentences with the meaning 'he', 'this', etc.)

	singular			plural		
	masculine	feminine	neuter	masculine	feminine	neuter
nominative	quī	quae	quod	quī	quae	quae
accusative	quem	quam	quod	quōs	quās	quae
genitive		cuius		quōrum	quārum	quōrum
dative		cui			quibus	
ablative	quō	quā	quō		quibus	

Notice again the use of the *connecting relative:*

tertiā hōrā dux advēnit. quem cum cōnspexissent, mīlitēs magnum clāmōrem sustulērunt.
At the third hour the leader arrived. When they caught sight of him, the soldiers raised a great shout.

deinde nūntiī locūtī sunt. quōrum verbīs obstupefactus, rēx diū tacēbat.
Then the messengers spoke. Stunned by their words, the king was silent for a long time.

pontifex ipse templum dēdicāvit. quō factō, omnēs plausērunt.
The chief priest himself dedicated the temple. When this had been done, everybody applauded.

9 Notice again how forms of the pronoun 'is' can be used as antecedents of the relative pronoun 'quī':

   1 is quī illam fābulam nārrāvit mentiēbātur.
      He who told that story was lying.
  or, The man who told that story was lying.
   2 eī quī fūgērunt mox capientur.
      Those who ran away will soon be caught.
   3 id quod nūntius dīxit nōs maximē perturbāvit.
      That which the messenger said alarmed us very much.
  or, What the messenger said alarmed us very much.
   4 eās vīllās vēndidī quae mē minimē dēlectābant.
      I sold those villas that least appealed to me.

Pick out the antecedent, relative pronoun and relative clause in each example.

In Stage 45, you met sentences in which the antecedent comes after the relative clause, or is omitted altogether:

   5 quī tē heri culpābat, is tē hodiē laudat.
      The person who was blaming you yesterday is praising you today.
   6 quae dominus iussit, ea servōs efficere oportet.
      What the master has ordered, the slaves must carry out.
  or, The slaves must carry out what the master has ordered.
   7 quod potuī, fēcī.
      I have done what I could.

Pick out the relative pronoun, relative clause and antecedent (if there is one) in each example.

10 quīdam ('one', 'a certain')

	singular			plural		
	masculine	feminine	neuter	masculine	feminine	neuter
nominative	quīdam	quaedam	quoddam	quīdam	quaedam	quaedam
accusative	quendam	quandam	quoddam	quōsdam	quāsdam	quaedam
genitive		cuiusdam		quōrundam	quārundam	quōrundam
dative		cuidam			quibusdam	
ablative	quōdam	quādam	quōdam		quibusdam	

Verbs

Indicative active

1

first conjugation	*second conjugation*	*third conjugation*	*fourth conjugation*
PRESENT (*'I carry'*, etc.)			
portō	doceō	trahō	audiō
portās	docēs	trahis	audīs
portat	docet	trahit	audit
portāmus	docēmus	trahimus	audīmus
portātis	docētis	trahitis	audītis
portant	docent	trahunt	audiunt
FUTURE (*'I shall carry'*, etc.)			
portābō	docēbō	traham	audiam
portābis	docēbis	trahēs	audiēs
portābit	*etc.*	trahet	*etc.*
portābimus		trahēmus	
portābitis		trahētis	
portābunt		trahent	
IMPERFECT (*'I was carrying'*, etc.)			
portābam	docēbam	trahēbam	audiēbam
portābās	docēbās	trahēbās	audiēbās
portābat	*etc.*	*etc.*	*etc.*
portābāmus			
portābātis			
portābant			

2 In Stage 44, you met the *historic present* tense, in which the present tense is used to describe events that happened in the past:

tābuerant cērae; nūdōs **quatit** ille lacertōs,
rēmigiōque carēns nōn ūllās **percipit** aurās.
The wax had melted; he **flaps** his bare arms, and being without wings he **fails** to get any grip on the air.

The historic present can be translated *either* by an English present tense (as in the example above), *or* by a past tense.

Notice again the use of the historic present tense in sentences containing 'dum' ('while . . .', 'at a moment when . . .'):

dum cēterī **labōrant**, duo servī effūgērunt.
While the rest **were working**, two slaves escaped.

3

first conjugation	second conjugation	third conjugation	fourth conjugation

PERFECT *('I have carried', 'I carried', etc.)*

portāvī	docuī	trāxī	audīvī
portāvistī	docuistī	trāxistī	audīvistī
portāvit	*etc.*	*etc.*	*etc.*
portāvimus			
portāvistis			
portāvērunt			

FUTURE PERFECT *('I shall have carried', etc., but often translated by an English present tense)*

portāverō	docuerō	trāxerō	audīverō
portāveris	docueris	trāxeris	audīveris
portāverit	*etc.*	*etc.*	*etc.*
portāverimus			
portāveritis			
portāverint			

PLUPERFECT *('I had carried', etc.)*

portāveram	docueram	trāxeram	audīveram
portāverās	docuerās	trāxerās	audīverās
portāverat	*etc.*	*etc.*	*etc.*
portāvcrāmus			
portāverātis			
portāverant			

4 In Unit IVB, you have met a new form of the 3rd person plural of the perfect tense:

portāvēre = portāvērunt   they (have) carried
trāxēre   = trāxērunt   they (have) dragged

Further examples:

audīvēre; recitāvēre; scrīpsēre; praebuēre.

Indicative passive

PRESENT *('I am carried', etc.)*			
portor	doceor	trahor	audior
portāris	docēris	traheris	audīris
portātur	docētur	trahitur	audītur
portāmur	docēmur	trahimur	audīmur
portāminī	docēminī	trahiminī	audīminī
portantur	docentur	trahuntur	audiuntur

FUTURE *('I shall be carried', etc.)*			
portābor	docēbor	trahar	audiar
portāberis	docēberis	trahēris	audiēris
portābitur	*etc.*	trahētur	*etc.*
portābimur		trahēmur	
portābiminī		trahēminī	
portābuntur		trahentur	

IMPERFECT *('I was being carried', etc.)*			
portābar	docēbar	trahēbar	audiēbar
portābāris	docēbāris	trahēbāris	audiēbāris
portābātur	*etc.*	*etc.*	*etc.*
portābāmur			
portābāminī			
portābantur			

2 Translate each word, then change it from the singular to the plural, so that it means 'we shall be . . .' instead of 'I shall be . . .':

1 portābor; laudābor; docēbor; monēbor.
2 trahar; cōgar; audiar; impediar.

Translate each word, then change it from the singular to the plural, so that it means 'you (pl.) will be . . .' instead of 'you (s.) will be . . .':

3 portāberis; cūrāberis; docēberis; movēberis.
4 trahēris; mittēris; audiēris; custōdiēris.

3 PERFECT *('I have been carried', 'I was carried', etc.)*

portātus sum	doctus sum	tractus sum	audītus sum
portātus es	doctus es	tractus es	audītus es
portātus est	*etc.*	*etc.*	*etc.*
portātī sumus			
portātī estis			
portātī sunt			

FUTURE PERFECT *('I shall have been carried', etc., but often translated by an English present tense)*

portātus erō	doctus erō	tractus erō	audītus erō
portātus eris	doctus eris	tractus eris	audītus eris
portātus erit	*etc.*	*etc.*	*etc.*
portātī erimus			
portātī eritis			
portātī erunt			

PLUPERFECT *('I had been carried', etc.)*

portātus eram	doctus eram	tractus eram	audītus eram
portātus erās	doctus erās	tractus erās	audītus erās
portātus erat	*etc.*	*etc.*	*etc.*
portātī erāmus			
portātī erātis			
portātī erant			

4 Translate each example; then, with the help of paragraph 1, change it from the perfect to the present tense, keeping the same person and number (i.e. 1st person singular, etc.), and translate again. For example, 'audītus sum' ('I have been heard', 'I was heard') would become 'audior' .('I am heard', 'I am being heard').

portātī sunt; audītus es; tractus est; doctī sumus; mūtātī estis; impedītus sum.

Subjunctive active

1 PRESENT SUBJUNCTIVE

portem	doceam	traham	audiam
portēs	doceās	trahās	audiās
portet	doceat	trahat	audiat
portēmus	doceāmus	trahāmus	audiāmus
portētis	doceātis	trahātis	audiātis
portent	doceant	trahant	audiant

IMPERFECT SUBJUNCTIVE

portārem	docērem	traherem	audīrem
portārēs	docērēs	traherēs	audīrēs
portāret	*etc.*	*etc.*	*etc.*
portārēmus			
portārētis			
portārent			

PERFECT SUBJUNCTIVE

portāverim	docuerim	trāxerim	audīverim
portāverīs	docuerīs	trāxerīs	audīverīs
portāverit	*etc.*	*etc.*	*etc.*
portāverīmus			
portāvcrītis			
portāverint			

PLUPERFECT SUBJUNCTIVE

portāvissem	docuissem	trāxissem	audīvissem
portāvissēs	docuissēs	trāxissēs	audīvissēs
portāvisset	*etc.*	*etc.*	*etc.*
portāvissēmus			
portāvissētis			
portāvissent			

2 For ways in which the subjunctive is used, see pp.207–8.

Subjunctive passive

1 The forms of the PRESENT tense of the subjunctive passive (introduced in Stage 41) are as follows:

porter	docear	trahar	audiar
portēris	doceāris	trahāris	audiāris
portētur	doceātur	trahātur	audiātur
portēmur	doceāmur	trahāmur	audiāmur
portēminī	doceāminī	trahāminī	audiāminī
portentur	doceantur	trahantur	audiantur

2 The IMPERFECT tense of the subjunctive passive (introduced in Stage 43):

portārer	docērer	traherer	audīrer
portārēris	docērēris	traherēris	audīrēris
portārētur	etc.	etc.	etc.
portārēmur			
portārēminī			
portārentur			

3 The PERFECT tense of the subjunctive passive (introduced in Stage 48):

portātus sim	doctus sim	tractus sim	audītus sim
portātus sīs	doctus sīs	tractus sīs	audītus sīs
portātus sit	etc.	etc.	etc.
portātī sīmus			
portātī sītis			
portātī sint			

4 The PLUPERFECT tense of the subjunctive passive (introduced in Stage 46):

portātus essem	doctus essem	tractus essem	audītus essem
portātus essēs	doctus essēs	tractus essēs	audītus essēs
portātus esset	etc.	etc.	etc.
portātī essēmus			
portātī essētis			
portātī essent			

Other forms

1   IMPERATIVE SINGULAR AND PLURAL (*'carry!' etc.*)

portā, portāte	docē, docēte	trahe, trahite	audī, audīte

2   PRESENT PARTICIPLE (*'carrying', etc.*)

portāns	docēns	trahēns	audiēns

Present participles change their endings in the same way as 'ingēns' (shown on p.181), except that their ablative singular sometimes ends in '-e', e.g. 'portante', 'docente'.

3   PERFECT PASSIVE PARTICIPLE (*'having been carried', etc.*)

portātus	doctus	tractus	audītus

For perfect *active* participles, see Deponent verbs, p.199.

4   FUTURE PARTICIPLE (*'about to carry', etc.*)

portātūrus	doctūrus	tractūrus	audītūrus

Perfect passive and future participles change their endings in the same way as 'bonus' (p.180).

For examples of ways in which participles are used, see p.211.

5 PRESENT ACTIVE INFINITIVE (*'to carry'*, etc.)

| portāre | docēre | trahere | audīre |

6 PRESENT PASSIVE INFINITIVE (*'to be carried'*, etc.)

| portārī | docērī | trahī | audīrī |

Another way of using the present active and passive infinitives is described on p.161, Stage 48.

7 PERFECT ACTIVE INFINITIVE (*'to have carried'*, etc.)

| portāvisse | docuisse | trāxisse | audīvisse |

8 PERFECT PASSIVE INFINITIVE (*'to have been carried'*, etc.)

| portātus esse | doctus esse | tractus esse | audītus esse |

9 FUTURE ACTIVE INFINITIVE (*'to be about to carry'*, etc.)

| portātūrus esse | doctūrus esse | tractūrus esse | audītūrus esse |

For examples of ways in which infinitives are used to express indirect statements, see pp.209–11.

10 GERUND (*'carrying'*, etc.)

The cases of the gerund are formed in the following way:

accusative	portandum	docendum	trahendum	audiendum
genitive	portandī	docendī	trahendī	audiendī
dative	portandō	docendō	trahendō	audiendō
ablative	portandō	docendō	trahendō	audiendō

Notice that the gerund changes its endings in the same way as second declension nouns such as 'templum'; but it has no nominative case and no plural.

For ways in which the gerund is used, see p.214.

11 GERUNDIVE (*'being carried'*, *'needing to be carried'*, etc.)

| portandus | docendus | trahendus | audiendus |

Gerundives change their endings in the same way as 'bonus' (p.180). For ways in which the gerundive is used, see pp.214–15.

Deponent verbs

Indicative

1 Study the forms of the deponent verbs 'cōnor' ('I try'), 'vereor' ('I fear'), 'loquor' ('I speak') and 'mentior' ('I lie', 'I tell a lie'):

first conjugation	*second conjugation*	*third conjugation*	*fourth conjugation*
PRESENT *('I try', etc.)*			
cōnor	vereor	loquor	mentior
cōnāris	verēris	loqueris	mentīris
cōnātur	verētur	loquitur	mentītur
cōnāmur	verēmur	loquimur	mentīmur
cōnāminī	verēminī	loquiminī	mentīminī
cōnantur	verentur	loquuntur	mentiuntur
FUTURE *('I shall try', etc.)*			
cōnābor	verēbor	loquar	mentiar
cōnāberis	verēberis	loquēris	mentiēris
cōnābitur	*etc.*	loquētur	*etc.*
cōnābimur		loquēmur	
cōnābiminī		loquēminī	
cōnābuntur		loquentur	
IMPERFECT *('I was trying', etc.)*			
cōnābar	verēbar	loquēbar	mentiēbar
cōnābāris	verēbāris	loquēbāris	mentiebaris
cōnābātur	*etc.*	*etc.*	*etc.*
cōnābāmur			
cōnābāminī			
cōnābantur			

2 In paragraph 1, find the Latin for:

he tries; you (pl.) speak; we fear; I lie; I shall fear; we shall speak; they were trying; you(s.) were lying.

What would be the Latin for the following?

he will fear; we shall lie; you(pl.) were fearing; they were lying.

3 Give the meaning of:

1 loquitur; verēris; mentīmur; cōnāminī.

2 cōnābor; verēbimur; loquar; mentientur.

3 loquēbāris; cōnābāmur; verēbar; mentiēbāminī.

4 PERFECT *('I have tried', 'I tried', etc.)*

cōnātus sum	veritus sum	locūtus sum	mentītus sum
cōnātus es	veritus es	locūtus es	mentītus es
cōnātus est	*etc.*	*etc.*	*etc.*
cōnātī sumus			
cōnātī estis			
cōnātī sunt			

FUTURE PERFECT *('I shall have tried', etc. but often translated by an English present tense)*

cōnātus erō	veritus erō	locūtus erō	mentītus erō
cōnātus eris	veritus eris	locūtus eris	mentītus eris
cōnātus erit	*etc.*	*etc.*	*etc.*
cōnātī erimus			
cōnātī eritis			
cōnātī erunt			

PLUPERFECT *('I had tried', etc.)*

cōnātus eram	veritus eram	locūtus eram	mentītus eram
cōnātus erās	veritus erās	locūtus erās	mentītus erās
cōnātus erat	*etc.*	*etc.*	*etc.*
cōnātī erāmus			
cōnātī erātis			
cōnātī erant			

5 Translate each example; then, with the help of paragraph 1, change it from the perfect to the present tense, keeping the same person and number (i.e. 1st person singular, etc.), and translate again. For example, 'mentītus sum' ('I have lied', 'I lied') would become 'mentior' ('I lie').

cōnātus es; locūtus sum; veritī sumus; mentītī estis; precātī sunt; secūtus est.

Subjunctive

Deponent verbs form their subjunctive in the following way. Compare these forms with those of the subjunctive passive, shown on p.193.

PRESENT SUBJUNCTIVE *(introduced in Stage 41)*

cōner	verear	loquar	mentiar
cōnēris	vereāris	loquāris	mentiāris
cōnētur	vereātur	loquātur	mentiātur
cōnēmur	vereāmur	loquāmur	mentiāmur
cōnēminī	vereāminī	loquāminī	mentiāminī
cōnentur	vereantur	loquantur	mentiantur

IMPERFECT SUBJUNCTIVE *(introduced in Stage 43)*

cōnārer	verērer	loquerer	mentīrer
cōnārēris	verērēris	loquerēris	mentīrēris
cōnārētur	*etc.*	*etc.*	*etc.*
cōnārēmur			
cōnārēminī			
cōnārentur			

PERFECT SUBJUNCTIVE *(introduced in Stage 48)*

cōnātus sim	veritus sim	locutus sim	mentītus sim
cōnātus sīs	veritus sīs	locutus sīs	mentītus sīs
cōnātus sit	*etc.*	*etc.*	*etc.*
cōnātī sīmus			
cōnātī sitis			
cōnātī sint			

PLUPERFECT SUBJUNCTIVE *(introduced in Stage 46)*

cōnātus essem	veritus essem	locutus essem	mentītus essem
cōnātus essēs	veritus essēs	locutus essēs	mentītus essēs
cōnātus esset	*etc.*	*etc.*	*etc.*
cōnātī essēmus			
cōnātī essētis			
cōnātī essent			

Other forms

1 PRESENT PARTICIPLE (*'trying'*, *etc.*)

| cōnāns | verēns | loquēns | mentiēns |

2 PERFECT ACTIVE PARTICIPLE (*'having tried'*, *etc.*)

| cōnātus | veritus | locūtus | mentītus |

3 FUTURE PARTICIPLE (*'about to try'*, *etc.*)

| cōnātūrus | veritūrus | locūtūrus | mentītūrus |

Perfect active and future participles change their endings in the same way as 'bonus' (shown on p.180).

4 PRESENT INFINITIVE (*'to try'*, *etc.*)

| cōnārī | verērī | loquī | mentīrī |

5 PERFECT INFINITIVE (*'to have tried'*, *etc.*)

| cōnātus esse | veritus esse | locūtus esse | mentītus esse |

6 FUTURE INFINITIVE (*'to be about to try'*, *etc.*)

| cōnātūrus esse | veritūrus esse | locūtūrus esse | mentītūrus esse |

Irregular verbs

1 *Indicative*

PRESENT *('I am', etc.)*

sum	possum	eō	volō	ferō	capiō
es	potes	īs	vīs	fers	capis
est	potest	it	vult	fert	capit
sumus	possumus	īmus	volumus	ferimus	capimus
estis	potestis	ītis	vultis	fertis	capitis
sunt	possunt	eunt	volunt	ferunt	capiunt

FUTURE *('I shall be', etc.)*

erō	poterō	ībō	volam	feram	capiam
eris	poteris	ībis	volēs	ferēs	capiēs
erit	poterit	ībit	*etc.*	*etc.*	*etc.*
erimus	poterimus	ībimus			
eritis	poteritis	ībitis			
erunt	poterunt	ībunt			

IMPERFECT *('I was', etc.)*

eram	poteram	ībam	volēbam	ferēbam	capiēbam
erās	poterās	ībās	volēbās	ferēbās	capiēbās
etc.	*etc.*	*etc.*	*etc.*	*etc.*	*etc.*

PERFECT *('I have been', etc.)*

fuī	potuī	iī	voluī	tulī	cēpī
fuistī	potuistī	iistī	voluistī	tulistī	cēpistī
etc.	*etc.*	*etc.*	*etc.*	*etc.*	*etc.*

FUTURE PERFECT *('I shall have been', etc.)*

fuerō	potuerō	ierō	voluerō	tulerō	cēperō
fueris	potueris	ieris	volueris	tuleris	cēperis
etc.	*etc.*	*etc.*	*etc.*	*etc.*	*etc.*

PLUPERFECT *('I had been', etc.)*

fueram	potueram	ieram	volueram	tuleram	cēperam
fuerās	potuerās	ierās	voluerās	tulerās	cēperās
etc.	*etc.*	*etc.*	*etc.*	*etc.*	*etc.*

2

In Stage 46, you met sentences in which forms of 'sum' (e.g. 'est', 'erat', etc.) were omitted:

iam hōra diēī prīma.
Now it was the first hour of the day.

3 Subjunctive

PRESENT SUBJUNCTIVE

sim	possim	eam	velim	feram	capiam
sīs	possīs	eās	velīs	ferās	capiās
sit	*etc.*	*etc.*	*etc.*	*etc.*	*etc.*
sīmus					
sītis					
sint					

IMPERFECT SUBJUNCTIVE

essem	possem	īrem	vellem	ferrem	caperem
essēs	possēs	īrēs	vellēs	ferrēs	caperēs
etc.	*etc.*	*etc.*	*etc.*	*etc.*	*etc.*

PERFECT SUBJUNCTIVE

fuerim	potuerim	ierim	voluerim	tulerim	cēperim
fuerīs	potuerīs	ierīs	voluerīs	tulerīs	cēperīs
etc.	*etc.*	*etc.*	*etc.*	*etc.*	*etc.*

PLUPERFECT SUBJUNCTIVE

fuissem	potuissem	iissem	voluissem	tulissem	cēpissem
fuissēs	potuissēs	iissēs	voluissēs	tulissēs	cēpissēs
etc.	*etc.*	*etc.*	*etc.*	*etc.*	*etc.*

4 Infinitives

PRESENT INFINITIVE (*'to be'*, *etc.*)

esse	posse	īre	velle	ferre	capere

PERFECT INFINITIVE (*'to have been'*, *etc.*)

fuisse	potuisse	iisse	voluisse	tulisse	cēpisse

FUTURE INFINITIVE (*'to be about to be'*, *etc.*)

futūrus esse	–	itūrus esse	–	lātūrus esse	captūrus esse
(*sometimes* fore)					

5 'ferō' and 'capiō' have the following *passive* forms:

Indicative	PRESENT (*'I am brought'*, etc.)	
	feror	capior
	ferris	caperis
	fertur	capitur
	ferimur	capimur
	feriminī	capiminī
	feruntur	capiuntur
	FUTURE (*'I shall be brought'*, etc.)	
	ferar	capiar
	ferēris *etc.*	capiēris *etc.*
	IMPERFECT (*'I was being brought'*, etc.)	
	ferēbar	capiēbar
	ferēbāris *etc.*	capiēbāris *etc.*
	PERFECT (*'I have been brought'*, *'I was brought'*, etc.)	
	lātus sum	captus sum
	lātus es *etc.*	captus es *etc.*
	FUTURE PERFECT (*'I shall have been brought'*, etc.)	
	lātus erō	captus erō
	lātus eris *etc.*	captus eris *etc.*
	PLUPERFECT (*'I had been brought'*, etc.)	
	lātus eram	captus eram
	lātus erās *etc.*	captus erās *etc.*
Subjunctive	PRESENT SUBJUNCTIVE	
	ferar	capiar
	ferāris *etc.*	capiāris *etc.*
	IMPERFECT SUBJUNCTIVE	
	ferrer	caperer
	ferrēris *etc.*	caperēris *etc.*
	PERFECT SUBJUNCTIVE	
	lātus sim	captus sim
	lātus sīs *etc.*	captus sīs *etc.*
	PLUPERFECT SUBJUNCTIVE	
	lātus essem	captus essem
	lātus essēs *etc.*	captus essēs *etc.*
	PERFECT PASSIVE PARTICIPLE (*'having been brought'*, etc.)	
	lātus	captus
	PRESENT PASSIVE INFINITIVE (*'to be brought'*, etc.)	
	ferrī	capī
	PERFECT PASSIVE INFINITIVE (*'to have been brought'*, etc.)	
	lātus esse	captus esse

6   In Stage 41, you met the irregular verb 'fīō' ('I am made', 'I become', etc.):

PRESENT		PRESENT INFINITIVE
fīō	*I am made*	fierī *to be made*
fīs	*you are made*	
fit	*he is made*	PRESENT SUBJUNCTIVE
fiunt	*they are made*	fīam
		fīās *etc.*

FUTURE (*'I shall be made'*, etc.)	
fīam	
fīēs	
fīet *etc.*	

IMPERFECT (*'I was being made'*, etc.)	IMPERFECT SUBJUNCTIVE
fīēbam	fierem
fīēbās *etc.*	fierēs *etc.*

The forms of 'fīō' are used as present, future and imperfect tenses of the passive of 'faciō' ('I make', 'I do', etc.):

servī nihil faciunt.   nihil fit.
The slaves are doing nothing.   Nothing is being done.
                                       or, Nothing is happening.

populus mē rēgem faciet.   rex fīam.
The people will make me a king. I shall be made king.
                                       or, I shall become king.

The other tenses of the passive of 'faciō' are formed in the usual way:

equitēs impetum fēcērunt.   impetus ab equitibus factus est.
The cavalry made an attack.   An attack was made by the
                                       cavalry.

PART TWO: SYNTAX

Uses of the cases

1 *nominative*
poēta recitābat.	The poet was reciting.

2 *vocative*
cavē, **domine!**	Be careful, master!

3 *accusative*

3a **amīcōs** prōdidistī.	You betrayed your friends.
3b **multās hōrās** iter faciēbam.	I was travelling for many hours. (Compare 6d)
3c per **aquam**; in **urbem**	through the water; into the city (Compare 6e)

For examples of the accusative used in indirect statements, see pp.209–11.

4 *genitive*

4a fidēs **sociōrum meōrum**	the loyalty of my companions
4b parum **cibī**	not enough food
4c eques **summae audāciae**	a horseman of extreme boldness (Compare 6b)

5 *dative*

5a **coniugī** pecūniam reddidī.	I returned the money to my wife.
5b **lēgibus** pārēmus.	We obey the laws.
5c faber **magnō auxiliō** erit.	The craftsman will be a great help.

5d In Stage 45, you met the dative used in sentences like this:

fūrēs **mihi** omnia abstulērunt.	The thieves stole everything from me.

5e Notice the following use of the dative:

est **nōbīs** nūlla spēs.   We have no hope.

Further examples:

1 est mihi vīlla.
2 erant nōbīs multae gemmae.
3 cōnsulēs, quibus est summa potestās, tē adiuvābunt.

6 *ablative*

6a **vulneribus** cōnfectus	overcome by wounds
6b homō **vultū sevērō**	a man with a stern expression (Compare 4c)
6c **clārā gente** nātus	born from a famous family
6d **tertiō mēnse** revēnit.	He returned in the third month. (Compare 3b)
6e ex **hortīs**; in **Britanniā**	from the gardens; in Britain (Compare 3c)
6f perītior **frātre** sum.	I am more skilful than my brother.

This use of the ablative is known as the *ablative of comparison*.

6g You have also met the ablative used with adjectives such as 'dignus' and verbs such as 'ūtor' and 'careō':

dignus **suppliciō**	worthy of punishment
nāvibus ūtēbātur.	He was using ships.

6h In some of the Latin verse in Unit IVB, you have met further ways of using the ablative. For example, in Stage 47 you met sentences like these:

exarsit dolor **ossibus**.	Indignation blazed in his bones.
pelagō dēcurrit **apertō**.	He races over the open sea.

For ablative absolute phrases, see p.211.

7 Study the following examples:

1 **Rōmae** manēbam.
I was staying in Rome.

2 **Londiniī** habitāmus.
We live in London.

3 **Neāpolī** mortuus est.
He died at Naples.

4 quid **Pompēiīs** accidit?
What happened at Pompeii?

The words in heavy print are in the *locative* case.

The locative case is used only in names of towns and small islands and a small number of other words; it is therefore not normally included in lists of cases such as the table on pp.178–9. In first and second declension singular nouns, the locative case has the same form as the genitive; in third declension singular nouns, it is the same as the dative; in plural nouns, it is the same as the ablative.

Notice the locative case of 'domus' ('home') and 'rūs' ('country'):

5 **domī** dormiēbat.
He was sleeping at home.

6 **rūrī** numquam labōrō.
I never work in the country.

Further examples:

7 hanc epistulam Ephesī scrībō.
8 Athēnīs manēbimus.
9 mīlitēs in castrīs Dēvae erant.
10 rūrī ōtiōsus sum.

Uses of the subjunctive

1 *with 'cum'*

cum prōvinciam circumīrem, incendium Nīcomēdīae coortum est.

When I was going around the province, a fire broke out at Nicomedia.

2 *indirect question*

mīlitēs cognōscere volunt ubi senex gemmās cēlāverit.

The soldiers want to find out where the old man has hidden the jewels.

Sometimes the verb of asking, etc. (e.g. 'rogō', 'scio') is placed *after* the indirect question:

utrum custōs esset an carnifex, nēmō sciēbat.

Whether he was a guard or an executioner, no one knew.

3 *purpose clause*

hīc manēbō, ut vīllam dēfendam.

I shall stay here, to defend the villa.

prīnceps Plīnium ēmīsit quī Bīthȳnōs regeret.

The Emperor sent Pliny out to rule the Bithynians.

tacēbāmus, nē ā centuriōne audīrēmur.

We kept quiet, in order not to be heard by the centurion.

4 *indirect command*

tē moneō ut lēgibus pāreās.

I advise you to obey the laws.

medicus nōbīs imperāvit nē ingrederēmur.

The doctor told us not to go in.

5 *result clause*

barbarī tot hastās coniēcērunt ut plūrimī equitēs vulnerārentur.

The barbarians threw so many spears that most horsemen were wounded.

6 *with 'priusquam' ('before') and 'dum' ('until')*

abībō, priusquam ā dominō agnōscar.

I shall go away, before I am recognised by the master.

7 *fear clause*

verēbāmur nē omnēs nāvēs dēlētae essent.

We were afraid that all the ships had been destroyed.

perīculum est nē occīdāris.

There is a risk that you may be killed.

8 In Stage 45, you met the *jussive* subjunctive:

lūdōs spectēmus!   epistulam statim recitet.

Let us watch the games!   Let him read out the letter at once.

9 Translate the following examples, referring if necessary to the
tables of subjunctive forms on pp.192–3 and 198:

1 senex mīlitibus persuāsit ut arma dēpōnerent.
2 fugite, priusquam ā custōdibus capiāminī.
3 amīcī tuī timēbant nē interfectus essēs.
4 proficīscāmur!
5 cum pecūniam repperissem, revēnī
6 rex captīvīs pepercit nē crūdēlis vidērētur.
7 tantus erat strepitus ut omnēs terrērēmur.
8 quārē Imperātor Agricolam revocāverit, nescio.
9 aquam ferte, quā flammās exstinguam!
10 Salvius nunc respondeat.

In each sentence, find the reason why a subjunctive is being used.

10 For examples of the subjunctive in conditional sentences, see
pp.212–13.

11 For examples of the subjunctive used with the accusative and
infinitive in indirect statements, see paragraphs 4 and 5 on p.217.

12 For examples of the subjunctive in direct and indirect
deliberative questions, see p.156, Stage 48.

Indirect statement

1   From Unit IVA onwards, you have met indirect statements, expressed by a noun or pronoun in the *accusative* case and one of the following *infinitive* forms of the verb. Some indirect statements are introduced by a verb in the *present* tense (e.g. 'dīcō', 'crēdunt'), while others are introduced by a verb in the *perfect* or *imperfect* tense (e.g. 'dīxī', 'crēdēbant'); notice again how this makes a difference to the translation of the infinitive.

1   *present active infinitive*
   crēdō prīncipem Agricolae invidēre.
   I believe that the Emperor is jealous of Agricola.

   crēdēbam prīncipem Agricolae invidēre.
   I believed that the Emperor was jealous of Agricola.

   (Compare this with the direct statement:
   'prīnceps Agricolae invidet.')

2   *present passive infinitive*
   scit multās prōvinciās ā latrōnibus vexārī.
   He knows that many provinces are troubled by bandits.

   sciēbat multās prōvinciās ā latrōnibus vexārī.
   He knew that many provinces were troubled by bandits.

   (Compare: 'multae prōvinciae ā latrōnibus vexantur.')

3   *perfect active infinitive*
   centuriō hostēs dīcit cōnstitisse.
   The centurion says that the enemy have halted.

   centuriō hostēs dīxit cōnstitisse.
   The centurion said that the enemy had halted.

   (Compare: 'hostēs cōnstitērunt.')

4   *perfect passive infinitive*
   fēmina marītum servātum esse putat.
   The woman thinks that her husband has been saved.

   fēmina marītum servātum esse putāvit.
   The woman thought that her husband had been saved.

   (Compare: 'marītus servātus est.')

5 *future active infinitive*

senātōrēs prō certō habent cīvēs numquam cessūrōs esse.
The senators are sure that the citizens will never give in.

senātōrēs prō certō habēbant cīvēs numquam cessūrōs esse.
The senators were sure that the citizens would never give in.

(Compare: 'cīvēs numquam cēdent.')

The verb of speaking, etc. (e.g. 'crēdō', 'dīcit', 'putat') can be placed either at the beginning of the sentence (as in example 1 above) or in the middle of the indirect statement (as in example 3) or at the end of the sentence (example 4).

2 Notice how the verb 'negō' is used with indirect statements:

iuvenis negāvit sē pecūniam perdidisse.
The young man denied that he had wasted the money.
or, The young man said that he had not wasted the money.

3 Further examples:

1 nauta dīcit sē nāvem mox refectūrum esse.
2 nauta dīxit sē nāvem mox refectūrum esse.
3 sciō magnum perīculum nōbīs imminēre.
4 sciēbam magnum perīculum nōbīs imminēre.
5 dux eum discessisse crēdit.
6 dux eum discessisse crēdēbat.
7 nūntiī vīllās negant dēlētās esse.
8 nūntiī vīllās negāvērunt dēlētās esse.
9 audiō multōs captīvōs ad mortem cotīdiē dūcī.
10 audīvī multōs captīvōs ad mortem cotīdiē dūcī.

4 Sometimes one indirect statement is followed immediately by another:

rēx dīxit Rōmānōs exercitum parāvisse; mox prīmōs mīlitēs adventūrōs esse.
The king said that the Romans had prepared an army; (he said that) the first soldiers would soon arrive.

Notice that the verb 'dīxit' is not repeated in the second half of the sentence; the use of the accusative ('prīmōs mīlitēs') and the infinitive ('adventūrōs esse') makes it clear that the sentence is still reporting what the king said.

Further examples:

1 servus nūntiāvit cōnsulem morbō gravī afflīgī; medicōs dē vītā eius dēspērāre.
2 fāma vagābātur decem captīvōs ē carcere līberātōs esse; Imperātōrem enim eīs ignōvisse.

5 For examples of the subjunctive used with the infinitive in indirect statements, see paragraphs 4 and 5 on p.217.

Uses of the participle

1 From Unit IIIA onwards, you have met participles used in sentences like these:

1 senex, multās iniūriās passus, auxilium ā patrōnō petīvit.
  The old man, having suffered many acts of injustice, sought help from his patron.
2 prīncipī ē Campāniā redeuntī complūrēs senātōrēs obviam iērunt.
  When the Emperor was returning from Campania, several senators went to meet him.
3 ingēns multitūdō fugientium viās omnēs complēvit.
  A huge crowd of (people) running away filled all the streets.
4 ab amīcīs incitātus, in Circō Maximō certāvit.
  Urged on by his friends, he competed in the Circus Maximus.
5 ānulum inventum ad dominum tulimus.
  When the ring had been found, we took it to the master.
6 ānulō inventō, omnēs gaudēbant. (*ablative absolute*)
  When the ring had been found, everyone was glad.

Conditional sentences

1 In Stage 42, you met conditional sentences in which *indicative* forms of the verb were used:

sī valēs, gaudeō.   If you are well, I am pleased.

Notice again that a Latin future perfect (or future) tense in a conditional clause is usually translated by an English present tense:

sī illud iterum **fēceris**, tē pūniam.
If you **do** that again, I shall punish you.

2 In Stage 46, you met conditional sentences in which *pluperfect subjunctive* forms of the verb were used:

sī dīligentius labōrāvissem, dominus mē līberāvisset.
If I had worked harder, the master would have freed me.

sī in eōdem locō mānsissēs, perīculum vītāvissēs.
If you had stayed in the same place, you would have avoided the danger.

3 Notice again how the word 'nisi' is used in conditional sentences:

nisi Imperātor novās cōpiās mīserit, opprimēmur.
If the Emperor does not send reinforcements, we shall be overwhelmed.

or, Unless the Emperor sends reinforcements, we shall be overwhelmed.

4 Further examples of conditional sentences containing indicative and pluperfect subjunctive forms of the verb:

1 sī illud putās, longē errās.
2 sī Milō cēterōs āthlētās superāvisset, cīvēs statuam eī posuissent.
3 nisi amīcī nōbīs subvēnerint, in carcerem coniciēmur.

4 nisi cliēns vehementer exclāmāvisset, patrōnus eum nōn animadvertisset.

5 sī diūtius in urbe morātī essētis, numquam effūgissētis.

5 You have also met the *imperfect* tense of the subjunctive in conditional sentences. For example:

sī Rōmae nunc habitārem, clientēs mē assiduē vexārent.
If I were living in Rome now, my clients would be continually pestering me.

sī Domitiānus nōs adhūc regeret, miserrimī essēmus.
If Domitian were still ruling us, we should be very unhappy.

Notice that the imperfect subjunctive in conditional sentences is usually translated by 'were . . .' followed by 'would be . . .' or 'should be . . .'.

Further examples:

1 sī Marcus hodiē vīveret, cum Imperātōre cēnāret.
2 sī rēx essem, nōn in hāc vīllā labōrārem.
3 sī ego tuum fundum administrārem, tū dīvitissimus essēs.

6 In the following conditional sentences, the *present* subjunctive is being used:

sī hanc medicīnam bibās, statim convalēscās.
If you were to drink this medicine, you would get better at once.

sī piscēs per āera volent, omnēs mīrentur.
If fish were to fly through the air, everybody would be amazed.

The present subjunctive in conditional sentences can usually be translated by 'were to . . .' followed by 'would . . .' or 'should . . .'.

Further examples:

1 sī Iuppiter ipse Lesbiam petat, illa eum spernat.
2 sī forte aurum in Britanniā inveniāmus, dīvitēs fīāmus.
3 sī mīlitēs urbem oppugnent, facile eam capiant.

Gerund and gerundive

1   In Unit IVB, you have met the *gerund*, e.g. 'portandum' ('carrying'), 'docendum' ('teaching'), etc. Notice again how the various cases of the gerund are used:

accusative (with 'ad', meaning 'for the purpose of')
multī hominēs ad **audiendum** aderant.
Many men were there for the purpose of listening.
  or, in more natural English:
Many men were there to listen.

genitive
optimam habeō occāsiōnem **cognōscendī** quid acciderit.
I have an excellent opportunity of finding out what has happened.

ablative
prūdenter **emendō** et **vēndendō**, pater meus dīvitissimus factus est.
By buying and selling sensibly, my father became very rich.

The cases of the gerund are listed in full on p.195.

Further examples:

1 senātor ad dīcendum surrēxit.
2 puer artem cantandī discere cōnābātur.
3 decem gladiātōrēs ad pugnandum ēlēctī sunt.
4 diū labōrandō, lībertātem adeptus sum.
5 senex nūllam spem convalēscendī habēbat.

2   You have also met sentences in which 'ad' ('for the purpose of') is used with the *gerundive*, e.g. 'portandus' ('being carried'), 'docendus' ('being taught'), etc.:

iuvenis ad epistulam **legendam** cōnsēdit.
The young man sat down for the purpose of the letter being read.
  or, in more natural English:
The young man sat down to read the letter.

Further examples:

1 multī clientēs advēnērunt ad nōs salūtandōs.
2 cīvēs in theātrum ad fābulam spectandam conveniēbant.
3 servus aquam ad flammās exstinguendās quaerēbat.

3 Notice again a rather different type of sentence, which you have met from Unit IIIA onwards, in which the gerundive ('portandus', 'docendus', etc.) has the meaning *needing* to be carried', *needing* to be taught', etc., and is used with some form of the verb 'esse' (e.g. 'est', 'sunt', 'erit', 'erat') to indicate that something *ought* to be done:

1 nōbīs vīlla aedificanda est.
  We must build a house.
  (Compare this with another way of expressing the same idea: necesse est nōbīs vīllam aedificāre.)
2 mīlitibus cōnsistendum erit.
  The soldiers will have to halt.
  (Compare: necesse erit mīlitibus cōnsistere.)
3 mihi longum iter faciendum erat.
  I had to make a long journey.
4 fūrēs pūniendī sunt.
  The thieves must be punished.

When the gerundive is used in this way, it is known as a *gerundive of obligation*.

Further examples:

5 tibi novae vestēs emendae sunt.
  (Compare: necesse est tibi novās vestēs emere.)
6 servīs currendum erat.
  (Compare: necesse erat servīs currere.)
7 mihi fundus īnspiciendus erit.
8 pecūnia reddenda est.

Longer sentences

1 From Unit I onwards, you have met sentences like these:

1 *coquus numquam labōrat,* **quod semper dormit.**
The cook never works, because he is always asleep.
2 *fūrēs,* **postquam canem excitāvērunt,** *fūgērunt.*
The thieves, after they woke the dog up, ran away.
or, The thieves ran away after they woke the dog up.

Each of these sentences is made up of:

(i) a group of words which would make a complete sentence on its own, e.g. 'coquus numquam labōrat' in example 1, and 'fūrēs fūgērunt' in example 2. Groups of words like these are known as *main clauses*.
(ii) a group of words introduced by a word like 'quod' or 'postquam', e.g. 'quod semper dormit' in example 1, and 'postquam canem excitāvērunt' in example 2. Groups of words like these are known as **subordinate clauses**. Notice that a subordinate clause on its own would not make a complete sentence.

2 There are many different kinds of subordinate clause. The commonest kind is the **relative** clause, which you have met from Unit IIA onwards in sentences like this:

servī **quī vīnum effundunt** *magnō pretiō ēmptī sunt.*
The slaves who are pouring out the wine were bought at a high price.

In this example, the main clause is 'servī magnō pretiō ēmptī sunt', and the subordinate clause is a relative clause: 'quī vīnum effundunt'.

3 Translate the following examples:

1 togae, quās ille senex vēndit, sunt sordidae.
2 amīcus meus currere nōn potest, quod pēs dolet.
3 hospitēs, postquam cibum gustāvērunt, vehementer plausērunt.
4 virgō quae senātōrī nūpsit trēdecim annōs nāta est.

Pick out the main clause and subordinate clause in each sentence.

4 Compare the Latin sentences in paragraphs 1 and 2, which were all *direct* statements, with the following examples, which are all *indirect* statements:

1 audiō coquum numquam labōrāre, **quod semper dormiat**.
I hear that the cook never works, because he is always asleep.
2 puer affirmāvit fūrēs, **postquam canem excitāvissent**, fūgisse.
The boy declared that the thieves, after they had woken the dog up, had run away.
3 mercātor respondit servōs **quī vīnum effunderent** magnō pretiō ēmptōs esse.
The merchant replied that the slaves who were pouring out the wine had been bought at a high price.

Notice in particular that when an indirect statement contains a subordinate clause, the verb in the subordinate clause is normally *subjunctive* (e.g. 'dormiat', 'excitāvissent', 'effunderent').

5 Translate the following examples:

1 servus dīcit togās, quās ille senex vēndat, sordidās esse.
2 praecō spērābat clientēs, simulac patrōnum salūtāvissent, abitūrōs esse.
3 iuvenis nūntiāvit patrem, quod morbō afflīgerētur, domī manēre.
4 cīvēs exīstimābant Agricolam, postquam Calēdoniōs vīcisset, iniūstē revocātum esse.

Pick out the subordinate clause in each sentence.

PART THREE: VOCABULARY

Notes

1   Nouns, adjectives, verbs and prepositions are listed as in the Language Information section of Unit IVA.

2   Verbs and adjectives which are often used with a noun or pronoun in the *dative* or *ablative* case are marked + *dat.* or + *abl.*

For example: careō, carēre, caruī + *abl.* – lack
dignus, digna, dignum + *abl.* – worthy
obstō, obstāre, obstitī + *dat.* – obstruct
similis, simile + *dat.* – similar
ūtor, ūtī, ūsus sum + *abl.* – use

pecūniā carēbam.   I lacked money, I had no money.
dignus ingentī praemiō   worthy of a huge reward
custōdēs nōbīs obstābant.   The guards were obstructing us.
similis patrī meō   similar to my father, like my father
gladiīs brevibus ūtēbantur.   They were using short swords.

3   Notice again the difference between the listed forms of deponent verbs and the forms of ordinary verbs:

deponent verbs   *ordinary verbs*
cōnor, cōnārī,   colloco, collocāre, collocāvī,
   cōnātus sum – try   collocātus – place, put
loquor, loquī,   vēndō, vēndere, vēndidī,
   locūtus sum – speak   vēnditus – sell

Pages 219–56 can be used to check whether a word with a passive ending (e.g. 'ēgrediuntur', 'custōdiuntur') comes from a deponent verb or not.

For example, 'ēgrediuntur' comes from a verb which is listed as 'ēgredior, ēgredī, ēgressus sum – go out'. It is clear from the listed forms that 'ēgredior' is a *deponent* verb; it therefore has an *active* meaning, and 'ēgrediuntur' must mean 'they go out'.

'custōdiuntur', on the other hand, comes from a verb which is listed as 'custōdiō, custōdīre, custōdīvī, custōdītus – guard'. It is clear from the listed forms that 'custōdiō' is *not* a deponent verb; 'custōdiuntur' must therefore have a *passive* meaning, i.e. 'they are being guarded'.

4 Translate the following sentences, using pages 219–56 to check whether the words in heavy print are deponent verbs or not:

1 centuriō mīlitēs **hortābātur**.
2 amīcus meus ab Imperātōre **commendābātur**.
3 cūr dē fortūnā tuā semper **quereris?**
4 cūr ā dominō tuō semper **neglegeris?**
5 puer dē perīculō **monitus est**.
6 mercātor multās gemmās facile **adeptus est**.

5 All words which are given in the vocabulary checklists for Stages 1–48 are marked with an asterisk.

a

* ā, ab + *abl.* – from; by
* abeō, abīre, abiī – go away
  abripiō, abripere, abripuī, abreptus – tear away from, remove by force
  abrumpō, abrumpere, abrūpī, abruptus – split, tear apart
  absēns, *gen.* absentis – absent
  abstulī *see* auferō
* absum, abesse, āfuī – be out, be absent, be away
* ac – and
  accēnsus, accēnsa, accēnsum – inflamed, on fire
* accidō, accidere, accidī – happen
* accipiō, accipere, accēpī, acceptus – accept, take in, receive
  accommodō, accommodāre, accommodāvī, accommodātus – fasten
* accūsō, accūsāre, accūsāvī, accūsātus – accuse
  ācer, ācris, ācre – eager, excited
* ācriter – keenly, eagerly, fiercely
  āctus *see* agō
  acūtus, acūta, acūtum – sharp
* ad + *acc.* – to, at
  ad convalēscendum – in order to get better
  ad praesēns – for the present, for the moment
  ad vigilandum – for keeping watch

* addō, addere, addidī, additus – add
  addere gradum – go forward step by step
  addūcō, addūcere, addūxī, adductus – lead, lead on, encourage, pull, draw up (to the chest)
  adēmptus, adēmpta, adēmptum – taken away
* adeō, adīre, adiī – approach, go up to
* adeō – so much, so greatly
  trēs adeō – as many as three, three entire
  adeptus *see* adipīscor
  adest, adfuī *see* adsum
  adhibeō, adhibēre, adhibuī, adhibitus – use, apply
  precēs adhibēre – offer prayers
* adhūc – up till now, still
  usque adhūc – up till now, until now
  adībō *see* adeō
* adipīscor, adipīscī, adeptus sum – receive, obtain
* aditus, aditūs, m. – entrance
* adiuvō, adiuvāre, adiūvī, adiūtus – help
  adligō, adligāre, adligāvī, adligātus – tie
* adloquor, adloquī, adlocūtus sum – speak to, address

* administrō, administrāre, administrāvī, administrātus – look after, manage
  rem administrāre – manage the task
admīror, admīrārī, admīrātus sum – admire
admittō, admittere, admīsī, admissus – admit, let in
admoneō, admonēre, admonuī, admonitus – warn, advise
adnītor, adnītī, adnīxus sum – strain, exert oneself
* adstō, adstāre, adstitī – stand by, stand
* adsum, adesse, adfuī – be here, be present, arrive
aduncus, adunca, aduncum – curved
adūrō, adūrere, adussī, adustus – burn
* adveniō, advenīre, advēnī – arrive
* adventus, adventūs, m. – arrival
* adversus, adversa, adversum – hostile, unfavourable, unfortunate, undesirable, opposite
* rēs adversae – misfortune
* adversus + acc. – against
* aedificium, aedificiī, n. – building
* aedificō, aedificāre, aedificāvī, aedificātus – build
* aeger, aegra, aegrum – sick, ill
aequātus, aequāta, aequātum – level, side by side
* aequor, aequoris, n. – sea
* aequus, aequa, aequum – equal, fair, calm
* aequō animō – calmly, in a calm spirit
aequō discrīmine – at an equal distance
āēr, āeris, m. – air
* aestās, aestātis, f. – summer
aestimō, aestimāre, aestimāvī, aestimātus – value
aestus, aestūs, m. – heat
aethēr, aetheris, m. – sky, heaven

afferō, afferre, attulī, adlātus – bring, bring news, report
* afficiō, afficere, affēcī, affectus – affect, treat
affīgō, affīgere, affīxī, affīxus – attach to, nail to
  cruce affīgere – nail to a cross, crucify
* affirmō, affirmāre, affirmāvī – declare
afflīgō, afflīgere, afflīxī, afflīctus – afflict, hurt, strike
affluō, affluere, afflūxī – flock to the spot
* ager, agrī, m. – field
* aggredior, aggredī, aggressus sum – assail, attack, make an attempt on
* agitō, agitāre, agitāvī, agitātus – chase, hunt
* agmen, agminis, n. – column (of men), procession
* agnōscō, agnōscere, agnōvī, agnitus – recognise
agnus, agnī, m. – lamb
* agō, agere, ēgī, āctus – do, act, drive
  agī – move, roll
* fābulam agere – act a play
* grātiās agere – thank, give thanks
  iter agere – make one's way, travel
* negōtium agere – do business, work
  officium agere – do one's duty
* agricola, agricolae, m. – farmer
ait – says, said
āla, ālae, f. – wing
āles, ālitis, m.f. – bird
* aliquandō – sometimes
aliquantō – somewhat, rather
aliquī, aliqua, aliquod – some
* aliquis, aliquid – someone, something
* alius, alia, aliud – other, another, else
* aliī . . . aliī – some . . . others
  in aliud – for any other purpose
alō, alere, aluī, altus – encourage
altē – high
* alter, altera, alterum – the other, another, a second, the second
  alter . . . alter – one . . . the other
  usque alter – yet another

altum, altī, n. – deep sea, open sea
* altus, alta, altum – high, deep
amāns, amantis, m. – lover
* ambō, ambae, ambō – both
* ambulō, ambulāre, ambulāvī – walk
amīca, amīcae, f. – friend, girl-friend,
mistress
* amīcitia, amīcitiae, f. – friendship
* amīcus, amīcī, m. – friend
* āmittō, āmittere, āmīsī, āmissus –
lose
* amō, amāre, amāvī, amātus – love,
like
* amor, amōris, m. – love
* amplector, amplectī, amplexus sum –
embrace, grasp, clasp
* amplius – more fully, at greater
length, any more
* amplissimus, amplissima,
amplissimum – very great
* an – or
* utrum . . . an – whether . . . or
* ancilla, ancillae, f. – slave-girl, maid
* angustus, angusta, angustum –
narrow
* animadvertō, animadvertere,
animadvertī, animadversus –
notice, take notice of
animal, animālis, n. – animal
* animus, animī, m. – spirit, soul, mind
* aequō animō – calmly, in a calm
spirit
furēns animī – furiously determined,
with furious eagerness
* in animō volvere – wonder, turn
over in the mind
* annus, annī, m. – year
* ante (1) + acc. – before, in front of
ante (2) – in front
* anteā – before
* antīquus, antīqua, antīquum – old,
ancient
* ānulus, ānulī, m. – ring
anus, anūs, f. – old woman
anxius, anxia, anxium – anxious
* aperiō, aperīre, aperuī, apertus –
open, reveal

* appāreō, appārēre, appāruī – appear
* appellō, appellāre, appellāvī,
appellātus – call, call out to
* appropinquō, appropinquāre,
appropinquāvī + dat. –
approach, come near to
* aptus, apta, aptum – suitable
* apud + acc. – among, at the house of
* aqua, aquae, f. – water
aquaeductus, aquaeductūs, m. –
aqueduct
aquilex, aquilegis, m. – water
engineer, hydraulic engineer
* āra, ārae, f. – altar
arātor, arātōris, m. – ploughman
arātrum, arātrī, n. – plough
arbitror, arbitrārī, arbitrātus sum –
think
* arbor, arboris, f. – tree
arca, arcae, f. – strong-box, chest,
coffin
* accessō, arcessere, accessīvī,
arcessītus – summon, send for
architectus, architectī, m. – builder,
architect
arcuātus, arcuāta, arcuātum – arched
arcus, arcūs, m. – arch
* ardeō, ardēre, arsī – burn, be on fire
ārea, āreae, f. – courtyard, building
site
arēna, arēnae, f. – arena; sand
* argenteus, argentea, argenteum –
made of silver
* arma, armōrum, n. pl. – arms,
weapons
armātus, armāta, armātum – armed
* arrogantia, arrogantiae, f. – cheek,
arrogance
* ars, artis, f. – art, skill
per artem – deliberately, by design
artē – closely
artus, artūs, m. – limb
as, assis, m. – as (smallest Roman
coin)
* ascendō, ascendere, ascendī – climb,
rise
aspectus, aspectūs, m. – sight

* aspiciō, aspicere, aspexī – look towards, catch sight of
assiduē – continually
assiduus, assidua, assiduum – continual
assignō, assignāre, assignāvī, assignātus – attribute, put down to
astrologus, astrologī, m. – astrologer
* at – but, yet
āter, ātra, ātrum – black
Athēnae, Athēnārum, f.pl. – Athens
āthlēta, āthlētae, m. – athlete
* atque – and
* ātrium, ātriī, n. – hall
ātrōx, *gen.* ātrōcis – violent, dreadful
attollō, attollere – lift, raise
sē attollere – raise itself, rise up
attollor, attollī – rise
* attonitus, attonita, attonitum – astonished
attulī *see* afferō
* auctor, auctōris, m. – creator, originator, person responsible
* auctōritās, auctōritatis, f. – authority
* audācia, audāciae, f. – boldness, audacity
* audāx, *gen.* audācis – bold, daring
* audeō, audēre – dare
* audiō, audīre, audīvī, audītus – hear
* auferō, auferre, abstulī, ablātus – take away, steal
* augeō, augēre, auxī, auctus – increase
* aula, aulae, f. – palace
aura, aurae, f. – breeze, air
* aureus, aurea, aureum – golden, made of gold
* auris, auris, f. – ear
* aurum, aurī, n. – gold
* aut – or
aut . . . aut – either . . . or
* autem – but
* auxilium, auxiliī, n. – help
* auxiliō esse – be a help, be helpful
* avārus, avārī, m. – miser
avē atque valē – hail and farewell
avēna, avēnae, f. – reed

* avidē – eagerly
avidus, avida, avidum – eager
* avis, avis, f. – bird
avunculus, avunculī, m. – uncle

b

baculum, baculī, n. – stick, staff
balneum, balneī, n. – bath
barba, barbae, f. – beard
barbarus, barbara, barbarum – barbarian
* barbarus, barbarī, m. – barbarian
bāsiō, bāsiāre, bāsiāvī – kiss
bāsium, bāsiī, n. – kiss
beātus, beāta, beātum – prosperous, wealthy
* bellum, bellī, n. – war
* bellum gerere – wage war, campaign
bellus, bella, bellum – pretty
* bene – well
bene velle – like, be friendly
* optimē – very well
* beneficium, beneficiī, n. – act of kindness, favour
benignitās, benignitātis, f. – kindness, concern, kindly interest
* benignus, benigna, benignum – kind
* bibō, bibere, bibī – drink
Bīthȳnī, Bīthȳnōrum, m.pl. – Bithynians
blanditiae, blanditiārum, f.pl. – flatteries
* bonus, bona, bonum – good
* bona, bonōrum, n.pl. – goods, property
* melior, melius – better
melius est – it would be better
* optimus, optima, optimum – very good, excellent, best
Boōtēs, Boōtae, m. – Bear-keeper (constellation)
* bracchium, bracchiī, n. – arm
* brevis, breve – short, brief, shallow
Britannia, Britanniae, f. – Britain

c

* cadō, cadere, cecidī – fall, die
* caecus, caeca, caecum – blind;
  invisible, unseen, impenetrable
* caedēs, caedis, f. – murder, slaughter
* caedō, caedere, cecīdī, caesus – kill
  caelebs, caelibis, m. – widower
* caelum, caelī, n. – sky, heaven
  caeruleus, caerulea, caeruleum –
  blue, from the deep blue sea,
  dark, dark blue, dark green
  Caesarēs, Caesarum, m.pl. – the
  Caesars (family of the first
  Roman emperors)
  Calēdoniī, Calēdoniōrum, m.pl. –
  Scots
  cālīgō, cālīginis, f. – darkness, gloom
  callidē – cleverly
  calliditās, calliditātis, f. – cleverness,
  shrewdness
* callidus, callida, callidum – clever,
  cunning, shrewd
  camera, camerae, f. – ceiling
* campus, campī, m. – plain, ground
  candēns, gen. candentis – gleaming
  white
* candidus, candida, candidum –
  bright, shining, gleaming white
* canis, canis, m. – dog
* cantō, cantāre, cantāvī – sing, chant
  capāx, gen. capācis – liable to, full of
* capillī, capillōrum, m.pl. – hair
* capiō, capere, cēpī, captus – take,
  catch, capture
  Capreae, Capreārum, f.pl. – Capri
* captīvus, captīvī, m. – prisoner,
  captive
  captō, captāre, captāvī, captātus –
  try to catch
* caput, capitis, n. – head
* carcer, carceris, m. – prison
* careō, carēre, caruī + abl. – lack, be
  without
  carīna, carīnae, f. – keel, ship
* carmen, carminis, n. – song

carpō, carpere, carpsī, carptus –
  pluck, seize, crop; hasten upon,
  hasten through, fly through
* cārus, cāra, cārum – dear
* castīgō, castīgāre, castīgāvī,
  castīgātus – scold
* castra, castrōrum, n.pl. – camp
* cāsus, cāsūs, m. – misfortune, chance
* catēna, catēnae, f. – chain
  caupō, caupōnis, m. – innkeeper
* causa, causae, f. – reason, cause; case
  (of law)
  causam īnferre – make an excuse,
  invent an excuse
* cautē – cautiously
* caveō, cavēre, cāvī – beware
  caverna, cavernae, f. – cave, cavern
  cavō, cavāre, cavāvī, cavātus –
  hollow out
  cecidī see cadō
* cēdō, cēdere, cessī – give in, give way
* celebrō, celebrāre, celebrāvī,
  celebrātus – celebrate
* celeriter – quickly, fast
  quam celerrimē – as quickly as
  possible
* cēlō, cēlāre, cēlāvī, cēlātus – hide
  celsus, celsa, celsum – high
* cēna, cēnae, f. – dinner
* cēnō, cēnāre, cēnāvī – dine, have
  dinner
* centum – a hundred
* centuriō, centuriōnis, m. – centurion
  cēnula, cēnulae, f. – little supper
  cēpī see capiō
* cēra, cērae, f. – wax, wax tablet
* certāmen, certāminis, n. – struggle,
  contest, fight
  certē – certainly, at least
* certō, certāre, certāvī – compete
* certus, certa, certum – certain,
  infallible
*   prō certō habēre – know for certain
* cēterī, cēterae, cētera – the others, the
  rest
  chorus, chorī, m. – chorus, choir

* cibus, cibī, m. – food
* cinis, cineris, m. – ash
circuit = circumit
* circum + *acc.* – around
circumeō, circumīre, circumiī – go round, go around
circumflectō, circumflectere, circumflexī, circumflexus – turn
circumflectere cursum – turn one's course round
circumsiliō, circumsilīre – hop around
circumsistō, circumsistere, circumstetī – take up positions around
* circumspectō, circumspectāre, circumspectāvī – look round
* circumveniō, circumvenīre, circumvēnī, circumventus – surround
circus, circī, m. – circus, stadium
citō – quickly
* cīvis, cīvis, m.f. – citizen
* clādēs, clādis, f. – disaster
* clam – secretly, in private
* clāmō, clāmāre, clāmāvī – shout
* clāmor, clāmōris, m. – shout, uproar
* clārus, clāra, clārum – famous, distinguished, splendid; clear, loud
* claudō, claudere, clausī, clausus – shut, close, block, conclude, complete, cut off
clāvus, clāvī, m. – tiller, helm
* cliēns, clientis, m. – client
clīvus, clīvī, m. – slope
* coepī – I began
coeptum, coeptī, n. – work, undertaking
* cōgitō, cōgitāre, cōgitāvī – think, consider
* cognōscō, cognōscere, cognōvī, cognitus – get to know, find out
* cōgō, cōgere, coēgī, coāctus – force, compel
* cohors, cohortis, f. – cohort
collēgium, collēgiī, n. – brigade, guild

* colligō, colligere, collēgī, collēctus – gather, collect, assemble
* collocō, collocāre, collocāvī, collocātus – place, put
* colloquium, colloquiī, n. – talk, chat
* comes, comitis, m.f. – comrade, companion
cōmiter – politely, courteously
* comitor, comitārī, comitātus sum – accompany
* commemorō, commemorāre, commemorāvī, commemorātus – talk about, mention, recall
* commendō, commendāre, commendāvī, commendātus – recommend
committō, committere, commīsī, commissus – commit, begin
* commodus, commoda, commodum – convenient
* commōtus, commōta, commōtum – moved, upset, affected, alarmed, excited, distressed, overcome
commūnis, commūne – shared (by two or more people)
* comparō, comparāre, comparāvī, comparātus – obtain; compare
compellō, compellere, compulī, compulsus – drive, compel
* compleō, complēre, complēvī, complētus – fill
complector, complectī, complexus sum – embrace
complexus, complexūs, m. – embrace
* complūrēs, complūra – several
* compōnō, compōnere, composuī, compositus – put together, arrange, settle, mix, compose, make up, construct
* comprehendō, comprehendere, comprehendī, comprehēnsus – arrest, seize
compulsus *see* compellō
cōnātur *see* cōnor
concidō, concidere, concidī – collapse
conclāve, conclāvis, n. – room
condiciō, condiciōnis, f. – status

condō, condere, condidī, conditus –
hide, bury

sē condere – bring oneself to rest

* condūcō, condūcere, condūxī,
conductus – hire

* cōnficiō, cōnficere, cōnfēcī,
cōnfectus – finish, finish off,
murder

* cōnfectus, cōnfecta, cōnfectum –
finished, worn out, exhausted,
overcome

* cōnfīdō, cōnfīdere + *dat.* – trust,
put trust; be sure, be confident

* coniciō, conicere, coniēcī, coniectus
– hurl, throw

* coniungō, coniungere, coniūnxī,
coniūnctus – join

* coniūnx, coniugis, f. – wife

* coniūrātiō, coniūrātiōnis, f. – plot,
conspiracy

* coniūrō, coniūrāre, coniūrāvī,
coniūrātus – plot, conspire

* cōnor, cōnārī, cōnātus sum – try

* cōnscendō, cōnscendere, cōnscendī –
climb on, embark on, go on
board, mount

cōnscientia, cōnscientiae, f. –
awareness, knowledge

cōnscius, cōnsciī, m. – accomplice,
member of the plot

cōnsēnsus, cōnsēnsūs, m. –
agreement

* cōnsentiō, cōnsentīre, cōnsēnsī –
agree

cōnsequor, cōnsequī, cōnsecūtus sum
– follow, chase

cōnsīdō, cōnsīdere, cōnsēdī – sit down

* cōnsilium, cōnsiliī, n. – plan, idea,
advice; council

* cōnsistō, cōnsistere, cōnstitī –
stand one's ground, stand firm,
halt, stop

cōnspectus, cōnspectūs, m. – sight

* cōnspiciō, cōnspicere, cōnspexī,
cōnspectus – catch sight of

* cōnspicor, cōnspicārī, cōnspicātus
sum – catch sight of

cōnstat, cōnstāre, cōnstitit – be
agreed

* satis cōnstat – it is generally agreed

* cōnstituō, cōnstituere, cōnstituī,
cōnstitūtus – decide; set up,
place

cōnsuētūdō, cōnsuētūdinis, f. –
custom

* cōnsul, cōnsulis, m. – consul (senior
magistrate)

* cōnsulātus, cōnsulātūs, m. –
consulship (rank of consul)

* cōnsulō, cōnsulere, cōnsuluī,
cōnsultus – consult, take thought
for, give consideration to

* cōnsūmō, cōnsūmere, cōnsūmpsī,
cōnsūmptus – eat

cōnsurgō, cōnsurgere, cōnsurrēxī –
jump up

* contemnō, contemnere, contempsī,
contemptus – reject, despise,
disregard

* contendō, contendere, contendī –
hurry

* contentus, contenta, contentum –
satisfied

contingō, contingere, contigī,
contāctus – touch

contigit nōbis ut . . . – it was our
good fortune that . . ., we had the
good fortune to . . .

continuō – immediately

* contrā (1) + *acc.* – against

contrā (2) – in reply, opposite, in the
opposite direction, on the other
hand

contrahō, contrahere, contrāxī,
contractus – draw together,
bring together, assemble

contrārius, contrāria, contrārium –
opposite, contrary

conturbō, conturbāre, conturbāvī,
conturbātus – mix up, lose count
of

contus, contī, m. – pole, rod

convalēscō, convalēscere, convaluī –
get better, recover

* conveniō, convenīre, convēnī –
    come together, gather, meet
* convertō, convertere, convertī,
    conversus – turn, divert
    sē convertere – turn
    convīvālis, convīvāle – for dining
    convocō, convocāre, convocāvī,
    convocātus – call together
    coorior, coorīrī, coortus sum – break
    out
* cōpiae, cōpiārum, f.pl. – forces
* coquō, coquere, coxī, coctus – cook
* coquus, coquī, m. – cook
* corōna, corōnae, f. – garland, wreath
* corpus, corporis, n. – body
    corripiō, corripere, corripuī,
    correptus – seize
    Cōrus, Cōrī, m. – North-west wind
* cotīdiē – every day
* crās – tomorrow
* crēdō, crēdere, crēdidī + dat. –
    trust, believe, have faith in
    cremō, cremāre, cremāvī, cremātus –
    cremate, burn, destroy by fire
* creo, creare, creavi, creatus – make,
    create
* crēscō, crēscere, crēvī, crētus – grow
* crīmen, crīminis, n. – charge
    crīnēs, crīnium, m.pl. – hair
* crūdēlis, crūdēle – cruel
    crux, crucis, f. – cross
    cruce affīgere – nail to a cross,
    crucify
* cubiculum, cubiculī, n. – bedroom
    cubitō, cubitāre, cubitāvī – lie down,
    rest
    culīna, culīnae, f. – kitchen
* culpa, culpae, f. – blame, fault
    illīus culpā – through her fault,
    thanks to her
* culpō, culpāre, culpāvī – blame
* cum (1) – when, since, because
* cum (2) + abl. – with
    cūnctor, cūnctārī, cūnctātus sum –
    delay, hesitate
    cūnctus, cūncta, cūnctum – all
    cupiditās, cupiditātis, f. – desire

    cupīdō, cupīdinis, f. – desire
    Cupīdō, Cupīdinis, m. – Cupid (god
    of love)
    cupidus, cupida, cupidum – eager,
    passionate
* cupiō, cupere, cupīvī – want
* cūr? – why?
* cūra, cūrae, f. – care, trouble, bother
*   cūrae esse – be a matter of concern
    cūrātor, cūrātōris, m. – supervisor,
    superintendent
* cūria, cūriae, f. – senate-house
* cūrō, cūrāre, cūrāvī – look after,
    supervise
    cūrandum est – steps must be
    taken
* currō, currere, cucurrī – run, race,
    row, go, fly
* cursus, cursūs, m. – course, flight
    circumflectere cursum – turn one's
    course round
    curvāmen, curvāminis, n. – curve
    cuspis, cuspidis, f. – point
* custōdiō, custōdīre, custōdīvī,
    custōdītus – guard
* custōs, custōdis, m. – guard

d

    dā, dabō see dō
* damnō, damnāre, damnāvī,
    damnātus – condemn
    damnōsus, damnōsa, damnōsum –
    ruinous, fatal
    datus see dō
* dē + abl. – from, down from; about,
    over
* dea, deae, f. – goddess
* dēbeō, dēbēre, dēbuī, dēbitus – owe;
    ought, should, must
* decem – ten
* decet, decēre, decuit – be proper
* dēcidō, dēcidere, dēcidī – fall down
* decimus, decima, decimum – tenth
* dēcipiō, dēcipere, dēcēpī, dēceptus –
    deceive, trick

* decōrus, decōra, decōrum – right, proper
décurrō, décurrere, décurrī – run down, speed, race
decus, decoris, n. – glory
dēdecus, dēdecoris, n. – disgrace
dedī *see* dō
* dēfendō, dēfendere, dēfendī, dēfēnsus – defend
* dēfessus, dēfessa, dēfessum – exhausted, tired out
dēflectō, dēflectere, dēflexī – turn aside, turn off the road
dēfūnctus, dēfūncta, dēfūnctum – dead
dēhīscō, dēhīscere – gape open
* dēiciō, dēicere, dēiēcī, dēiectus – throw down, throw
dein = deinde
* deinde – then
* dēlectō, dēlectāre, dēlectāvī, dēlectātus – delight, please
* dēleō, dēlēre, dēlēvī, dēlētus – destroy
dēliciae, dēliciārum, f.pl. – darling
dēligō, dēligāre, dēligāvī, dēligātus – bind, tie, tie up, moor
dēligō, dēligere, dēlēgī, dēlēctus – choose, select
dēmānō, dēmānāre, dēmānāvī – flow down
dēmissus, dēmissa, dēmissum – low
* dēmittō, dēmittere, dēmīsī, dēmissus – let down, lower
* dēmōnstrō, dēmōnstrāre, dēmōnstrāvī, dēmōnstrātus – point out, show
* dēmum – at last
*   tum dēmum – then at last, only then
* dēnique – at last, finally
dēns, dentis, m. – tooth, tusk
* dēnsus, dēnsa, dēnsum – thick
* dēpōnō, dēpōnere, dēposuī, dēpositus – put down, take off, give up, abandon
* dērīdeō, dērīdēre, dērīsī, dērīsus – mock, jeer at

* dēscendō, dēscendere, dēscendī – go down, come down
* dēserō, dēserere, dēseruī, dēsertus – desert, leave behind
dēsīderium, dēsīderiī, n. – loss, longing
* dēsiliō, dēsilīre, dēsiluī – jump down
* dēsinō, dēsinere – end, cease
* dēspērō, dēspērāre, dēspērāvī – despair, give up
dēstinātus, dēstināta, dēstinātum – determined
dēstringō, dēstringere, dēstrīnxī, dēstrictus – draw out, draw (a sword), unsheathe
dēstruō, dēstruere, dēstrūxī, dēstrūctus – pull down, demolish
dēsum, dēesse, dēfuī – be lacking, be missing, be unavailable
dētineō, dētinēre, dētinuī, dētentus – hold back, strand
dētrahō, dētrahere, dētrāxī, dētractus – pull down, take off
dēturbō, dēturbāre, dēturbāvī, dēturbātus – push, send flying
* deus, deī, m. – god
*   dī immortālēs! – heavens above!
dī mānēs – the spirits of the dead
nē illud deī sinant! – heaven forbid!
Dēva, Dēvae, f. – Chester
dēvorō, dēvorāre, dēvorāvī, dēvorātus – devour, eat up
dēvoveō, dēvovēre, dēvōvī, dēvōtus – curse
dexter, dextra, dextrum – right, on the right
* dextra, dextrae, f. – right hand
dī *see* deus
* dīcō, dīcere, dīxī, dictus – say, call, name
male dīcere – insult
sacrāmentum dīcere – take the military oath
* dictō, dictāre, dictāvī, dictātus – dictate
didicī *see* discō

* diēs, diēī, m.f. – day
  diēs fēstus, diēī fēstī, m. – festival,
    holiday
* diēs nātālis, diēī nātālis, m. –
    birthday
  differō, differre, distulī, dīlātus –
    postpone
* difficilis, difficile – difficult, obstinate
  diffīdō, diffīdere + dat. – distrust
* dignitās, dignitātis, f. – dignity,
    importance, honour, prestige
* dignus, digna, dignum + abl. –
    worthy, appropriate
* dīligenter – carefully
* dīligentia, dīligentiae, f. – industry,
    hard work
* dīligō, dīligere, dīlēxī – be fond of
* dīmittō, dīmittere, dīmīsī, dīmissus –
    send away, dismiss, turn, direct
  dīrigō, dīrigere, dīrēxī, dīrēctus –
    steer
* dīrus, dīra, dīrum – dreadful
* discēdō, discēdere, discessī – depart,
    leave
  discernō, discernere, discrēvī,
    discrētus – distinguish
* discipulus, discipulī, m. – disciple,
    follower, pupil, student
* discō, discere, didicī – learn
  discordia, discordiae, f. – strife
* discrīmen, discrīminis, n. –
    boundary, dividing line,
    distance; crisis
    aequō discrīmine – at an equal
      distance
  disiciō, disicere, disiēcī, disiectus –
    scatter, disperse
  dispār, gen. disparis – of different
    length
  dispergō, dispergere, dispersī,
    dispersus – scatter
  dispiciō, dispicere, dispexī, dispectus
    – consider
* dissentiō, dissentīre, dissēnsī –
    disagree, argue
  dissolūtiō, dissolūtiōnis, f. –
    disintegration, break-up

  dissolvō, dissolvere, dissolvī,
    dissolūtus – disperse, dissolve
  distribuō, distribuere, distribuī,
    distribūtus – distribute
  distringō, distringere, distrīnxī,
    districtus – distract, divert
  distulī see differō
* diū – for a long time
  diūtius – any longer
* dīversus, dīversa, dīversum –
    different
* dīves, gen. dīvitis – rich
  dīvidō, dīvidere, dīvīsī, dīvīsus –
    separate
* dīvitiae, dīvitiārum, f.pl. – riches
  dīvortium, dīvortiī, n. – divorce
* dīvus, dīvī, m. – god
  dīxī see dīcō
* dō, dare, dedī, datus – give, put
    forward
* poenās dare – pay the penalty, be
    punished
* doceō, docēre, docuī, doctus – teach
* doctus, docta, doctum – learned,
    educated, skilful, clever
* doleō, dolēre, doluī – hurt, be in
    pain; grieve, be sad
* dolor, dolōris, m. – pain; grief
* domina, dominae, f. – mistress
* dominus, dominī, m. – master, owner
* domus, domūs, f. – home, house, family
    domī – at home
    domum revenīre – return home
* dōnec – until
* dōnō, dōnāre, dōnāvī, dōnātus –
    give
* dōnum, dōnī, n. – present, gift
* dormiō, dormīre, dormīvī – sleep,
    sleep through
* dubitō, dubitāre, dubitāvī –
    hesitate, doubt, be doubtful
* dubium, dubiī, n. – doubt
  dubius, dubia, dubium – uncertain,
    doubtful
  ducem see dux
* ducentī, ducentae, ducenta – two
    hundred

* dūcō, dūcere, dūxī, ductus – lead;
     consider, marry
  dulce – sweetly
* dulcis, dulce – sweet
* dum – while, until, so long as,
     provided that
  dumtaxat – not exceeding
* duo, duae, duo – two
*   duo mīlia – two thousand
* duodecim – twelve
* duodēvīgintī – eighteen
* dūrus, dūra, dūrum – harsh, hard
* dux, ducis, m. – leader
  dūxī see dūcō

e

* ē, ex + abl. – from, out of
* ecce! – see! look!
* efferō, efferre, extulī, ēlātus – bring
     out, carry out, carry away
*   ēlātus, ēlāta, ēlātum – thrilled,
     excited, carried away
* efficiō, efficere, effēcī, effectus – carry
     out, accomplish
     efficere ut – bring it about that, see
     to it that
     rem efficere – accomplish the task
* effigiēs, effigiēī, f. – image, statue
  efflāgitō, efflāgitāre, efflāgitāvī –
     demand justice
  effringō, effringere, effrēgī, effrāctus –
     break down
* effugiō, effugere, effūgī – escape
* effundō, effundere, effūdī, effūsus –
     pour out
  ēgī see agō
* ego, meī – I, me
     mēcum – with me
     meī locō – my place
  ēgredior, ēgredī, ēgressus sum – go
     out
  ēgregius, ēgregia, ēgregium –
     excellent, outstanding
* ēheu! – alas!
* ēiciō, ēicere, ēiēcī, ēiectus – throw out

  ēlābor, ēlābī, ēlāpsus sum – escape
  ēlegāns, gen. ēlegantis – tasteful,
     elegant
  ēliciō, ēlicere, ēlicuī, ēlicitus –
     lure, entice
* ēligō, ēligere, ēlēgī, ēlēctus – choose
  ēmineō, ēminēre, ēminuī – project
* ēmittō, ēmittere, ēmīsī, ēmissus –
     throw, send out
* emō, emere, ēmī, ēmptus – buy
* enim – for
  ēnsis, ēnsis, m. – sword
  ēnumerō, ēnumerāre, ēnumerāvī,
     ēnumerātus – count
  eō – therefore, for this reason
* eō, īre, iī – go
*   obviam īre + dat. – meet, go to meet
  Ephesius, Ephesia, Ephesium – of
     Ephesus
* epistula, epistulae, f. – letter
  epulae, epulārum, f.pl. – dishes,
     feast, banquet
* eques, equitis, m. – horseman; man of
     equestrian rank
  equidem – indeed
* equitō, equitāre, equitāvī – ride
* equus, equī, m. – horse
  eram see sum
* ergō – therefore
* ēripiō, ēripere, ēripuī, ēreptus –
     snatch, tear, rescue, snatch away
* errō, errāre, errāvī – make a mistake;
     wander
     longē errāre – make a big mistake
  ērudiō, ērudīre, ērudiī, ērudītus –
     teach
  est see sum
* et – and
*   et ... et – both ... and
* etiam – even, also
     nōn modo . . . sed etiam – not only
     . . . but also
  Etruscus, Etruscī, m. – Etruscan
  etsī – although, even if
* euge! – hurray!
  euntem see eō
* ēvādō, ēvādere, ēvāsī – escape

229

ēvānēscō, ēvānēscere, ēvānuī –
    vanish, die away
ēveniō, ēvenīre, ēvēnī – occur
ēvertō, ēvertere, ēvertī, ēversus –
    overturn
* ex, ē + abl. – from, out of
* exanimātus, exanimāta, exanimātum
    – unconscious
exanimis, exanime – out of one's
    mind
exardeō, exardēre, exarsī – blaze up
* excipiō, excipere, excēpī, exceptus –
    receive, take over
* excitō, excitāre, excitāvī, excitātus –
    arouse, wake up, awaken
* exclāmō, exclāmāre, exclāmāvī –
    exclaim, shout
excōgitō, excōgitāre, excōgitāvī,
    excōgitātus – invent, think up
excruciō, excruciāre, excruciāvī,
    excruciātus – torture, torment
excutiō, excutere, excussī, excussus –
    examine, investigate; shake off,
    drive violently off
* exemplum, exemplī, n. – example
    pertinēre ad exemplum – involve a
    precedent
* exeō, exīre, exiī – go out
exequiae, exequiārum, f.pl. – funeral
    rites
* exerceō, exercēre, exercuī,
    exercitus – exercise, practise,
    train
* exercitus, exercitūs, m. – army
exigō, exigere, exēgī, exāctus –
    demand, spend
* exilium, exiliī, n. – exile
* exīstimō, exīstimāre, exīstimāvī,
    exīstimātus – think, consider
* exitium, exitiī, n. – ruin,
    destruction
expediō, expedīre, expedīvī,
    expedītus – bring out, get out
    sēsē expedīre – prepare oneself,
    get ready
expingō, expingere, expīnxī, expictus
    – paint, put paint onto

expleō, explēre, explēvī, explētus –
    complete, put final touch to
* explicō, explicāre, explicāvī,
    explicātus – explain
expōnō, expōnere, exposuī,
    expositus – unload; set out,
    explain
exsequor, exsequī, exsecūtus sum –
    carry out
* exspectō, exspectāre, exspectāvī,
    exspectātus – wait for
* exstinguō, exstinguere, exstīnxī,
    exstīnctus – extinguish, put out,
    destroy
* exstruō, exstruere, exstrūxī,
    exstrūctus – build
exsultō, exsultāre, exsultāvī –
    exult, be triumphant, get excited
exta, extōrum, n.pl. – entrails
extendō, extendere, extendī,
    extentus – stretch out
exterreō, exterrēre, exterruī,
    exterritus – frighten away
* extrā + acc. – outside
* extrahō, extrahere, extrāxī,
    extractus – drag out, pull out,
    take out
* extrēmus, extrēma, extrēmum –
    furthest
    extrēma scaena – the edge of the stage

f

* faber, fabrī, m. – craftsman,
    carpenter, workman, fireman
* fābula, fābulae, f. – play, story
*   fābulam agere – act a play
* facile – easily
* facilis, facile – easy
* facinus, facinoris, n. – crime
* faciō, facere, fēcī, factus – make, do
    impetum facere – charge, make an
    attack
    ō factum male! – O dreadfully
    done! O dreadful deed!
factiō, factiōnis, f. – organised group

* factum, factī, n. – deed, achievement
factus *see* faciō, fīō
facultās, facultātis, f. – opportunity
* fallō, fallere, fefellī, falsus – deceive,
escape notice of, slip by
fidem fallere – break one's word
* falsus, falsa, falsum – false, untrue,
dishonest
* fāma, fāmae, f. – rumour
* familia, familiae, f. – household
* familiāris, familiāris, m. – close
friend, relation, relative
familiāritās, familiāritātis, f. –
friendliness
fās, m. – right
faucēs, faucium, f.pl. – throat
fauce – by hunger
* faveō, favēre, fāvī + *dat.* – favour,
support
* favor, favōris, m. – favour
* fax, facis, f. – torch
febricula, febriculae, f. – slight fever
fēcī *see* faciō
fēcunditās, fēcunditātis, f. – fertility
fēcundus, fēcunda, fēcundum –
fertile, rich
* fēlīx, *gen.* fēlīcis – lucky, happy
* fēmina, fēminae, f. – woman
feriō, ferīre – strike
* ferō, ferre, tulī, lātus – bring, carry
* ferōciter – fiercely
* ferōx, *gen.* ferōcis – fierce, ferocious
ferrātus, ferrāta, ferrātum – tipped
with iron
ferreus, ferrea, ferreum – iron, made
of iron
* ferrum, ferrī, n. – iron, sword
* fessus, fessa, fessum – tired
* festīnō, festīnāre, festīnāvī – hurry
* fēstus, fēsta, fēstum – festival, holiday
fīam *see* fīō
fictus *see* fingō
* fidēlis, fidēle – faithful, loyal, reliable,
trustworthy
fidēliter – faithfully, loyally, reliably
* fidēs, fideī, f. – loyalty, trust-
worthiness

fidem fallere – break one's word
(medius) fidius! – for goodness sake!
* fīdus, fīda, fīdum – loyal, trustworthy
figūra, figūrae, f. – figure, shape
* fīlia, fīliae, f. – daughter
* fīlius, fīliī, m. – son
* fingō, fingere, fīnxī, fictus – pretend,
invent, forge
* fīnis, fīnis, m. – end; starting-place
* fīō, fierī, factus sum – be made,
be done, become, occur
fistula, fistulae, f. – pipe
* flamma, flammae, f. – flame
flāvus, flāva, flāvum – yellow, golden
flectō, flectere, flexī, flexus – bend
* fleō, flēre, flēvī – weep (for)
flētus, flētūs, m. – weeping, tears
* flōreō, flōrēre, flōruī – flourish
* flōs, flōris, m. – flower
* flūctus, flūctūs, m. – wave
* flūmen, flūminis, n. – river
* fluō, fluere, flūxī – flow
fluēns, *gen.* fluentis – dripping,
streaming
foedus, foeda, foedum – foul, horrible
* fōns, fontis, m. – fountain, spring
fore = futūrum esse (*future infinitive of*
sum)
forēs, forium, f.pl. – door
fōrma, fōrmae, f. – beauty,
appearance
formīdō, formīdinis, f. – fear, terror
formīdolōsus, formīdolōsa,
formīdolōsum – alarming
fors – perhaps
* fortasse – perhaps
* forte – by chance
* fortis, forte – brave
* fortiter – bravely
fortuita, fortuitōrum, n.pl. –
accidents
* fortūna, fortūnae, f. – fortune, luck
* forum, forī, n. – forum, market-place
* fossa, fossae, f. – ditch
* fragor, fragōris, m. – crash, shout
* frangō, frangere, frēgī, frāctus – break
* frāter, frātris, m. – brother

frāternus, frāterna, frāternum – of a
brother, fraternal
* fraus, fraudis, f. – trick
fremitus, fremitūs, m. – noise, din
frēna, frēnōrum, n.pl. – reins
frētum, frētī, n. – water, sea
frīgidus, frīgida, frīgidum – cold
frondēns, *gen.* frondentis – leafy
frōns, frontis, f. – front, prow
* frūmentum, frūmentī, n. – grain
fruor, fruī, fructus sum + *abl.* – enjoy
* frūstrā – in vain
fūdī *see* fundō
* fuga, fugae, f. – escape
* fugiō, fugere, fūgī – run away, flee
(from)
fuī *see* sum
fulciō, fulcīre, fulsī, fultus – prop up,
wedge
* fulgeō, fulgēre, fulsī – shine, glitter
fulgur, fulguris, n. – lightning
fūmus, fūmī, m. – smoke
* fundō, fundere, fūdī, fūsus – pour,
pour out
* fundus, fundī, m. – farm; depth
fūnus, fūneris, n. – funeral, funeral
procession
* fūr, fūris, m. – thief
* furēns, *gen.* furentis – furious, in a
rage
furēns animī – furiously
determined, with furious
eagerness
fūstis, fūstis, m. – club, stick
futūrus, futūra, futūrum – future

g

* gaudeō, gaudēre – be pleased, rejoice,
be delighted
* gaudium, gaudiī, n. – joy
per gaudium – joyfully
* geminī, geminōrum, m.pl. – twins
geminus, gemina, geminum – twin,
the two, twofold, double
* gemitus, gemitūs, m. – groan

* gemma, gemmae, f. – jewel, gem
gena, genae, f. – cheek
gener, generī, m. – son-in-law
* gēns, gentis, f. – family, tribe, race
* genū, genūs, n. – knee
* genus, generis, n. – race
* gerō, gerere, gessī, gestus – wear;
achieve
*   bellum gerere – wage war,
campaign
sē gerere – behave, conduct oneself
Gerūsia, Gerūsiae, f. – the Gerusia
(club for wealthy, elderly men)
gestiō, gestīre, gestīvī – become
restless
gladiātor, gladiātōris, m. – gladiator
* gladius, gladiī, m. – sword
* glōria, glōriae, f. – glory
gnātus = nātus
gradus, gradūs, m. – step
addere gradum – go forward step
by step
grātiae, grātiārum, f.pl. – thanks
*   grātiās agere – thank, give thanks
grātificor, grātificārī, grātificātus
sum – do favours
grātulor, grātulārī, grātulātus sum –
congratulate
* grātus, grāta, grātum – acceptable,
pleasing
* gravis, grave – heavy, serious, severe
* graviter – heavily, soundly, seriously
gravō, gravāre, gravāvī – load, weigh
down
gremium, gremiī, n. – lap
gubernāculum, gubernāculī, n. –
helm, steering-oar
gurges, gurgitis, m. – whirlpool,
swirling water
* gustō, gustāre, gustāvī – taste

h

* habeō, habēre, habuī, habitus –
have, regard
*   prō certō habēre – know for certain

* habitō, habitāre, habitāvī – live
* haereō, haerēre, haesī – stick, cling,
  linger
* haesitō, haesitāre, haesitāvī – hesitate
  hama, hamae, f. – fire-bucket
  harundō, harundinis, f. – reed, rod
* haruspex, haruspicis, m. –
  soothsayer
* hasta, hastae, f. – spear
* haud – not
* haudquāquam – not at all
* hauriō, haurīre, hausī, haustus –
  drain, drink up
  haustus, haustūs, m. – drinking,
  drinking-place
  Helicē, Helicēs, f. – Great Bear
  (constellation)
* hercle! – by Hercules!
* hērēs, hērēdis, m.f. – heir
* heri – yesterday
  hetaeria, hetaeriae, f. – political club
  heu! = ēheu!
  hībernus, hīberna, hībernum –
  wintry, of winter
* hic, haec, hoc – this
  hī . . . aliī – some . . . others
  hī . . . hī – some . . . others
* hīc – here
* hiems, hiemis, f. – winter, storm
* hinc – from here; then, next
* hodiē – today
* homō, hominis, m. – man
* honor, honōris, m. – honour, official
  position
* honōrō, honōrāre, honōrāvī,
  honōrātus – honour
* hōra, hōrae, f. – hour
  horrendus, horrenda, horrendum –
  horrifying
* horreum, horreī, n. – barn, granary
* hortor, hortārī, hortātus sum –
  encourage, urge
* hortus, hortī, m. – garden
* hospes, hospitis, m. – guest, host
* hostis, hostis, m.f. – enemy
* hūc – here, to this place

  hūc . . . illūc – this way . . . that
  way, one way . . . another way,
  here and there, up and down
  humilis, humile – low-born, of low
  class; low-lying
  humus, humī, f. – ground
*   humī – on the ground

i

* iaceō, iacēre, iacuī – lie
* iaciō, iacere, iēcī, iactus – throw
* iactō, iactāre, iactāvī, iactātus –
  throw
* iam – now
  iam iamque – at any moment now
  nec iam – no longer
  nunc iam – now however, as things
  are now
* iānua, iānuae, f. – door
* ibi – there, then, in those days
  ībō see eō
  ictus, ictūs, m. – blow
* īdem, eadem, idem – the same
  in idem – for a common purpose,
  for the same purpose
* identidem – repeatedly
* ideō – for this reason
*   ideō . . . quod – for the reason that,
  because
* igitur – therefore, and so
* ignārus, ignāra, ignārum – not
  knowing, unaware,
  unsuspecting
* ignāvus, ignāva, ignāvum – lazy,
  cowardly
* ignis, ignis, m. – fire, lightning, heat
  of sun
* ignōrō, ignōrāre, ignōrāvī – not know
  of
* ignōscō, ignōscere, ignōvī + dat. –
  forgive
  ignōtus, ignōta, ignōtum – unknown
  iī see eō
  īlex, īlicis, f. – oak tree

īlia, īlium, n.pl. – groin
illāc – by that way
* ille, illa, illud – that, he, she
nē illud deī sinant! – heaven forbid!
* illūc – there, to that place
hūc . . . illūc – this way . . . that
way, one way . . . another way,
here and there, up and down
illūstris, illūstre – bright
imber, imbris, m. – rain, storm-cloud
imitor, imitārī, imitātus sum – copy,
imitate, mime
* immemor, gen. immemoris – forgetful
immēnsus, immēnsa, immēnsum –
vast
* immineō, imminēre, imminuī + dat. –
hang over
immītis, immīte – cruel
* immortālis, immortāle – immortal
* dī immortālēs! – heavens above!
* immōtus, immōta, immōtum – still,
motionless
* impediō, impedīre, impedīvī,
impedītus – delay, hinder
impellō, impellere, impulī,
impulsus – push, force
impendium, impendiī, n. – expense,
expenditure
impendō, impendere, impendī,
impēnsus – spend, make use of
impēnsē – strongly, violently
* imperātor, imperātōris, m. –
emperor
imperfectus, imperfecta,
imperfectum – unfinished
* imperium, imperiī, n. – power,
empire, rule, reign
* imperō, imperāre, imperāvī + dat. –
order, command; be emperor
* impetus, impetūs, m. – attack
impetum facere – charge, make an
attack
* impōnō, impōnere, imposuī,
impositus – impose, put into, put
onto
impotēns, gen. impotentis – helpless,
powerless

improbus, improba, improbum –
wicked, relentless
imprūdenter – stupidly, foolishly
impulī, impulsus see impellō
īmus, īma, īmum – lowest, bottom
* in (1) + acc. – into, onto
in aliud – for any other purpose
in idem – for a common purpose,
for the same purpose
in mentem venīre – occur, come to
mind
in perpetuum – for ever
in rem subitam – to meet the
sudden crisis
* in (2) + abl. – in, on
* in animō volvere – wonder, turn
over in the mind
in prīmīs – in the first place, in
particular
in proximō – nearby
* inānis, ināne – empty, meaningless
* incēdō, incēdere, incessī – march,
stride
* incendium, incendiī, n. – fire, blaze
* incendō, incendere, incendī,
incēnsus – burn, set fire to
* incēnsus, incēnsa, incēnsum –
inflamed, angered
incertus, incerta, incertum –
uncertain
* incidō, incidere, incidī – fall
* incipiō, incipere, incēpī, inceptus –
begin
* incitō, incitāre, incitāvī, incitātus –
urge on, encourage
inclīnō, inclīnāre, inclīnāvī,
inclīnātus – lean
incohō, incohāre, incohāvī,
incohātus – begin
* incolumis, incolume – safe
incurrō, incurrere, incurrī – run onto,
collide with, bump into
* inde – then
* indicium, indiciī, n. – sign, evidence
indignē – unfairly
indignor, indignārī, indignātus sum –
feel shame, think it shameful

*induō, induere, induī, indūtus – put on

inedia, inediae, f. – starvation

ineptiō, ineptīre – be silly, be a fool

ineptus, inepta, ineptum – silly

ineram *see* īnsum

inertia, inertiae, f. – laziness, idleness

*īnfāns, īnfantis, m. – child, baby

*īnfēlīx, *gen.* īnfēlīcis – unlucky

īnferiae, īnferiārum, f.pl. – tribute to the dead

īnferior, īnferius – lower, further down-stream

*īnferō, īnferre, intulī, inlātus – bring in, bring on, bring against
causam īnferre – make an excuse, invent an excuse

*īnfestus, īnfesta, īnfestum – hostile, dangerous

ingeminō, ingemināre, ingemināvī – redouble

*ingenium, ingeniī, n. – character

*ingēns, *gen.* ingentis – huge

*ingredior, ingredī, ingressus sum – enter

inhorrēscō, inhorrēscere, inhorruī – shudder

*iniciō, inicere, iniēcī, iniectus – throw in

*inimīcus, inimīcī, m. – enemy

inīquus, inīqua, inīquum – unfair, narrow, dangerous

*initium, initiī, n. – beginning

*iniūria, iniūriae, f. – injustice, injury

iniūstē – unfairly

iniūstus, iniūsta, iniūstum – unjust

inlēctus, inlēcta, inlēctum – unread

innītor, innītī, innīxus sum – lean on, lean, rest

innocēns, *gen.* innocentis – innocent

*inopia, inopiae, f. – shortage, scarcity, poverty

inquiētus, inquiēta, inquiētum – unsettled

*inquit – says, said
inquam – I said
inquis – you say

*īnsānus, īnsāna, īnsānum – mad, crazy, insane

*īnsidiae, īnsidiārum, f.pl. – trap, ambush

*īnspiciō, īnspicere, īnspexī, īnspectus – look at, inspect, examine, search

īnstīgō, īnstīgāre, īnstīgāvī, īnstīgātus – urge on

īnstituō, īnstituere, īnstituī, īnstitūtus – set up

īnstrūmentum, īnstrūmentī, n. – equipment

*īnstruō, īnstruere, īnstrūxī, īnstrūctus – draw up, set up, equip, fit (with wings)

*īnsula, īnsulae, f. – island; block of flats

*īnsum, inesse, īnfuī – be in, be inside

*intellegō, intellegere, intellēxī, intellēctus – understand

*intentē – intently

intentus, intenta, intentum – intent

*inter + *acc.* – among, during
inter sē – among themselves, with each other

*intereā – meanwhile

intereō, interīre, interiī, interitus – wear away, wear out

*interficiō, interficere, interfēcī, interfectus – kill

*interim – meanwhile

interior – on the inside

*intrā + *acc.* – inside

*intrō, intrāre, intrāvī – enter

intulī *see* īnferō

inultus, inulta, inultum – unavenged

invalēscō, invalēscere, invaluī – become strong

*inveniō, invenīre, invēnī, inventus – find

investīgō, investīgāre, investīgāvī, investīgātus – investigate

*invideō, invidēre, invīdī + *dat.* – envy, be jealous of, begrudge, cast an evil eye

*invidia, invidiae, f. – jealousy, envy, unpopularity
*invītō, invītāre, invītāvī, invītātus – invite
*invītus, invīta, invītum – unwilling, reluctant
involvō, involvere, involvī, involūtus – envelop, swallow up
iocōsum, iocōsī, n. – moment of fun, moment of pleasure
*iocus, iocī, m. – joke
Iovis *see* Iuppiter
*ipse, ipsa, ipsum – himself, herself, itself; master, mistress
*īra, īrae, f. – anger
*īrātus, īrāta, īrātum – angry
irrigō, irrigāre, irrigāvī, irrigātus – water
*irrumpō, irrumpere, irrūpī – burst in, burst into
*is, ea, id – he, she, it; that
id quod – what
*iste, ista, istud – that
it *see* eō
*ita – in this way, so
*ita vērō – yes
*itaque – and so
*iter, itineris, n. – journey, progress
iter agere – make one's way, travel
*iterum – again
nōn iterum – never again
*iubeō, iubēre, iussī, iussus – order
*iūdex, iūdicis, m. – judge
*iūdicō, iūdicāre, iūdicāvī, iūdicātus – judge
*iungō, iungere, iūnxī, iūnctus – join
iūnctus – side by side
Iūnōnius, Iūnōnia, Iūnōnium – sacred to Juno
Iuppiter, Iovis, m. – Jupiter (god of the sky, greatest of Roman gods)
iūrgium, iūrgiī, n. – argument, dispute
iūs, iūris, n. – right, privilege
iussī *see* iubeō
*iussum, iussī, n. – order, instruction
iūstus, iūsta, iūstum – proper, right, fair

iūstius erat – it would have been fairer, more proper
iuvencus, iuvencī, m. – bullock, young bull
iuvenīlis, iuvenīle – youthful
*iuvenis, iuvenis, m. – young man
*iuvō, iuvāre, iūvī, iūtus – help, assist, please
*iuxtā + *acc.* – next to
iuxtā – side by side

k

Kal. = Kalendās
Kalendae, Kalendārum, f.pl. – Kalends, 1st day of each month

l

labellum, labellī, n. – lip
*labor, labōris, m. – work
*lābor, lābī, lāpsus sum – fall, glide; pass by, slide by
*labōrō, labōrāre, labōrāvī – work
lacerō, lacerāre, lacerāvī, lacerātus – tear apart
lacertus, lacertī, m. – arm, muscle
*lacrima, lacrimae, f. – tear
*lacrimō, lacrimāre, lacrimāvī – weep, cry
lacus, lacūs, m. – lake
*laedō, laedere, laesī, laesus – harm
*laetus, laeta, laetum – happy
laevus, laeva, laevum – left
laevā parte – on the left hand
lagōna, lagōnae, f. – bottle
lāniger, lānigerī, m.f. – woolly one, lamb
*lapis, lapidis, m. – stone
lātē – widely
latebrae, latebrārum, f.pl. – hiding-place
*lateō, latēre, latuī – lie hidden
*latrō, latrōnis, m. – robber
lātrō, lātrāre, lātrāvī – bark

* latus, lateris, n. – side
* lātus, lāta, lātum – wide
* laudō, laudāre, laudāvī, laudātus –
    praise
* laus, laudis, f. – praise, fame
* lavō, lavāre (*sometimes* lavere), lāvī,
    lautus – wash
* lectīca, lectīcae, f. – sedan-chair
* lectus, lectī, m. – couch, bed
* lēgātus, lēgātī, m. – commander
    lēgem *see* lēx
* legiō, legiōnis, f. – legion
* legō, legere, lēgī, lēctus – read;
    choose, conscript, gather up
    lēgō, lēgāre, lēgāvī, lēgātus –
    bequeath
    lēniō, lēnīre, lēnīvī, lēnītus – soothe,
    calm down
* lēniter – gently
* lentē – slowly
    lentus, lenta, lentum – supple
    lēnunculus, lēnunculī, m. – small
    boat
* leō, leōnis, m. – lion
* levis, leve – light, slight, trivial,
    changeable, inconsistent,
    worthless
    levō, levāre, levāvī, levātus – raise,
    lift up
* lēx, lēgis, f. – law
* libenter – gladly
* liber, librī, m. – book
* līberālis, līberāle – generous
* līberī, līberōrum, m.pl. – children
* līberō, līberāre, līberāvī, līberātus –
    free, set free
* lībertās, lībertātis, f. – freedom
* lībertus, lībertī, m. – freedman,
    ex-slave
    lībrō, lībrāre, lībrāvī, lībrātus –
    balance
    librum *see* liber
* licet, licēre – be allowed
*   mihi licet – I am allowed
    licet – although
* līmen, līminis, n. – threshold,
    doorway

līmes, līmitis, m. – course
* lingua, linguae, f. – tongue, language
    līnum, līnī, n. – thread
    liqueō, liquēre, līquī – flow
    liquor, liquōris, m. – water
* littera, litterae, f. – letter (of
    alphabet)
*   litterae, litterārum, f.pl. – letter,
    letters (correspondence),
    literature
* lītus, lītoris, n. – sea-shore, shore
* locus, locī, m. – place
    meī locō – in my place
    locus nātālis, locī nātālis, m. –
    place of birth, native land
* longē – far, a long way
    longē errāre – make a big mistake
* longus, longa, longum – long
* loquor, loquī, locūtus sum – speak
    lūcem *see* lūx
    Lucrīnus lacus, Lucrīnī lacūs, m. –
    the Lucrine lake
    lūctor, lūctārī, lūctātus sum – struggle
* lūdō, lūdere, lūsī, lūsus – play
* lūdus, lūdī, m. – game
* lūgeō, lūgēre, lūxī – lament, mourn
* lūmen, lūminis, n. – light
    lūmina, lūminum, n.pl. – eyes
* lūna, lūnae, f. – moon
    lupus, lupī, m. – wolf
    lūsus, lūsūs, m. – play, games
* lūx, lūcis, f. – light, daylight

m

máchināmentum, máchināmentī, n.
    – machine, contraption
madēscō, madēscere, maduī –
    become wet
madidus, madida, madidum –
    soaked through
* magister, magistrī, m. – master,
    foreman, pilot
* magistrātus, magistrātūs, m. –
    magistrate (elected official of
    Roman government)

magnificus, magnifica, magnificum –
  splendid, magnificent
* magnopere – greatly
*   magis – more
*   maximē – very greatly, very much,
      most of all
* magnus, magna, magnum – big,
    large, great
    maior, maius – bigger, larger,
      greater
*   maximus, maxima, maximum –
      very big, very large, very great,
      greatest
* male – badly, unfavourably
    male dīcere – insult
    ō factum male! – O dreadfully
      done! O dreadful deed!
    vōbīs male sit – curses on you
* mālō, mālle, māluī – prefer
* malus, mala, malum – evil, bad
*   pessimus, pessima, pessimum –
      very bad, worst
* mandātum, mandātī, n. –
    instruction, order
* mandō, mandāre, mandāvī,
    mandātus – order, entrust,
    hand over
* māne – in the morning
* maneō, manēre, mānsī – remain, stay
    mānēs, mānis, m. – departed spirit
    dī mānēs – the spirits of the dead
    manifestus, manifesta, manifestum –
      clear
    mānō, mānāre, mānāvī – flow, be wet
    multum mānāns – drenched
* manus, manūs, f. – hand; band
    manus ultima – final touch
* mare, maris, n. – sea
    margarītum, margarītī, n. – pearl
    maritīmus, maritīma, maritīmum –
      seaside, by the sea
* marītus, marītī, m. – husband
    Massicus, Massica, Massicum –
      Massic
* māter, mātris, f. – mother
    mātrimōnium, mātrimōniī, n. –
      marriage

    mātrōna, mātrōnae, f. – lady
    maximē see magnopere
    maximus see magnus
    mē see ego
    medicāmentum, medicāmentī, n. –
      ointment, medicine, drug
* medicus, medicī, m. – doctor
* meditor, meditārī, meditātus sum –
      consider
* medius, media, medium – middle
    medius fidius! – for goodness sake!
    meī see ego
    mel, mellis, n. – honey
    melior see bonus
    mellītus, mellīta, mellītum – sweet as
      honey
* meminī, meminisse – remember
    memoria, memoriae, f. – memory
* mendāx, mendācis, m. – liar
* mēns, mentis, f. – mind
    in mentem venīre – occur, come to
      mind
* mēnsa, mēnsae, f. – table
* mēnsis, mēnsis, m. – month
    mēnsor, mēnsoris, m. – surveyor
    mēnsūra, mēnsūrae, f. –
      measurement
* mentior, mentīrī, mentītus sum – lie,
      tell a lie
* mercātor, mercātōris, m. – merchant
    mereō, merēre, meruī – deserve
*   meritus, merita, meritum –
      deserved, well-deserved
    mēta, mētae, f. – turning-point
* metuō, metuere, metuī – be afraid,
      fear
* metus, metūs, m. – fear
* meus, mea, meum – my, mine
    mī Secunde – my dear Secundus
    mī = mihi
    mihi see ego
* mīles, mīlitis, m. – soldier
    mīlitō, mīlitāre, mīlitāvī – be a
      soldier
* mīlle – a thousand
*   mīlia – thousands
* minimē – no, least, very little

minister, ministrī, m. – servant, agent

* minor, minārī, minātus sum + *dat.* – threaten

minus *see* paulum

* mīrābilis, mīrābile – marvellous, strange, wonderful

* mīror, mīrārī, mīrātus sum – admire, wonder at

mīrus, mīra, mīrum – extraordinary

misellus, misella, misellum – wretched little

* miser, misera, miserum – miserable, wretched, sad

misericors, *gen.* misericordis – tender-hearted, full of pity

* mittō, mittere, mīsī, missus – send

modicus, modica, modicum – ordinary, little

* modo – just, now, only, just now

* modo ... modo – now ... now, sometimes ... sometimes

nōn modo ... sed etiam – not only ... but also

* modus, modī, m. – manner, way, kind

* quō modō? – how? in what way?

moechus, moechī, m. – lover, adulterer

mōlēs, mōlis, f. – bulk; embankment, sea-wall

* molestus, molesta, molestum – troublesome

molliō, mollīre, mollīvī, mollītus – soothe, soften

* mollis, molle – soft, gentle

* moneō, monēre, monuī, monitus – warn, advise

monitus, monitūs, m. – warning, advice

* mōns, montis, m. – mountain

* mora, morae, f. – delay

* morbus, morbī, m. – illness

mordeō, mordēre, momordī, morsus – bite

* morior, morī, mortuus sum – die

* mortuus, mortua, mortuum – dead

* moror, morārī, morātus sum – delay, hold steady

* mors, mortis, f. – death

mortem obīre – die

morsus, morsūs, m. – bite, fangs

mortālis, mortāle – mortal

* mōs, mōris, m. – custom

mōtus, mōtūs, m. – movement

* moveō, movēre, mōvī, mōtus – move, influence

mōtus, mōta, mōtum – moved, moving

* mox – soon

* mulier, mulieris, f. – woman

* multitūdō, multitūdinis, f. – crowd

* multō – much

multum – much

multum mānāns – drenched

* multus, multa, multum – much

* multī – many

* plūrimī, plūrimae, plūrima – very many

* plūrimus, plūrima, plūrimum – most

* plūs, *gen.* plūris – more

quid plūra? – why say more?

mūniō, mūnīre, mūnīvī, mūnītus – protect, immunise

* mūnus, mūneris, n. – gift

* mūrus, mūrī, m. – wall

* mūtō, mūtāre, mūtāvī, mūtātus – change

mūtus, mūta, mūtum – silent

n

* nam – for

* nārrō, nārrāre, nārrāvī, nārrātus – tell, relate

* nāscor, nāscī, nātus sum – be born

trēdecim annōs nāta – thirteen years old

nat *see* nō

nātālis, nātāle – native

* diēs nātālis, diēī nātālis, m. – birthday

locus nātālis, locī nātālis, m. – place of birth, native land

natō, natāre, natāvī – swim
nātūra, nātūrae, f. – nature
nātus *see* nāscor
nātus, nātī, m. – son
naufragium, naufragiī, n. – shipwreck
* nauta, nautae, m. – sailor
nauticus, nautica, nauticum – made
    by sailors
nāvigātiō, nāvigātiōnis, f. – voyage
* nāvigō, nāvigāre, nāvigāvī – sail
* nāvis, nāvis, f. – ship
* nē – that . . . not, so that . . . not, in
    order that . . . not
    nē deī illud sinant! – heaven forbid!
*   nē quid – lest anything, in case
    anything
*   nē . . . quidem – not even
*   nē quis – lest anyone, in case
    anyone, that anyone, that
    nobody
nebula, nebulae, f. – mist
* nec – and not, nor
    nec iam – no longer
*   nec . . . nec – neither . . . nor
necessārius, necessāria, necessārium
    – necessary
* necesse – necessary
necessitās, necessitātis, f. – need
* necō, necāre, necāvī, necātus – kill
* neglegēns, *gen.* neglegentis – careless
neglegentia, neglegentiae, f. –
    carelessness
* neglegō, neglegere, neglēxī,
    neglēctus – neglect
* negō, negāre, negāvī, negātus – deny,
    say that . . . not
* negōtium, negōtiī, n. – business
*   negōtium agere – do business,
    work
* nēmō – no one, nobody
* neque – and not, nor
*   neque . . . neque – neither . . . nor
nēquīquam – in vain
Nēreis, Nēreidis, f. – sea-nymph
* nescio, nescīre, nescīvī – not know
nēve – and that . . . not
nex, necis, f. – slaughter

nī = nisi
Nīcomēdēnsēs, Nīcomēdēnsium,
    m.pl. – people of Nicomedia
nīdus, nīdī, m. – nest
* niger, nigra, nigrum – black
* nihil – nothing
    nihil opus est – there is no need
    nihil vōcis – no voice
* nihilōminus – nevertheless
nimbus, nimbī, m. – rain-cloud
* nimis – too
* nimium – too much
* nisi – except, unless
nītor, nītī, nīxus sum – lean
nix, nivis, f. – snow
nō, nāre, nāvī – swim
* nōbilis, nōbile – noble, of noble birth
nōbīs *see* nōs
* noceō, nocēre, nocuī + *dat.* – hurt
nocte *see* nox
* nōlō, nōlle, nōluī – not want
    nōlī, nōlīte – do not, don't
    nōllem – I should not want
* nōmen, nōminis, n. – name
* nōn – not
    nōn iterum – never again
    nōn sī – not even if
* nōnāgintā – ninety
* nōndum – not yet
* nōngentī, nōngentae, nōngenta –
    nine hundred
* nōnne? – surely?
* nōnnūllī, nōnnūllae, nōnnūlla –
    some, several
* nōnus, nōna, nōnum – ninth
nōrat = nōverat
* nōs – we, us
nōscitō, nōscitāre, nōscitāvī –
    recognise
nōsse = nōvisse
* noster, nostra, nostrum – our
nōtitia, nōtitiae, f. – notice
* nōtus, nōta, nōtum – known,
    well-known, famous
Notus, Notī, m. – South wind
* novem – nine
* nōvī – I know

novō, novāre, novāvī, novātus –
  change, revolutionise
* novus, nova, novum – new
* nox, noctis, f. – night, darkness
* nūbēs, nūbis, f. – cloud
* nūbō, nūbere, nūpsī + *dat.* – marry
  nūdus, nūda, nūdum – bare
* nūllus, nūlla, nūllum – not any, no,
    not at all
* num? – (1) surely . . . not?
* num – (2) whether
* numerō, numerāre, numerāvī,
    numerātus – count
* numerus, numerī, m. – number
    numerī, numerōrum, m.pl. –
    military units
* numquam – never
* nunc – now
    nunc iam – now however, as things
    are now
* nūntiō, nūntiāre, nūntiāvī, nūntiātus
    – announce
* nūntius, nūntiī, m. – messenger,
    message, news
* nūper – recently
    nūpsī *see* nūbō
    nūptiae, nūptiārum, f.pl. – wedding,
    marriage
* nusquam – nowhere

O

    obdūrō, obdūrāre, obdūrāvī – be firm
    obeō, obīre, obiī – meet, go to meet
    mortem obīre – die
    obēsus, obēsa, obēsum – fat
* obiciō, obicere, obiēcī, obiectus –
    present, put in the way of,
    expose to
    oblīdō, oblīdere, oblīsī, oblīsus –
    crush
* oblīvīscor, oblīvīscī, oblītus sum –
    forget
* obscūrus, obscūra, obscūrum –
    dark, gloomy

    observō, observāre, observāvī,
      observātus – notice, observe
    obstinātē – stubbornly
    obstinātus, obstināta, obstinātum –
      stubborn
    obstipēscō, obstipēscere, obstipuī –
      gape in amazement
* obstō, obstāre, obstitī + *dat.* –
      obstruct, block the way
    obstringō, obstringere, obstrīnxī,
      obstrictus – bind (with oath of
      loyalty)
    obstruō, obstruere, obstrūxī,
      obstrūctus – block the way
      through
* obstupefaciō, obstupefacere,
      obstupefēcī, obstupefactus –
      amaze, stun
    obterō, obterere, obtrīvī, obtrītus –
      trample to death
    obtulī *see* offerō
* obviam eō, obviam īre, obviam iī
      + *dat.* – meet, go to meet
* occāsiō, occāsiōnis, f. – opportunity
* occīdō, occīdere, occīdī, occīsus – kill
    occidō, occidere, occidī – set
* occupātus, occupāta, occupātum –
      busy
* occupō, occupāre, occupāvī,
      occupātus – seize, take over
* occurrō, occurrere, occurrī – meet
    ocellus, ocellī, m. – poor eye, little eye
* octāvus, octāva, octāvum – eighth
* octingentī, octingentae, octingenta –
      eight hundred
* octō – eight
    Octōber, Octōbris, Octōbre –
      October
* octōgintā – eighty
* oculus, oculī, m. – eye
* ōdī – I hate
* odium, odiī, n. – hatred
*   odiō esse – be hateful
    odōrātus, odōrāta, odōrātum – sweet-
      smelling
* offendō, offendere, offendī, offēnsus –
      displease, offend

* offerō, offerre, obtulī, oblātus – offer
* officium, officiī, n. – duty, task
    officium agere – do one's duty
* ōlim – once, some time ago,
    sometimes
    omittō, omittere, omīsī, omissus –
    drop, leave out, omit, abandon
* omnīnō – completely
* omnis, omne – all, every
    omnia – all, everything
    opera, operae, f. – work, attention
    tuā operā – by your doing, because
    of you
    operiō, operīre, operuī, opertus –
    cover, bury
    operis see opus
* opēs, opum, f.pl. – money, wealth
    opifex, opificis, m. – inventor,
    craftsman
* oportet, oportēre, oportuit – be right
    nōs oportet – we must
* oppidum, oppidī, n. – town
* opprimō, opprimere, oppressī,
    oppressus – crush
* oppugnō, oppugnāre, oppugnāvī,
    oppugnātus – attack
    optimē see bene
    optimus see bonus
* optō, optāre, optāvī, optātus – pray
    for, long for
* opus, operis, n. – work, construction,
    building
    nihil opus est – there is no need
*   opus est + abl. – there is need of
    testāceum opus – brick work
    ōra see ōs
* ōrātiō, ōrātiōnis, f. – speech
    ōrātor, ōrātōris, m. – speaker
    (in court), pleader
    orba, orbae, f. – (female) orphan
* orbis, orbis, m. – globe
*   orbis terrārum – world
    orbitās, orbitātis, f. – childlessness
    orbus, orba, orbum – bereaved,
    orphaned
    Orcus, Orcī, m. – the Underworld,
    Hell

* ōrdō, ōrdinis, m. – row, line
    Ōriōn, Ōriōnis, m. – Orion, the
    hunter (constellation)
* orior, orīrī, ortus sum – rise, rise up,
    arise
* ōrnō, ōrnāre, ōrnāvī, ōrnātus –
    decorate
    ōrnātus, ōrnāta, ōrnātum –
    decorated, elaborately furnished
* ōrō, ōrāre, ōrāvī – beg
* ōs, ōris, n. – face, mouth
    os, ossis, n. – bone
* ōsculum, ōsculī, n. – kiss
* ostendō, ostendere, ostendī,
    ostentus – show
* ōtiōsus, ōtiōsa, ōtiōsum – idle, on
    holiday, on vacation
* ōtium, ōtiī, n. – leisure
    per ōtium – at leisure, free from
    care
    ovis, ovis, f. – sheep

p

    pacīscor, pacīscī, pactus sum –
    exchange, bargain
    pācō, pācāre, pācāvī, pācātus –
    make peaceful
* paene – nearly, almost
    paenitentia, paenitentiae, f. –
    repentance, change of heart
* pallēscō, pallēscere, palluī – grow
    pale
* pallidus, pallida, pallidum – pale
    palma, palmae, f. – palm, hand
* pār, gen. paris – equal
* parātus, parāta, parātum – ready,
    prepared
* parcō, parcere, pepercī + dat. –
    spare
* parēns, parentis, m.f. – parent
    parentēs, parentum, m.f.pl. –
    ancestors, forefathers
* pāreō, pārēre, pāruī + dat. – obey
    pariēs, parietis, m. – wall, side
    (of couch)

pariō, parere, peperī, partus – gain, win

pariter – equally, at the same time

* parō, parāre, parāvī, parātus – prepare

* pars, partis, f. – part, direction
  laevā parte – on the left hand
  summā suī parte – from its highest part, from the top downwards

* parum – too little, not . . . enough

* parvus, parva, parvum – small

*   minimus, minima, minimum – very little, least

passer, passeris, m. – sparrow

passus, passa, passum – loose, dishevelled

passus see patior

pāstor, pāstōris, m. – shepherd

* patefaciō, patefacere, patefēcī, patefactus – reveal

pateō, patēre, patuī – lie open

* pater, patris, m. – father

patientia, patientiae, f. – patience

* patior, patī, passus sum – suffer, endure, allow

* patria, patriae, f. – country, homeland

patrius, patria, patrium – of the father

patrō, patrāre, patrāvī, patrātus – accomplish, commit

* patrōnus, patrōnī, m. – patron

* paucī, paucae, pauca – few, a few

* paulātim – gradually

* paulīsper – for a short time

* paulō – a little

* paulum – a little, slightly, to a slight extent

*   minus – less

* pauper, gen. pauperis – poor

* pavor, pavōris, m. – panic

* pāx, pācis, f. – peace

peccō, peccāre, peccāvī – do wrong, be to blame

* pectus, pectoris, n. – chest, breast, heart

* pecūnia, pecūniae, f. – money, sum of money

pedem see pēs

* peditēs, peditum, m.pl. – foot soldiers, infantry

pelagus, pelagī, n. – sea

* pendeō, pendēre, pependī – hang

penes + acc. – with

penna, pennae, f. – feather, wing

pepercī see parcō

* per + acc. – through, along
  per artem – deliberately, by design
  per gaudium – joyfully
  per ōtium – at leisure, free from care

percipiō, percipere, percēpī, perceptus – take hold of, get a grip on

percussor, percussōris, m. – assassin

* perdō, perdere, perdidī, perditus – destroy, waste, lose
  perditus, perdita, perditum – completely lost, gone for ever

perdūcō, perdūcere, perdūxī, perductus – bring, carry, continue

* pereō, perīre, periī – die, perish

perferō, perferre, pertulī, perlātus – bring, endure

* perficiō, perficere, perfēcī, perfectus – finish

* perfidia, perfidiae, f. – treachery

* perfidus, perfida, perfidum – treacherous, untrustworthy

* perīculōsus, perīculōsa, perīculōsum – dangerous

* perīculum, perīculī, n. – danger

periī see pereō

* perītus, perīta, perītum – skilful

permisceō, permiscēre, permiscuī, permixtus – mix with

* permōtus, permōta, permōtum – alarmed, disturbed

perōsus, perōsa, perōsum – hating

perpetuus, perpetua, perpetuum – perpetual
  in perpetuum – for ever

persevērō, persevērāre, persevērāvī – continue

perstō, perstāre, perstitī – persist

* persuādeō, persuādēre, persuāsī
  + *dat.* – persuade
* perterritus, perterrita, perterritum –
  terrified
pertinācia, pertināciae, f. – obstinacy,
  determination
pertineō, pertinēre, pertinuī –
  concern
  pertinēre ad exemplum – involve a
  precedent
* perturbō, perturbāre, perturbāvī,
  perturbātus – disturb, alarm
* perveniō, pervenīre, pervēnī –
  reach, arrive at
* pēs, pedis, m. – foot, paw
pessimus *see* malus
* pestis, pestis, f. – pest, scoundrel
* petō, petere, petīvī, petītus – make
  for, attack; seek, beg for, ask for
* pietās, pietātis, f. – duty, piety, family
  feeling (respect for (1) the gods,
  (2) homeland, (3) family)
pinguis, pingue – plump
pīnus, pīnī, f. – pine tree, boat
  (made of pine wood)
pīpiō, pīpiāre, pīpiāvī – chirp
piscis, piscis, m. – fish
pius, pia, pium – good, pious,
  respectful to the gods
* placeō, placēre, placuī + *dat.* –
  please, suit
placidus, placida, placidum – calm,
  peaceful
plānus, plāna, plānum – level, flat
* plaudō, plaudere, plausī, plausus –
  applaud, clap
* plaustrum, plaustrī, n. – wagon, cart
* plēnus, plēna, plēnum – full
* plērīque, plēraeque, plēraque – most,
  the majority
plūma, plūmae, f. – feather
plumbum, plumbī, n. – lead
plūra, plūs *see* multus
* pōculum, pōculī, n. – wine-cup
* poena, poenae, f. – punishment
*   poenās dare – pay the penalty, be
  punished

* poēta, poētae, m. – poet
* polliceor, pollicērī, pollicitus sum –
  promise
pollex, pollicis, m. – thumb
* pompa, pompae, f. – procession
* pondus, ponderis, n. – weight
* pōnō, pōnere, posuī, positus – put,
  place, put up, serve
* pōns, pontis, m. – bridge
* pontifex, pontificis, m. – priest
pontus, pontī, m. – sea
* populus, populī, m. – people
* porta, portae, f. – gate
* portō, portāre, portāvī, portātus –
  carry
* portus, portūs, m. – harbour
* poscō, poscere, poposcī – demand,
  ask for
positus *see* pōnō
* possideō, possidēre, possēdī,
  possessus – possess
* possum, posse, potuī – can, be able
* post + *acc.* – after, behind
* posteā – afterwards
' postquam – after, when
* postrēmō – finally, lastly
postrēmus, postrēma, postrēmum –
  last
* postrīdiē – on the next day
* postulō, postulāre, postulāvī,
  postulātus – demand
posuī *see* pōnō
* potēns, *gen.* potentis – powerful
potes *see* possum
* potestās, potestātis, f. – power
potis, pote – possible
  quī potis est? – how is that
  possible? how can that be?
potius – rather
potuī *see* possum
prae + *abl.* – instead of, rather than
* praebeō, praebēre, praebuī,
  praebitus – provide
* praeceps, *gen.* praecipitis –
  headlong
praeceptum, praeceptī, n. –
  instruction

praecipiō, praecipere, praecēpī,
    praeceptus – instruct, order
praecipuē – especially
* praecō, praecōnis, m. – herald,
    announcer
praecurrō, praecurrere, praecucurrī –
    go on ahead, run ahead
praedium, praediī, n. – estate,
    property
* praefectus, praefectī, m. –
    commander
* praeficiō, praeficere, praefēcī,
    praefectus – put in charge
* praemium, praemiī, n. – prize,
    reward, profit
* praesēns, *gen.* praesentis – present,
    ready
    ad praesēns – for the present, for
    the moment
* praesertim – especially
* praesidium, praesidiī, n. – protection
* praestō, praestāre, praestitī – show,
    display
* praesum, praeesse, praefuī + *dat.* – be
    in charge of
praesūmō, praesūmere, praesūmpsī,
    praesūmptus – take in advance
* praeter + *acc.* – except
* praetereā – besides
* praetereō, praeterīre, praeteriī –
    pass by, go past
praetōriānus, praetōriāna,
    praetōriānum – praetorian
    (belonging to emperor's
    bodyguard)
praevaleō, praevalēre, praevaluī –
    prevail, be uppermost
prātum, prātī, n. – meadow
* prāvus, prāva, prāvum – evil
* precēs, precum, f.pl. – prayers
    precēs adhibēre – offer prayers
* precor, precārī, precātus sum – pray
    (to)
* premō, premere, pressī, pressus –
    push, press, crush
* pretiōsus, pretiōsa, pretiōsum –
    expensive, precious

* pretium, pretiī, n. – price
prīmō – at first
prīmum – first, for the first time
* prīmus, prīma, prīmum – first
    in prīmīs – in the first place, in
    particular
* prīnceps, prīncipis, m. – chief,
    chieftain, emperor
prīncipātus, prīncipātūs, m. –
    principate, reign
* prīncipia, prīncipiōrum, n.pl. –
    headquarters
* prior, prius – first, in front, earlier
prīscus, prīsca, prīscum – ancient
* prius – earlier, before now
* priusquam – before, until
prīvātus, prīvāta, prīvātum – private
* prō + *abl.* – in front of, for, in return
    for, as
*   prō certō habēre – know for certain
* probō, probāre, probāvī, probātus –
    prove, examine (e.g. at time of
    enrolment)
* prōcēdō, prōcēdere, prōcessī –
    advance, proceed
* procul – far off
* prōcumbō, prōcumbere, prōcubuī –
    fall down
prōcurrō, prōcurrere, prōcurrī –
    project
prōdesse *see* prōsum
prōditor, prōditōris, m. – betrayer,
    informer
* prōdō, prōdere, prōdidī, prōditus –
    betray
prōdūcō, prōdūcere, prōdūxī,
    prōductus – bring forward, bring
    out, prolong, continue
* proelium, proeliī, n. – battle
* proficīscor, proficīscī, profectus sum
    – set out
profiteor, profitērī, professus sum –
    declare
* prōgredior, prōgredī, prōgressus sum
    – advance
* prohibeō, prohibēre, prohibuī,
    prohibitus – prevent

prōiciō, prōicere, prōiēcī, prōiectus –
cast (as an offering)
prōlēs, prōlis, f. – offspring, brood
prōmissum, prōmissī, n. – promise
* prōmittō, prōmittere, prōmīsī,
prōmissus – promise
prōmptus, prōmpta, prōmptum –
quick
prōmunturium, prōmunturiī, n. –
promontory
prōnus, prōna, prōnum – easy
* prope – near
propinquus, propinquī, m. – relative
prōpōnō, prōpōnere, prōposuī,
prōpositus – propose, put
forward
prōpositum, prōpositī, n. – intention,
resolution
proprius, propria, proprium – right,
proper; one's own, that belongs
to one
* propter + *acc.* – because of
proptereā – for that reason
prōra, prōrae, f. – prow
prōsequor, prōsequī, prōsecūtus sum
– follow, escort
prōsiliō, prōsilīre, prōsiluī – leap
forward, jump
prōsum, prōdesse, prōfuī + *dat.* –
benefit
quid prōderit? – what good will it
do?
prōtegō, prōtegere, prōtēxī,
prōtēctus – protect
prōtendō, prōtendere, prōtendī,
prōtentus – thrust forward
* prōvincia, prōvinciae, f. – province
* proximus, proxima, proximum –
nearest, next to, last
in proximō – nearby
prūdēns, *gen.* prūdentis – shrewd,
intelligent, sensible
* prūdentia, prūdentiae, f. – prudence,
good sense, shrewdness
Prūsēnsēs, Prūsēnsium, m.pl. –
people of Prusa
* pūblicus, pūblica, pūblicum – public

pudīcitia, pudīcitiae, f. – chastity,
virtue, purity
pudīcus, pudīca, pudīcum – chaste,
virtuous
* puella, puellae, f. – girl
* puer, puerī, m. – boy
pugiō, pugiōnis, m. – dagger
* pugna, pugnae, f. – fight
* pugnō, pugnāre, pugnāvī – fight
* pulcher, pulchra, pulchrum –
beautiful
pulchritūdō, pulchritūdinis, f. –
beauty
* pulsō, pulsāre, pulsāvī, pulsātus – hit,
knock at, thump, punch
* pūniō, pūnīre, pūnīvī, pūnītus –
punish
puppis, puppis, f. – poop, stern
pūriter – decently, with clean water
pūrus, pūra, pūrum – pure, clean,
spotless
* puto, putāre, putāvī – think

q

* quadrāgintā – forty
quadrātus, quadrāta, quadrātum –
squared, in blocks
* quadringentī, quadringentae,
quadringenta – five hundred
quaedam *see* quīdam
* quaerō, quaerere, quaesīvī, quaesītus
– search for, look for
* quālis, quāle – what sort of
* quam – (1) how
tam . . . quam – as . . . as
* quam – (2) than
quam celerrimē – as quickly as
possible
* quamquam – although
quamvīs – although
* quandō? – when?
quandoquidem – seeing that, since
* quantus, quanta, quantum – how big
quantum – as, as much as, as far as
quantum est – as much as there is

* quārē? – why?
   quārē – and so, wherefore
* quārtus, quārta, quārtum – fourth
* quasi – as if
   quassō, quassāre, quassāvī,
      quassātus – shake violently
   quater – four times
   quatiō, quatere – shake, flap
* quattuor – four
* quattuordecim – fourteen
* -que – and
   -que . . . -que – both . . . and
* queror, querī, questus sum – lament,
      complain about
   questus, questūs, m. – lamentation,
      cry of grief
* quī, quae, quod – who, which, some
   id quod – what
   quī? quae? quod? – which? what?
      how?
      quī potis est? – how is that
         possible? how can that be?
* quia – because
   quicquam see quisquam
   quicquid see quisquis
   quīcumque, quaecumque,
      quodcumque – whoever,
      whatever, any whatever
   quid see quis
* quīdam, quaedam, quoddam – one, a
      certain
* quidem – indeed
*   nē . . . quidem – not even
   quidquid see quisquis
* quiēs, quiētis, f. – rest
   quiētus, quiēta, quiētum – quiet,
      peaceful
   quīlibet, quaelibet, quodlibet –
      anyone at all, anything at all
* quīndecim – fifteen
* quīngentī, quīngentae, quīngenta –
      five hundred
* quīnquāgintā – fifty
* quīnque – five
* quīntus, quīnta, quīntum – fifth
* quis? quid? – who? what?
      quid plūra? – why say more?

quid prōderit? – what good will it
   do?
quis, quid – anyone, anything
*   nē quid – lest anything, in case
      anything
*   nē quis – lest anyone, in case
      anyone, that anyone, that
      nobody
*   sī quid – if anything
*   sī quis – if anyone
* quisquam, quicquam or quidquam –
      anyone, anything
* quisque, quaeque, quodque – each
      one, every one
   usque quāque – on every possible
      occasion
   ut quisque – as soon as each one
* quisquis – whoever
*   quidquid or quicquid – whatever,
      whatever possible
   quidquid est – whatever is
      happening
* quō? – where? where to?
* quō modō? – how? in what way?
* quod – because
*   ideō quod – for the reason that,
      because
   quodcumque see quīcumque
* quondam – one day, once, sometimes
* quoniam – since
* quoque – also, too
   quōsdam see quīdam
* quot? – how many?
* quotiēns – whenever

r

rapidus, rapida, rapidum – rushing,
   racing, blazing, consuming
* rapiō, rapere, rapuī, raptus – seize,
   grab
   rārus, rāra, rārum – occasional
* ratiōnēs, ratiōnum, f.pl. – accounts
   ratis, ratis, f. – boat
* recipiō, recipere, recēpī, receptus –
   recover, take back

* recitō, recitāre, recitāvī, recitātus –
recite, read out
* rēctē – rightly, properly
rēctor, rēctōris, m. – helmsman
* recumbō, recumbere, recubuī – lie
down, recline
* recūsō, recūsāre, recūsāvī, recūsātus
– refuse
* reddō, reddere, reddidī, redditus –
give back, make
sibi reddī – be restored to one's
senses, be restored to oneself
* redeō, redīre, rediī – return, go back,
come back
* redūcō, redūcere, redūxī, reductus –
lead back
* referō, referre, rettulī, relātus –
bring back, carry, deliver, tell,
report
rem referre – report the event
rēfert, rēferre, rētulit – make a
difference
* reficiō, reficere, refēcī, refectus –
repair
* rēgīna, rēgīnae, f. – queen
* regiō, regiōnis, f. – region
rēgis see rēx
* rēgnum, rēgnī, n. – kingdom
* regō, regere, rēxī, rēctus – rule
* regredior, regredī, regressus sum –
go back, return
* relēgō, relēgāre, relēgāvī, relēgātus –
exile
* relinquō, relinquere, relīquī,
relictus – leave
* reliquus, reliqua, reliquum –
remaining, the rest
relūcēscō, relūcēscere, relūxī –
become light again
rem see rēs
remaneō, remanēre, remānsī – stay
behind
* remedium, remediī, n. – cure
rēmigium, rēmigiī, n. – oars, wings
remittō, remittere, remīsī, remissus –
send back
rēmus, rēmī, m. – oar

renīdeō, renīdēre – grin, smirk, smile
repellō, repellere, reppulī, repulsus –
repel, push back
repulsus, repulsa, repulsum –
repelled, taken aback
* repente – suddenly
* reperiō, reperīre, repperī, repertus –
find
repetō, repetere, repetīvī, repetītus –
seek again, repeat, claim
repudiō, repudiāre, repudiāvī,
repudiātus – divorce, reject
* requīrō, requīrere, requīsīvī,
requīsītus – ask, seek, search for,
go looking for
* rēs, reī, f. – thing, business
in rem subitam – to meet the
sudden crisis
* rē vērā – in fact, truly, really
rem administrāre – manage the
task
rem efficere – accomplish the task
rem referre – report the event
* rēs adversae – misfortune
resīdō, resīdere, resēdī – sit down,
sink down
* resistō, resistere, restitī + dat. – resist
resonō, resonāre, resonāvī – resound
resorbeō, resorbēre – suck back
respectō, respectāre, respectāvī – look
towards, count on
* respiciō, respicere, respexī – look at,
look upon, look back, look up
respīrō, respīrāre, respīrāvī –
recover, revive, recover one's
breath, get one's breath back
* respondeō, respondēre, respondī –
reply
respōnsum, respōnsī, n. – answer
rēspūblica, reīpūblicae, f. – 'the
republic'
restituō, restituere, restituī,
restitūtus – restore
* retineō, retinēre, retinuī,
retentus – keep, hold back,
restrain, check
rettulī see referō

reus, reī, m. – defendant
   vōtī reus – bound by one's vow, in
   payment of one's vow
* reveniō, revenīre, revēnī – come back,
   return
* revertor, revertī, reversus sum – turn
   back, return
* revocō, revocāre, revocāvī, revocātus
   – recall, call back, recover
revomō, revomere, revomuī – vomit
   up
* rēx, rēgis, m. – king
rhētor, rhētoris, m. – teacher
* rīdeō, rīdēre, rīsī – laugh, smile
* rīpa, rīpae, f. – river bank
rīsus, rīsūs, m. – smile
rīte – properly
rīvus, rīvī, m. – stream
* rogō, rogāre, rogāvī, rogātus – ask
rogus, rogī, m. – pyre
Rōma, Rōmae, f. – Rome
Rōmānī, Rōmānōrum, m.pl. –
   Romans
Rōmānus, Rōmāna, Rōmānum –
   Roman
rōstrum, rōstrī, n. – prow
rubeō, rubēre – be red
ruīna, ruīnae, f. – ruin, wreckage,
   collapse
rūmor, rūmōris, m. – rumour
rūmōrēs, rūmōrum, m.pl. –
   gossip, rumours
* rumpō, rumpere, rūpī, ruptus –
   break, split, burst, rupture
* ruō, ruere, ruī – rush, collapse
rūpēs, rūpis, f. – rock, crag
* rūrsus – again
* rūs, rūris, n. – country, countryside
rūsticus, rūstica, rūsticum –
   country, in the country, of a
   countryman

S

Sabīnus, Sabīnī, m. – Sabine
* sacer, sacra, sacrum – sacred

* sacerdōs, sacerdōtis, m. – priest
sacrāmentum, sacrāmentī, n. – oath
   sacrāmentum dīcere – take the
   military oath
sacrificium, sacrificiī, n. – offering,
   sacrifice
sacrificō, sacrificāre, sacrificāvī,
   sacrificātus – sacrifice
* saepe – often
* saeviō, saevīre, saeviī – be in a rage
* saevus, saeva, saevum – savage, cruel
* sagitta, sagittae, f. – arrow
salsus, salsa, salsum – salty
* saltō, saltāre, saltāvī – dance
salūbris, salūbre – comfortable
* salūs, salūtis, f. – safety, health
* salūtō, salūtāre, salūtāvī, salūtātus –
   greet
* salvē! salvēte! – hello!
* sānē – obviously
* sanguis, sanguinis, m. – blood
* sapiēns, gen. sapientis – wise
* satis – enough
*   satis cōnstat – it is generally agreed
* saxum, saxī, n. – rock
scapha, scaphae, f. – small boat
* scelestus, scelesta, scelestum –
   wicked, wretched
* scelus, sceleris, n. – crime
* scindō, scindere, scidī, scissus – tear,
   tear up, cut up, cut open, carve
* sciō, scīre, scīvī – know
scopulus, scopulī, m. – reef, rock
* scrībō, scrībere, scrīpsī, scrīptus –
   write
* sē – himself, herself, themselves
   inter sē – among themselves, with
   each other
   sēcum – with him, with her, with
   them
* secō, secāre, secuī, sectus – cut
sector, sectārī, sectātus sum – chase
   after
* secundus, secunda, secundum –
   second
sēcūritās, sēcūritātis, f. – unconcern,
   lack of anxiety

* secūrus, secūra, secūrum – without a
care
secūtus *see* sequor
* sed – but
* sēdecim – sixteen
* sedeō, sedēre, sēdī – sit
* sēdēs, sēdis, f. – seat
sēgnis, sēgne – timid, unenterprising
* sella, sellae, f. – chair
semel – once
* semper – always
* senātor, senātōris, m. – senator
* senex, senis, m. – old man
senīlis, senīle – old
senior, senius – older, elder, elderly
sēnsus, sēnsūs, m. – feeling, sense
* sententia, sententiae, f. – opinion,
sentence
* sentiō, sentīre, sēnsī, sēnsus – feel,
notice
* sepeliō, sepelīre, sepelīvī, sepultus –
bury
* septem – seven
* septendecim – seventeen
* septimus, septima, septimum –
seventh
* septingentī, septingentae,
septingenta – seven hundred
* septuāgintā – seventy
* sepulcrum, sepulcrī, n. – tomb
sepultūra, sepultūrae, f. – burial
sepultus, sepultī, m. – one who is
buried
* sequor, sequī, secūtus sum – follow
* serēnus, serēna, serēnum – calm, clear
* sermō, sermōnis, m. – conversation
sērō – late, after a long time
* serviō, servīre, servīvī + *dat.* – serve
(as a slave)
* servō, servāre, servāvī, servātus –
save, look after
* servus, servī, m. – slave
* sescentī, sescentae, sescenta – six
hundred
sēsē = sē
sēstertius, sēstertiī, m. – sesterce
(coin)

Sētīnus, Sētīna, Sētīnum – Setian
sevērē – severely
sevēritās, sevēritātis, f. – strictness,
severity
* sevērus, sevēra, sevērum – severe,
strict
* sex – six
* sexāgintā – sixty
* sextus, sexta, sextum – sixth
* sī – if
nōn sī – not even if
*   sī quid – if anything
*   sī quis – if anyone
sibi *see* sē
* sīc – thus, in this way, in the same
way
siccus, sicca, siccum – dry
* sīcut – like
* sīdus, sīderis, n. – star
* signum, signī, n. – sign, seal, signal
* silentium, silentiī, n. – silence
sileō, silēre, siluī – be silent
* silva, silvae, f. – wood
sim *see* sum
* similis, simile + *dat.* – similar
* simul – at the same time, as soon as
* simulac, simulatque – as soon as
simulātiō, simulātiōnis, f. – pretence,
play-acting
* simulō, simulāre, simulāvī,
simulātus – pretend
* sine + *abl.* – without
sinō, sinere, sīvī, situs – allow
nē illud deī sinant! – heaven forbid!
sīpō, sīpōnis, m. – fire-pump
sitiō, sitīre, sitīvī – be thirsty
sitis, sitis, f. – thirst
* socius, sociī, m. – companion, partner
* sōl, sōlis, m. – sun, day
* soleō, solēre – be accustomed
solitus, solita, solitum – common,
usual
sōlitūdō, sōlitūdinis, f. – lonely place
* sollicitus, sollicita, sollicitum –
worried, anxious
* sōlus, sōla, sōlum – alone, lonely,
only, on one's own

* solvō, solvere, solvī, solūtus – loosen, untie, cast off
* somnus, somnī, m. – sleep
* sonitus, sonitūs, m. – sound
  sonō, sonāre, sonuī – sound
* sordidus, sordida, sordidum – dirty
* soror, sorōris, f. – sister
* sors, sortis, f. – lot, fate, one's lot
* spargō, spargere, sparsī, sparsus – scatter, spread
  spatiōsus, spatiōsa, spatiōsum – huge
* spatium, spatiī, n. – space, distance
  spē see spēs
* speciēs, speciēī, f. – appearance
* spectāculum, spectāculī, n. – show, spectacle
* spectō, spectāre, spectāvī, spectātus – look at, watch
* spernō, spernere, sprēvī, sprētus – despise, reject, ignore, disobey, disregard
* spērō, spērāre, spērāvī – hope, expect
* spēs, speī, f. – hope
  spoliō, spoliāre, spoliāvī, spoliātus – deprive
  spūmō, spūmāre, spūmāvī – foam
  stābam see stō
* statim – at once
* statiō, statiōnis, f. – post
  statua, statuae, f. – statue
* sternō, sternere, strāvī, strātus – lay low, knock over
* stilus, stilī, m. – pen (pointed stick for writing on wax tablet)
  stīva, stīvae, f. – plough-handle
* stō, stāre, stetī – stand, lie at anchor
* stola, stolae, f. – dress
* strēnuē – hard, energetically
* strepitus, strepitūs, m. – noise, din
  stringō, stringere, strīnxī, strictus – draw, unsheathe
* studeō, studēre, studuī – study
* studium, studiī, n. – enthusiasm, keenness, shout of support, cheer; study
* stultus, stulta, stultum – stupid, foolish

* suādeō, suādēre, suāsī + dat. – advise, suggest
* suāvis, suāve – sweet
* suāviter – sweetly
* sub (1) + acc. – under, to the depths of
* sub (2) + abl. – under, beneath
  subeō, subīre, subiī – approach, come up, take over
  subinde – regularly
* subitō – suddenly
  subitus, subita, subitum – sudden
  in rem subitam – to meet the sudden crisis
  sublevō, sublevāre, sublevāvī, sublevātus – remove, relieve
  subrīdeō, subrīdēre, subrīsī – smile, smirk
  subsellium, subselliī, n. – bench (for prisoner in court)
  subsistō, subsistere, substitī – halt, stop
  suburgeō, suburgēre – drive up close
* subveniō, subvenīre, subvēnī + dat. – help, come to help
  successus, successūs, m. – success
  sufficiēns, gen. sufficientis – enough, sufficient
  suī see sē
  sulcō, sulcāre, sulcāvī – plough through
* sum, esse, fuī – be
  summa, summae, f. – full responsibility, supreme command
  summergō, summergere, summersī, summersus – sink, dip
* summus, summa, summum – highest, greatest, top
  summā suī parte – from its highest part, from the top downwards
* sūmptuōsus, sūmptuōsa, sūmptuōsum – expensive, lavish, costly
  suōpte = suō
* superbus, superba, superbum – arrogant, proud
  superior, superius – higher, further up-stream

* superō, superāre, superāvī, superātus
  – overcome, overpower, surpass,
  achieve, win
superstes, superstitis, m. – survivor
* supersum, superesse, superfuī –
  survive, remain, be left
* supplicium, suppliciī, n. –
  punishment, penalty
  supplicium ultimum – death
  penalty
* suprā + *acc.* – over, on top of
suprēmus, suprēma, suprēmum – last
* surgō, surgere, surrēxī – get up, rise,
  grow up, be built up
* suscipiō, suscipere, suscēpī,
  susceptus – undertake, take on
suspīciōsus, suspīciōsa, suspīciōsum
  – suspicious
* suspicor, suspicārī, suspicātus sum –
  suspect
sustulī *see* tollere
* suus, sua, suum – his, her, their, his
  own
  suī, suōrum, m.pl. – his men, his
  family, their families

t

* taberna, tabernae, f. – shop, inn
tābēscō, tābēscere, tābuī – melt
tablīnum, tablīnī, n. – study
* taceō, tacēre, tacuī – be silent, be
  quiet
* tacitē – quietly, silently
* tacitus, tacita, tacitum – quiet, silent,
  in silence
* taedet, taedēre – be tiring
* tālis, tāle – such
* tam – so
  tam . . . quam – as . . . as
* tamen – however
* tamquam – as, like
* tandem – at last
  vix tandem – at long last
* tangō, tangere, tetigī, tāctus – touch,
  move

* tantum – only
* tantus, tanta, tantum – so great, such
  a great
  tantum – so much, such a great
  number
tardē – late, slowly
* tardus, tarda, tardum – late, slow
taurus, taurī, m. – bull
tē *see* tū
* tēctum, tēctī, n. – ceiling, roof,
  building
* tegō, tegere, tēxī, tēctus – cover
* tellūs, tellūris, f. – land, earth
* tempestās, tempestātis, f. – storm
* templum, templī, n. – temple
* temptō, temptāre, temptāvī,
  temptātus – try, put to the test
* tempus, temporis, n. – time
tendō, tendere, tetendī, tentus –
  strain, strive, stretch out
* tenebrae, tenebrārum, f.pl. –
  darkness
tenebricōsus, tenebricōsa,
  tenebricōsum – dark, shadowy
* teneō, tenēre, tenuī, tentus – hold,
  keep to, hold on to, occupy,
  possess, be upon, hold back
tener, tenera, tenerum – tender,
  helpless
* tenuis, tenue – thin, subtle
tenuō, tenuāre, tenuāvī, tenuātus –
  thin out
* tergum, tergī, n. – back
* terra, terrae, f. – ground, land
  orbis terrārum – world
* terreō, terrēre, terruī, territus –
  frighten
terrestris, terrestre – on land
terror, terrōris, m. – terror
* tertius, tertia, tertium – third
testāceum opus, testāceī operis, n. –
  brick work
* testāmentum, testāmentī, n. – will
* testis, testis, m.f. – witness
tētē = tē
Teucrī, Teucrōrum, m.pl. – Trojans
theātrum, theātrī, n. – theatre

tibi *see* tū
Tīburs, Tīburtis, m. – man from Tibur
* timeō, timēre, timuī – be afraid, fear
timidē – fearfully
timidus, timida, timidum – fearful, frightened
* timor, timōris, m. – fear
tintinō, tintināre, tintināvī – ring
tīrō, tīrōnis, m. – recruit
toga, togae, f. – toga
* tollō, tollere, sustulī, sublātus – raise, lift up, hold up; remove, do away with
tōnsor, tōnsōris, m. – barber
torpeō, torpēre – be paralysed
torqueō, torquēre, torsī, tortus – torture, twist, turn
* tot – so many
totidem – the same number
* tōtus, tōta, tōtum – whole
tractō, tractāre, tractāvī, tractātus – handle, touch
* trādō, trādere, trādidī, trāditus – hand over
* trahō, trahere, trāxī, tractus – drag, draw on, urge on, draw, derive
tranquillum, tranquillī, n. – calm weather
* trāns + *acc.* – across
* trānseō, trānsīre, trānsiī, trānsitus – cross
trānsferō, trānsferre, trānstulī, trānslātus – transfer, put
* trecentī, trecentae, trecenta – three hundred
* trēdecim – thirteen
tremō, tremere, tremuī – tremble, shake
tremor, tremōris, m. – trembling, tremor
tremulus, tremula, tremulum – quivering
* trēs, tria – three
trēs adeō – as many as three, three entire
* tribūnus, tribūnī, m. – tribune (high-ranking officer)

triclīnium, triclīniī, n. – dining-room
triērarchus, triērarchī, m. – naval captain
* trīgintā – thirty
* trīstis, trīste – sad
triumphus, triumphī, m. – triumph
trudis, trudis, f. – pole
* tū, tuī – you (singular)
* tuba, tubae, f. – trumpet
tueor, tuērī, tuitus sum – watch over, protect
tulī *see* ferō
* tum – then
* tum dēmum – then at last, only then
tumidus, tumida, tumidum – swollen
* tumultus, tumultī, m. – riot
tunc – then
tundō, tundere – beat, buffet
* turba, turbae, f. – crowd
turbātus, turbāta, turbātum – confused
turbulentus, turbulenta, turbulentum – rowdy, disorderly, disturbed, muddy
turgidulus, turgidula, turgidulum – swollen
* tūtus, tūta, tūtum – safe
* tuus, tua, tuum – your (singular), yours

u

* ubi – where, when
ubicumque – wherever
* ubīque – everywhere
* ulcīscor, ulcīscī, ultus sum – avenge, take revenge on, take vengeance
* ūllus, ūlla, ūllum – any
* ultimus, ultima, ultimum – furthest, last, at the edge
manus ultima – final touch
supplicium ultimum – death penalty
* ultiō, ultiōnis, f. – revenge
* ultrā – more, further, beyond
ululātus, ululātūs, m. – shriek
Umber, Umbrī, m. – Umbrian

* umbra, umbrae, f. – shadow, ghost
* umerus, umerī, m. – shoulder
ūmidus, ūmida, ūmidum – rainy,
    stormy
* umquam – ever
ūnā – with him
*   ūnā cum + *abl.* – together with
* unda, undae, f. – wave
* unde – from where
* ūndecim – eleven
* ūndēvīgintī – nineteen
* undique – on all sides
* unguō, unguere, ūnxī, ūnctus –
    anoint, smear
ūnicus, ūnica, ūnicum – one and only
ūnivira, ūnivirae, f. – woman who has
    had only one husband
* ūnus, ūna, ūnum – one, a single
urbānus, urbāna, urbānum – smart,
    fashionable, refined; city-
    dweller, man from Rome
* urbs, urbis, f. – city
urgeō, urgēre – pursue, press upon
ūrō, ūrere, ussī, ustus – burn
usquam – anywhere
usque (1) – continually
    usque quāque – on every possible
    occasion
usque (2) + *acc.* – as far as
    usque adhūc – up till now, until
    now
    usque alter – yet another
ūsus, ūsūs, m. – use
ūsus *see* ūtor
* ut – (1) as, as soon as, when
    ut quisque – as soon as each one
* ut – (2) that, so that, in order that
* uterque, utraque, utrumque – each,
    both, each of two
    utrīque – both groups of people
uterus, uterī, m. – womb
* ūtilis, ūtile – useful
ūtilitās, ūtilitātis, f. – usefulness
* ūtor, ūtī, ūsus sum + *abl.* – use
* utrum – whether
*   utrum . . . an – whether . . . or
* uxor, uxōris, f. – wife

V

vacō, vacāre, vacāvī – be unoccupied
* vacuus, vacua, vacuum – empty
vadum, vadī, n. – water
vae tē! – alas for you!
vāgītus, vāgītūs, m. – wailing, crying
vagor, vagārī, vagātus sum – spread,
    go round
vagus, vaga, vagum – wandering
* valdē – very much, very
* valē – goodbye, farewell
    avē atque valē – hail and farewell
valeō, valēre, valuī – be well, feel well,
    thrive, prosper
* validus, valida, validum – strong
varius, varia, varium – different,
    various
vāstus, vāsta, vāstum – great, large
-ve – or
* vehementer – violently, loudly
vehiculum, vehiculī, n. – carriage
* vehō, vehere, vexī, vectus – carry
vehor, vehī, vectus sum – be carried
    (e.g. by horse or ship), travel
* vel – or
*   vel . . . vel – either . . . or
velim, vellem *see* volō
* velut – like
vēnālīcius, vēnālīciī, m. – slave-dealer
* vēnātiō, vēnātiōnis, f. – hunt
* vēndō, vēndere, vēndidī,
    vēnditus – sell
* venēnum, venēnī, n. – poison
* venia, veniae, f. – mercy
* veniō, venīre, vēnī – come, come
    forward
    in mentem venīre – occur, come to
    mind
venter, ventris, m. – stomach, womb
ventitō, ventitāre – often go, go
    repeatedly
* ventus, ventī, m. – wind
Venus, Veneris, f. – Venus (goddess
    of love)
venustus, venusta, venustum –
    tender-hearted, loving

* verberō, verberāre, verberāvī,
    verberātus – strike, beat
* verbum, verbī, n. – word
  vērē – truly
* vereor, verērī, veritus sum – be afraid,
    fear
  vēritās, vēritātis, f. – truth
* vērō – indeed
* vertō, vertere, vertī, versus – turn,
    churn up
    sē vertere – turn round
* vērum, vērī, n. – truth
* vērus, vēra, vērum – true, real
*   rē vērā – in fact, truly, really
* vester, vestra, vestrum – your
    (plural)
* vestīmenta, vestīmentōrum, n.pl. –
    clothes
* vestis, vestis, f. – clothing
* vetus, gen. veteris – old
  vetustās, vetustātis, f. – length,
    duration
* vexō, vexāre, vexāvī, vexātus – annoy
    vexātus, vexāta, vexātum –
    confused, in chaos
* via, viae, f. – street, way
  viātor, viātōris, m. – traveller
  vicārius, vicāriī, m. – substitute
  vīcīnia, vīcīniae, f. – nearness
* vīcīnus, vīcīnī, m. – neighbour
  victima, victimae, f. – victim
* victor, victōris, m. – victor, winner
  victus see vincere
* videō, vidēre, vīdī, vīsus – see
* videor, vidērī, vīsus sum – seem
  vigilō, vigilāre, vigilāvī – stay awake,
    keep watch
* vīgintī – twenty
  vīlicus, vīlicī, m. – bailiff, manager
* vīlis, vīle – cheap
* vīlla, vīllae, f. – house, villa
* vinciō, vincīre, vīnxī, vīnctus – bind,
    tie up
* vincō, vincere, vīcī, victus – conquer,
    win, be victorious
* vinculum, vinculī, n. – fastening,
    chain

* vīnum, vīnī, n. – wine
  violentia, violentiae, f. – violence
  vīpera, vīperae, f. – viper
* vir, virī, m. – man
* virgō, virginis, f. – virgin
  viridis, viride – green
* virtūs, virtūtis, f. – courage, virtue
* vīs, f. – force, violence
*   vīrēs, vīrium, f.pl. – forces, strength
  vīsitō, vīsitāre, vīsitāvī, vīsitātus –
    visit
  vīsō, vīsere, vīsī – come to visit
  vīsus see videō
* vīta, vītae, f. – life
* vitium, vitiī, n. – sin, fault, failure,
    vice
* vītō, vītāre, vītāvī, vītātus – avoid
* vituperō, vituperāre, vituperāvī,
    vituperātus – blame, curse
* vīvō, vīvere, vīxī – live, be alive
* vīvus, vīva, vīvum – alive, living
* vix – hardly, scarcely, with difficulty
    vix tandem – at long last
  vōbīs see vōs
  vōcem see vōx
* vocō, vocāre, vocāvī, vocātus – call
  volātus, volātūs, m. – flying, flight
* volō, velle, voluī – want
    bene velle – like, be friendly
    velim – I should like
    vellem – I should be willing
  volō, volāre, volāvī – fly
  volt = vult
  volucer, volucris, volucre –
    winged, swift
  voluntārius, voluntāriī, m. –
    volunteer
* volvō, volvere, volvī, volūtus –
    turn, set rolling, turn to
    billows, send rolling upwards
*   in animō volvere – wonder, turn
    over in the mind
  vōmer, vōmeris, m. – ploughshare
* vōs – you (plural)
  vōtum, vōtī, n. – vow
    vōtī reus – bound by one's vow,
    in payment of one's vow

* vōx, vōcis, f. – voice

vulgō, vulgāre, vulgāvī, vulgātus –
    make known

vulgus, vulgī, n. – the ordinary
    man, common man

* vulnerō, vulnerāre, vulnerāvī,
    vulnerātus – wound, injure

* vulnus, vulneris, n. – wound

vult *see* volō

* vultus, vultūs, m. – expression, face